D1568637

Founding editor: J. R. MULRYNE
General editors:
JAMES C. BULMAN, CAROL CHILLINGTON RUTTER

The *Henry VI* plays

Manchester University Press

Shakespeare in Performance

The *Henry VI* plays

STUART HAMPTON-REEVES and
CAROL CHILLINGTON RUTTER

Manchester
University Press
Manchester and New York

Distributed exclusively in the USA by Palgrave

Published by Manchester University Press
Oxford Road, Manchester M13 9NR, UK
and Room 400, 175 Fifth Avenue,
New York, NY 10010, USA
www.manchesteruniversitypress.co.uk

Distributed exclusively in the USA by
Palgrave, 175 Fifth Avenue,
New York, NY 10010, USA

Distributed exclusively in Canada by
UBC Press, University of British Columbia,
2029 West Mall, Vancouver, BC
Canada V6T 1Z2

British Library Cataloguing-in-Publication Data
A catalogue record for this book is available
from the British Library

Library of Congress Cataloging-in-Publication Data
applied for

ISBN 0 7190 5677 2 *hardback*
EAN 978 0 7190 5677 2

This edition first published 2006

15 14 13 12 11 10 09 08 07 06   10 9 8 7 6 5 4 3 2 1

Typeset in New Aster
by Koinonia, Manchester
Printed in Great Britain
by Bell & Bain Ltd, Glasgow

CONTENTS

LIST OF ILLUSTRATIONS

SERIES EDITORS' PREFACE

Recently, the study of Shakespeare's plays as scripts for performance in the theatre has grown to rival the reading of Shakespeare as literature among university, college and secondary-school teachers and their students. The aim of the present series is to assist this study by describing how certain of Shakespeare's texts have been realised in production.

The series is not concerned to provide theatre history in the traditional sense. Rather, it employs the more contemporary discourses of performance criticism to explore how a multitude of factors work together to determine how a play achieves meaning for a particular audience. Each contributor to the series has selected a number of productions of a given play and analysed them comparatively. These productions – drawn from different periods, countries and media – were chosen not only because they are culturally significant in their own right but also because they represent something of the range and variety of the possible interpretations of the play in hand. They illustrate how the convergence of various material conditions helps to shape a performance: the medium for which the text is adapted; stage-design and theatrical tradition; the acting company itself; the body and abilities of the individual actor; and the historical, political and social contexts which condition audience reception of the play.

We hope that theatregoers, by reading these accounts of Shakespeare in performance, may enlarge their understanding of what a playtext is and begin, too, to appreciate the complex ways in which performance is a collaborative effort. Any study of a Shakespeare text will, of course, reveal only a small proportion of the play's potential meaning; but by engaging issues of how a text is translated in performance, our series encourages a kind of reading that is receptive to the contingencies that make theatre a living art.

J. R. Mulryne, Founding editor
James C. Bulman, Carol Chillington Rutter, General editors

ACKNOWLEDGMENTS

We wish to thank the following people: Paul Allain, Michael Bogdanov, Michael Boyd, Jim Bulman, Gabriel Egan, Matthew Frost, Joy Leslie Gibson, Jack Hall, Terry Hands, Michael Hattaway, Barbara Hodgdon, Peter Holland, Tony Howard, John J. Joughin, Steve Longstaffe, George and Emma Mackay, Randall Martin, Katie Mitchell, J. R. Mulryne, Lucy Nicholson, Michael Poulton, Elizabeth Shafer, Robert Shaughnessy, Margaret Shewring, Debbie Williams and Richard Wilson. We are also grateful to the librarians at the Theatre Museum, the Shakespeare Centre in Stratford-upon-Avon, the British Film Institute, Birmingham City Library, the Victoria & Albert Museum, the BBC and the archives of the Oregon Shakespeare Festival in Ashland. We have benefited from funding from the Arts and Humanities Research Council, the British Academy, the University of Central Lancashire and the University of Warwick. Authorship of the chapters was divided as follows: Stuart Hampton-Reeves, Introduction, Chapters I–II and V–IX; Carol Chillington Rutter, Chapters III and IV. However, our comments on and editing of one another's work were so constant and pervasive that the reader should think of the book as genuinely collaborative. Although all chapters are published here for the first time, there is some overlap with two articles previously published by Hampton-Reeves: 'Alarums and Defeats: *Henry VI* on Tour' in *Early Modern Literary Studies* 5.2 (September 1999) and 'Shakespeare and the Festival of Britain' in *The Blackwell Companion to Shakespeare and Performance* (Oxford: Blackwell, 2005), and we are grateful to the publishers and to Lisa Hopkins, Barbara Hodgdon and William B. Worthen for letting us reproduce excerpts from those essays. All quotations from Shakespeare (unless otherwise stated) are from *The Norton Shakespeare*, ed. Stephen Greenblatt (New York: Norton, 1997).

INTRODUCTION

Henry VI and national culture

The *Henry VI* plays are arguably Shakespeare's most English works. Of all the canon, they are the plays least performed outside of England, and, even today, though there have been some notable international attempts to stage the plays, any spectators outside of England who have seen the plays on stage are likely to have seen them performed by an English company on tour. As long ago as 1944, E. M. W. Tillyard seemed to settle the trilogy's Englishness by arguing that the plays' main character is England itself. Yet *Henry VI*'s place in English culture remains a paradox. For on the English stage, these three history plays are among the most marginal and least seen of all Shakespeare's plays. Nevertheless, some of the most important Shakespeare productions of the last fifty years have been versions of *Henry VI*. The problems that circulate around the plays, particularly questions of textual authenticity, are perhaps symptoms of a wider anxiety about the nature and authenticity of Englishness itself, which, as Perry Anderson has noted, has been in crisis since the *de facto* end of Empire after the Second World War. And Englishness continues to remain a problem now – when 'England' has been unshackled from the imperial concept of 'Great Britain', as Wales, Scotland and Ireland have, in turn, sought devolution and distinct identities. The arc of this historic crisis in articulating an authentic national identity has been precisely echoed by the strange, certainly unexpected revival of the *Henry VI* plays in the 1950s after centuries of neglect. These are not just plays about England, of course; these are plays that put England at the edge of chaos and contemplate questions of national identity from the marginal position of imminent disaster.

The history of the *Henry VI* plays since the 1950s is bound up with issues of nationhood and national culture as seen from the perspective of the Royal Shakespeare Company. It was the RSC which, in 1963, dragged the plays from the obscure margins of the postwar repertoire into the centre of national culture. It is, of course, true that no account of the plays' performance history can afford to ignore the brilliant staging of the cycle at the Birmingham Rep the previous decade, which in turn inspired Peter Hall to mount his own productions at the rebranded Royal Shakespeare Theatre (it had, until Hall's tenure, been known as the Shakespeare Memorial Theatre). Those earlier stagings, produced by the impresario Sir Barry Jackson and directed by Douglas Seale, made their own tentative negotiations with the rapidly forming sense of nationhood after the war. But it was Peter Hall and his co-director (and adapter) John Barton who made the plays central to questions of national culture. *The Wars of the Roses*, as Hall and Barton renamed the trilogy (now incorporating *Richard III*), linked Shakespeare's earliest plays about England to questions about the current crisis in national identity and in doing so coincidentally established an artistic rationale for the RSC as England's *de facto* national theatre for staging Shakespeare. This link between the plays and national culture has been a hard one to break and has cast its shadow over all subsequent British productions of the *Henry VI* trilogy.

Jackson headed the company briefly after the war, when it was still the Shakespeare Memorial Theatre. His *Henry VIs* were the realisation of a long-cherished ambition, and they were staged at his local Birmingham Rep. Hall and Barton's *Wars* was the next important staging. Terry Hands staged the trilogy in 1977 and became RSC Joint Artistic Director the following year (and eventually sole Artistic Director). His successor, Adrian Noble, more or less wrote his job application with a stunning history play cycle, *The Plantagenets* (another adaptation of the plays) – he was appointed Artistic Director not long after it closed. In 2003, Michael Boyd succeeded Noble – not long after receiving a brace of awards for his *Henry VI* trilogy, staged at the RSC's Swan theatre in 2000–1. This curious tradition, almost a rite of passage, has put the *Henry VI* plays – so rarely performed, so little read, so marginal in the canon that some would like to deny that Shakespeare had any hand in them – in a surprisingly central place in modern British theatre history. When they come along, they are frequently heralds of change in performance practice. Jackson, ahead of his time, used the Rep as a way of showing what subsidised theatre could be like (although the Rep's only subsidy was Jackson's own personal fortune), and Hall's RSC cycle opened a decade of political theatre governed by large directorial concepts. Hands's sparsely designed trilogy went the other way, as if Hands had taken to heart John

Russell Brown's call to 'free Shakespeare' from over-conceptual directorial imposition. Noble's *The Plantagenets* heralded a return to big, spectacular, costume-drama Shakespeare; a decade later, Boyd's trilogy introduced new (or returned to old) working practices – an ensemble, short-contract, themed-season model that the RSC has since used to pattern changes to its repertory structure.

In a sense, it is the continuing marginality of the *Henry VI* plays that has made them so central. More than any other Shakespeare plays, these three allow directors to put their own stamp on them. Sometimes this is done literally, as directors since Hall and Barton have cut-and-pasted the texts to suit their vision, even writing 'new' Shakespeare. But by leaving the texts relatively intact, directors also have made their mark, for trilogies are so rarely performed that they make their own statement about Shakespeare. Playing them 'all', playing them in sequence offers a form of adaptation by association.

The rationale behind these textual choices can often be as revealing as the texts themselves. Hall would later recant his decision to reduce the three plays to two, but at the time he made a persuasive argument that the plays were not up to the standard of Shakespeare's later works and that, in any case, they were collaborations, written by many hands. His co-director, John Barton (who never recanted), wrote the adaptation and added much of his own material. Justifying this particular project, he said he would never treat Shakespeare's later plays to this sort of adaptation; with the *Henry*s, he imagined himself being given Shakespeare's texts as unfinished works in need of editing – removing those other 'hands' – and polishing. Barton rewrote the plays, as he thought, in the style of mature Shakespeare: he expunged the work of inferior playwrights from the RSC stage and, by doing so, he introduced a new classic to the canon. For his part, Hall disarmingly and cannily labelled the adaptation in pre-production publicity a 'literary heresy', glossing over the centuries-old tradition of rewriting Shakespeare for the stage while creating vital media interest in the 'heretical' project. Barton went on radio and took part in newspaper debates to defend his adaptation, and eventually the British Library even exhibited the promptbook so that the public could decide for itself whether the heretics should be canonised or burnt at the stake. If nothing else, Hall had succeeded in putting the RSC and its right to edit Shakespeare into people's minds.

Engineered or not, the debate over the adaptation proved to

[3]

be a timely one. Never before had the texts of the plays been the subject of so much public interest, which was fortunate for the RSC because, at that very moment, it was struggling to keep its head above water as it experienced the first of several periodic financial crises that were to dog (and maybe define) the institution over the next decades. The Shakespeare Memorial Theatre that Peter Hall took charge of in 1959 had until then always been funded through box office receipts and private donations. The new RSC was dependent on public subsidy, but, for various reasons connected with the National Theatre project, that subsidy was suddenly withdrawn in 1962, plunging the fledgling institution into crisis. Responding to the crisis, Hall insisted that the RSC was a national theatre in all but name. It was entitled to government subsidy because it served national culture and because only the RSC had the experience and the authority to perform 'definitive' Shakespeare. To make the point, Hall took the argument to the national press. Editorials, letter pages, interviews, radio shows and feature articles all appeared to defend the subsidy. The British public rose up to defend its national heritage (forgetting that the RSC was only a few years old and had never before received subsidy). This was the backdrop for *Wars*: the production *needed* to succeed, both as a box office hit (to make up for a lacklustre first RSC season) and, almost as important, as a statement of national culture and the RSC's role within it. Hall had to persuade the public that only the RSC had the authority to stage these plays; only the RSC could be trusted to improve the texts and play them as Shakespeare would have 'intended'. *Wars* was a major cultural statement that looked both inwards, to the kind of Shakespeare that Hall wanted the company to produce, and outwards, to connect with a public that had to be made to feel that the RSC's work was a part of its heritage and therefore worthy of public subsidy. As a 'state of the nation' work, *Wars* underpinned Hall's commitment to making Shakespeare relevant. He looked to Europe for cues. Bertolt Brecht, whose Berliner Ensemble had shaken up British theatre when it visited in 1957, was referred to when the production 'quoted' *Mother Courage* by putting a lookalike cart onstage for the Jack Cade rebellion. Famously, between rehearsals, Hall read the proofs of Polish critic Jan Kott's *Shakespeare Our Contemporary* and, in interviews, talked about the 'pressure of now', the need to make Shakespeare speak directly to the present moment. Hall won his war: the subsidy was restored, and

[4]

the National Theatre, established shortly afterwards, has rarely tackled Shakespeare's history plays – and has never attempted to stage the *Henry VI* plays.

From these beginnings, the performance history of the plays has been shaped by institutional politics and changing perceptions of nationhood. For history plays lacking a history, this has been a remarkable realignment. When Hands started directing the plays in 1977 (a 'reward' for bringing the RSC through its latest financial crisis), his rejection of directorial theatre was a big statement about not making a big statement. In some respects, the rehearsal process was more important than the performance, some accounts making rehearsals sound almost as if a kind of communion with Shakespeare was going on. A decade later, suffering yet another crisis, the RSC returned again to the *Henry VI* plays. This time, Adrian Noble stressed that the plays were written by a young man – just the right material, then, for the RSC, currently in the process of reinventing itself as a young company. Going back to the beginning of Shakespeare's writing career was also a way of returning to the origins of the company to re-imagine both 'histories' – of the playwright, of the RSC – to serve the needs of a new decade. Noble's trilogy, titled *The Plantagenets*, was, like the RSC's earlier *Wars*, a state-of-the-nation production, a wide-ranging consideration of England after a decade of Thatcherism. But, as we shall see in Chapter VII, it was also a self-mythologising production, with both company and audiences aware that a statement was being made about the future of the RSC, a future that, as in 1962, was in doubt. In performance, *The Plantagenets'* high production values looked back to the glory days of the Shakespeare Memorial Theatre rather than to the political theatre of the 1960s; but, as we shall see in Chapter VII, this interplay of tradition and nationhood was much more complex than it first seemed. Thereafter, to celebrate the millennium, the RSC returned again to Shakespeare's history plays, this time staging all eight 'Wars of the Roses' plays from *Richard II* to *Richard III* in full texts. This time, however, the issue of national culture was approached somewhat differently. Rather than making a great statement by assigning the double tetralogy to one directorial vision, Noble (as Artistic Director, in overall charge of the season) created what was in effect a devolved artistic structure, assigning different directors to each play. He gave the *Henry VI* trilogy to Michael Boyd – who directed the plays as a nightmare vision of a Balkanised England on the brink

[5]

of absolute chaos. Boyd's was not so much a 'state of the nation' production as a meditation on the meaning of nationhood in a world caught between the forces of globalisation and local fragmentation. Rather than insist on one vision of the past, Boyd challenged his audiences to acknowledge the strange histories onstage as their own national story.

These five productions, each by an Artistic Director (or former Artistic Director) of the RSC/SMT, frame our stage history, making the question of England, of nationhood and the role of cultural institutions which aspire to be thought of as 'national', a central preoccupation.

Henry VI's strange histories

Three other productions, each by talented directors who are known for oppositional or anti-institutional work (and who are known, too, for not, or not yet, aspiring to run the RSC) are also studied in detail. The work of Jane Howell (1981–83), Michael Bogdanov (1987–89) and Katie Mitchell (1994–95) constitutes a counter-history of the plays in performance, but one that is nevertheless informed by an urgent interrogation of nationhood and culture. Howell, directing the trilogy for the BBC, was as alive as Hall and Noble were to the plays' power to speak to contemporary conflicts, but her productions also made visual references to a national performance culture in which the BBC played a key role, including state funerals and royal weddings. Her directorial vision picked apart the politics of such representations and contrasted them with vivid images of disorder, of the nation breaking apart. Michael Bogdanov's *House of Lancaster* and *House of York* (an adaptation in two parts) was part of an ambitious history play cycle, *The Wars of the Roses*, that he used to launch his alternative national theatre, the English Shakespeare Company. Bogdanov turned the histories into contemporary political satires, irreverently savaging Thatcherism. But he and his company had a broader ambition to reconstitute an alternative sense of nationhood, one rooted in and representing England's regional diversity. In short, he and the English Shakespeare Company challenged directly the RSC's and the NT's claims to be the 'true' national theatre by offering a different model of what such a theatre could be. Bogdanov's vision was a touring repertory theatre, a theatre that would take Shakespeare *to* the nation, not with tuppenceha'penny scaled-down shows but with ambitious productions that would talk to audiences in their own voices, in their own regional accents, not in the plummy accents of the British ruling classes – or (most) drama school graduates.

Although oppositional, neither Howell nor Bogdanov departed from the strong, political line first developed by Hall and Barton. Although more about war than about power politics (as Hall and Barton had conceived them), these 1980s *Henry VI*s were yet mobilised to perform a materialist history, concerned only with human actions and class politics. In the 1950s, Jackson and Seale enjoyed exploiting the theatrical possibilities of scenes involving witches and demons. But after Hall, directors were reluctant to present history as anything other than a massive political force. The designer for the RSC's *Wars*, John Bury, set the plays in a world of steel, with massive doors symbolising the dominance of history over men, much like Jan Kott's idea of the 'grand staircase of history'. But evocative as it is, Kott's influential reading of Shakespeare's history plays concentrated too much on materialist politics and conveniently sidestepped Shakespeare's equally fascinating use of madness, demons and prophecies to decentre such an absolute notion of history.

Howell and Bogdanov inherited the legacy of Hall and Barton's Kottian interpretation of Shakespearean history. The supernatural, when it did appear, was nothing more than a fraudulent device by which either the powerful kept control or popular entertainers pulled the wool over their masters' eyes. As an example, consider for a moment the problems of staging the spirit scene from *Part Two*, when the ambitious Duchess of Gloucester visits the conjuror Bolingbroke and the witch Margery Jourdain. As Shakespeare wrote the scene, Jourdain and Bolingbroke summon a spirit who gives to them a series of cryptic prophecies, most of which come true later in the play. If the future is foreseeable and there really are spirits capable of seeing it, then history is inevitable and inescapable. Indeed, the moral of any prophecy is that you cannot escape the future. In this play, Suffolk believes he is invincible on land because he 'knows' he will die by water, but in the end he is killed on land, on a beach – by a man called Walter. No 'modern' history would include such a scene, or if it did, its tone would be deliberately ironic. But in Shakespeare's order of things, history can be providential, mysterious: history is only one aspect of a reality that reaches well beyond the human into the religious and the supernatural. Not far beneath the surface of Shakespeare's apparently 'modern' political dramas – dramas that, in Hall's terms, were all about the 'pressure of now' – are the traces of late medieval morality plays, *The Castle of Persever-ance*, for one, in which Mankind's story is set at the centre of an arena with devils and angels looking on. To an Elizabethan audi-ence, this is too obvious even to note; for a modern audience, the presence of the supernatural is an uncomfortable anachronism. Pursuing a much more materialist representation of history than they could encounter in Shakespeare's text, Bogdanov and Howell transformed the spirit scene into a fairground con-trick. Bogdanov cast Jourdain as a Gypsy mystic with a crystal ball. Howell went even further by showing us the conjurors preparing the stage for their show and placing a sound-effects man out of the Duchess's view. No real spirits appeared in either; the whole thing was just an elaborate ruse.

In 1988, Noble's *The Plantagenets* re-examined what Barbara Hodgdon helpfully calls 'Shakespeare-history' by making the supernatural a real part of the playworld. Consequently, Boling-broke and Jourdain conjured a real spirit, and there was no ambi-guity about Joan at all: she gabbled Latin incantations as she burnt at the stake. Hell apparently rumbled beneath the stage, occasion-ally spilling out in the form of pantomime smoke. In 1994, Katie Mitchell brought the supernatural on to centre stage in her version of *Part Three* – interestingly, the only play in the trilogy which does not bring spirits onstage. Mitchell invented one, an angel of death leading the souls of the fallen off the stage. Yet Mitch-ell's elegiac jeremiad for a lost England was no less political than Hall's, Howell's or Bogdanov's work. In fact, Mitchell's is the most topical production here discussed, being conceived as a response to the civil wars then taking place in Bosnia, as well as issuing an indictment to Britain for failing to intervene. Rather than presenting history in Kottian terms, Mitchell turned to another Polish artist and writer, Wlodzimierz Staniewski. His company, the Gardzienice Theatre Association, recovers disappearing or lost folk culture in Eastern Europe. By taking inspiration from them, Mitchell in effect repositioned *Part Three* as a folk play about the tragedy of civil war. Rather than celebrating or critiquing England, this production mourned it; the characters who spoke to the audi-ence did so as voices of the dead.

Although very different, Michael Boyd's strange, haunted

England in his *Henry VI* trilogy sustained Noble's and Mitchell's varying reinterpretations of Shakespeare's England in crisis. This, to date the most recent staging of the full texts, made a decisive break with the materialist interpretative tradition started by the RSC's *Wars*, a tradition that Boyd called a burden. (Looking back, reviewers of Boyd's trilogy did not draw by-now standard comparisons with Hall but rather linked Boyd to another luminary of the 1960s RSC, Peter Brook – a link Boyd himself played down.) Staged in the Swan, an annexe to the Royal Shakespeare Theatre that is much more flexible and intimate than the main stage, the trilogy was performed with insistent, almost brazen, theatricality. Actors ran up and down ladders, swung from the ceiling, hung from trapezes, played from the back of the stalls – and even from outside the auditorium. Just as he refused to accept the conventional limitations of the performance space, Boyd also rejected the strait-jacket of history. Controversially at the time, his Henry VI was played by David Oyelowo, a black actor (the first to play an English king at the RSC). But stranger still, ghosts crowded this stage, stalking England as it fell further towards anarchy, and usurpers were driven not just by ambition but by transgressive sexual obsessions.

What accounts for this seemingly untimely interest in the darker corners of the *Henry VI* plays? Why this turn away from power politics to spectres, haunting, magic and mourning? The return of the apparition to the history plays is contemporaneous with the postmodern response to the end of the Cold War in the late 1980s, when Francis Fukuyama went so far as to declare the 'end of history'. With the collapse of communism and, earlier in the century, fascism, the great ideological projects of the twentieth century – those that defined the goals of history in Western states – were at an end. The commodified cultures of the leading democracies in the world were, as Fredric Jameson complained, characterised by a 'waning of historicity', where 'historicity' is something different than 'history'. 'History', as we know, has thrived as a commodity: in historical films, novels, television serials, reality television and, especially, heritage. The recent renaissance in the British theatre is a reflection of its new position in the heritage economy, one which Adrian Noble was shrewd enough to anticipate when he directed *The Plantagenets*. But 'historicity' implies a sense of historical destiny, of where things are headed, as well as where we come from. Jameson's prophetic comment has now been borne out: as a commodity, 'history' is a series of fictions which do not address either the present or the future. As ideologies have waned, and as the *grands recits* of the Enlightenment have given way to the localised stories of postmodernism, those who do not wish to call a premature end to history have revisited notions of the future, of prophecy and of the 'spirit' of history. Among them, Jacques Derrida, roundly rejecting Fukuyama's position, introduced his political philosophy by outlining what he called the 'logic of the spectre' or hauntology. Jean Baudrillard, the arch-philosopher of the postmodern, sees the modern representational economy as one based on the simulacrum, itself a kind of ghost, a present absence. Ghosts, mourning, prophecies and hauntologies have become surprisingly important to modern historicity. As John Joughin puts it, 'these days, of course, haunting and history are never that far removed' (Joughin 17).

The question of nationhood following the end of the Cold War is now more commonly framed by discussions of globalisation and localisation, for the representation of England has moved beyond questions of post-imperialism, a fact reflected in the much more European sensibilities of Mitchell's and Boyd's work. Depicting a Balkanised England, a move that situated her work in a post-Cold-War context where the break-up of Yugoslavia was one of the signs heralding the end of history, Mitchell sounded the resonance between England's forgotten history and the then-current plight of the citizens of Sarajevo. Staging 'England' in the wake of devolution, when the breaking-up of Great Britain was inviting questions about national identity, Boyd saw a nation of ghosts. England was strange and dark, as if, brought into the light, 'This England' flinched and scurried back to the shadows, still haunted by its past transgressions.

Other national cultures

The productions which we will focus on have also had a global reach, influencing other productions around the world. The Birmingham Rep productions influenced the BBC serial *An Age of Kings* (see Chapters II and V), which was sold widely abroad; and the RSC and the BBC teamed up to broadcast *The Wars of the Roses* as a television production in 1965, with the script published soon after. Many people around the world, especially in America, will know the plays best from Jane Howell's 1983 BBC televisation (see

[10]

Chapter V); and for a lot of people in Asia, Australia and America the only time they have ever had the opportunity to see *Henry VI* onstage is when the English Shakespeare Company toured them in these regions in the late 1980s (see Chapter VI). Even the RSC's 1988 *The Plantagenets* (which never toured beyond England) gave rise to several American imitations following the publication of its script (see Chapter VII); Katie Mitchell's *Henry VI – The Battle for the Throne* (see Chapter VIII) toured Europe, North America and South America in 1994–95; and in 2001, Michael Boyd's full-text first tetralogy was taken on a brief American tour. These productions' international dissemination has made them central to the creation of a performance vocabulary for the *Henry VI* plays. In both their national and international afterlives, the statement that began this chapter remains true: the *Henry VI*s *are* fully implicated in notions of Englishness, even though – in fact, *because* – they present England in defeat.

One problem is that the plays' Englishness is partly defined in sharp contrast to the French, who are outrageously depicted as waspish, corrupt, devil-worshipping, self-serving fornicators. Naturally, the plays have had a difficult life in France, where they are rarely staged. Jean-Louis Barrault was mystified when audiences stayed away from his four-hour-long adaptation of *Henry VI*. He felt the production represented 'the best I am capable of doing' but from audiences and critics, he says, 'all we got was insults' (Barrault 299–300). In *Kings ou les adieux à Shakespeare* (Kings, or goodbye to Shakespeare), Denis Llorca played down Shakespeare's nationalism and focused instead on the commons to create what Jean-Michel Déprats describes as 'a ritualistic enactment, a poetic recreation about fleeting time' rather than 'a historical spectacle' (Déprats 235–6). Although Llorca had some success, *Henry VI* remains an unwelcome stranger to the French stage. Only two countries have seen past Shakespeare's apparent xenophobia to create rival traditions of performance: Germany and the United States.

Several German directors in the nineteenth and early twentieth century saw similarities between their own national situation and that depicted in the *Henry VI* plays. The composer Richard Wagner, one of the cultural prophets of German nationalism, was a *Henry VI* enthusiast. He would patiently read the play out loud to his wife Cosima, who wrote of his one-man performances, 'In the face of that, mortals can only be silent.' Cosima then criticised the 'buffoon' who would adapt the plays into two parts, and demanded to know, 'what is the point of genius when after centuries it can command no respect, and its manifestations become the prey of charlatans' (Wagner 47–8). The buffoon she referred to was Franz Dingelstedt, a Wagnerian director who had reduced the *Henry VI* plays to two parts and staged them along with Shakespeare's history plays in Weimar in 1864. Like the Wagners, Dingelstedt saw a potent analogy between the Wars of the Roses as depicted by Shakespeare and Germany's struggle to develop its own national culture. In a small way, then, the *Henry VI* plays found themselves part of the weft-and-weave of Germany's nascent nationalism and it has been claimed that the plays were staged repeatedly through the nineteenth century.

The rise and fall of the Nazi Party transformed the Wagnerian impulse in Germany. Bertolt Brecht cast Richard Gloucester as an Adolf Hitler figure in his play *The Resistable Rise of Arturo Ui*, and in 1967 one of Brecht's protégés, Peter Palitzsch of the Berliner Ensemble, staged *Henry VI* (*Der Rosenkrieg*) as a political fable about the destructive nature of power politics. The set was dominated by a pile of skeletons piled on broken wheels at the back of the stage. They could have represented the remains of a charnel house in a German concentration camp or the aftermath of the bombing of Dresden; either way, they were a strikingly morbid and difficult image for post-fascist German audiences. Heroism was undercut at every turn. In his excellent account of the production, Christopher Innes describes one episode where a single centre section opened to show Talbot and his son riding hobbyhorses towards the audience and shouting, 'To rescue England we give our lives.' The panel closed and then reopened to show Talbot still riding but now carrying his wounded son and saying, 'together we will tear the Fury, war, from her throne, hack her to pieces'. The panel closed and then opened again to show Talbot on foot, wounded and still carrying the body of his son. Then, in a final image, the panel closed and opened to reveal a 'field of death' (Innes 145). This and other such scenes were acutely resonant for an audience that lived still with the memory of war and defeat; Wagner would have been horrified at the liberties taken with Shakespeare's text, but he apparently cared little for Talbot's final scenes which he thought 'monotonous and sentimental' (Wagner 998).[1]

While Germany has recognised itself in Shakespeare's England, the United States has avoided questions of national culture altogether in many of its productions.[2] One production which highlights the ambivalent presence of the *Henry VI* plays in American culture is the fictional one attended by the President in the television series *The West Wing*. In this parallel universe, *Henry VI* is not only on Broadway, it is also a musical. Although a very traditional performance, some of its scenes (such as Margaret killing York) cause the President to reflect on the nature of political violence as he ponders his order to assassinate a diplomat. Outside the theatre one of the President's bodyguards is shot down in a drugstore and as he falls he knocks over a display of red and white roses which tumble on to the floor. *The West Wing* made its point through such ironic juxtaposition and selective quoting from *Henry VI*, but not from the performance watched by the President, which was an insipid, stodgy costume drama. A similar ambivalence attended *The Wars of the Roses*, a 1970 production in Central Park for the New York Shakespeare Festival. Before the performance, the Artistic Director, Joseph Papp, addressed the audience directly and, reflecting on the company's own financial crisis and its political tussles with the Mayor of New York, drew parallels with Shakespeare's depiction of political factionalism. However, those expecting a 'reflection of the current political climate' were, says one critic, severely disappointed by the 'undaunted conservatism' of the performance which followed (Hirsch 477).

Henry VI has been successfully played by American companies who put theatrical daring before textual authenticity. In the best of them, the audience's lack of historical identification with the divided England of *Henry VI* has not been a failing but an organising idea which has transformed the plays into absurdist tragicomedies. Of note here is the production of *Part Two* staged by Birnam Wood, a Californian Gypsy company who, in the 1970s, specialised in performing obscure works in unexpected locations. Their 1975 adaptation (which was idiosyncratically billed as *Part One*) was taken by some as 'a campy comment on Elizabethan horror chronicles' for it was full of ludicrous exaggerations: for example, Stephen Booth remembers, each time a character was killed they were wheeled offstage, their expressions frozen. The actors performed like puppets and, in the middle of a key climactic scene, the action stopped, and an actor abruptly sent the audience home (Booth 104). More recently, Karin Coonrod made up for the New York Shakespeare Festival's disappointing *Henry VI* with a lively production at the Joseph Papp Public Theater in 1997.

Coonrod staged history as a circus: for Joan's execution, Joan was represented by a paper cut-out burning in a cylinder; Henry often sat on a swing suspended in mid-air; wooden chairs were lowered from the ceiling on long red ribbons; bearded ladies attended the French King. According to Nina da Vinci Nichols, these wild theatrics represented 'the eclipse of our own historical consciousness' (Nichols 12).

However, in productions like this Shakespeare's text is usually treated irreverently, as if staging *Henry VI* in a modern theatre is itself part of the joke. Another example is Michael Khan's 1996 adaptation which cut the three plays into one fast-moving performance; in response, one reviewer wrote, 'I'm not sure a modern American audience actually wants any more of these plays than we get here' (*The Washington Post* 5 September 1996).

Viewed from the wider stage of Shakespeare's global revivals, the *Henry VI* plays remain Shakespeare's most English plays in part because they are the least appropriated by other nations. In Britain, the rediscovery of the *Henry VI* plays has seen them placed at the heart of British Shakespearean performance. Their heyday is indebted to the passing fashion for Brechtian-style epic theatre, the same fashion that the large 1970s London theatres (the Olivier, the Barbican) were designed to accommodate. Their recent history owes more to postmodern preoccupations with fragmentation, marginality and the limitations of reason. But whether they are staged as rational plays about politics or haunted plays about the terror of fractured identity, the persistence of these, Shakespeare's most Elizabethan plays, on the modern stage is remarkable. This is the story we wish to tell.

CHAPTER 1

Playing *Henry VI* in the early modern period

A question that dogs the *Henry VI* plays is whether they are best approached as a trilogy or as three single plays. Their textual history offers few clues. They were first published by the printer Thomas Millington in 1594, although he printed only versions of *Part Two* and *Part Three* and with different, cumbersome titles: *The First Part of the Contention of the two Famous Houses of York and Lancaster with the Death of Good Duke Humphrey* and *The True Tragedy of Richard, Duke of York, and the Death of Good King Henry the Sixth, with the whole contention between the houses Lancaster and York*. *Part One* was not published until 1623 (seven years after Shakespeare's death), when it was presented with its now traditional title with fuller versions of the other two parts, now renamed to construct a sequence. In recent years, textual criticism has tended to stress the differences among the three plays and there is currently a prevailing view that *Part One* was written last. Until recently, a single editor would oversee the publication of all three plays in a series (as Norman Sanders did for Penguin, Michael Hattaway for Cambridge); however, new series editors for Arden and Oxford have appointed different editors for each play. In the Oxford Complete Works it is not even possible to read the plays as a trilogy, for *Part One* comes after the other two plays, to which the original Quarto titles have been restored. But if textual critics are doing all that they can to interrupt trilogy-thinking, theatre has gone the other way. In the theatre, a mixture of artistic and logistical priorities has created a tradition of performing the plays together even if, by doing so, much has to be cut or rearranged to fit the trilogy into a more commercially viable two- or one-play show. As a way in to talking about the little we can say about the plays' first performance, maybe it is time to approach the question of their origin from a theatrical rather than a textual perspective.

So used are we to thinking of the *Henry VI* plays as inferior examples of Shakespeare at the start of his career that we over-look just what a bold (even preposterous) enterprise it was to stage them in the early 1590s. Shakespeare's many biographers skirt over what an audacious and unprecedented project it must have been and instead linger on the plays as 'crude' works by the 'very young Shakespeare' (Bloom 43), his 'first dramatic job' (Chambers *Elizabethan Stage* vol. 2, 129–30), at best a 'laboratory' in which Shakespeare experimented with ideas he would later develop in his 'mature' works (Bloom 50). Some like the plays: Park Honan is impressed with Shakespeare's attempt to 'respond imagina-tively to history's chaos' (Honan 139) and Peter Thomson thinks them masterpieces of Elizabethan epic theatre (Thomson 60); but neither asks why an untested dramatist was put to work on the most ambitious theatre work yet seen on the London stage.

To our knowledge, there was only one precedent for a *trilogy* of history plays, and this was Thomas Legge's *Richardus Tertius*. Legge was twice Vice-Chancellor of Cambridge University and it was there in 1579, in St John's College hall, that he staged his remarkable dramatisation of the reign of Richard III over three successive evenings. Even though written in Latin, the play was well known in the 1590s: Shakespeare used it as a source for his own Richard III play (Richard's seduction of Lady Anne is based on Legge), and in 1598 Francis Meres (himself a Cambridge man) praised 'Doctor Legge' alongside Shakespeare as 'our best for tragedy' in his commonplace book *Palladis Tamia: Wit's Treasury*. It is highly probable that in the audience for *Richardus Tertius* in 1579 was the future playwright Robert Greene, who graduated from St John's College the following year and was, like Legge, a Norwich man. Many years later he saw *Henry VI*: we know this because he quotes from it in his posthumously published *A Groatsworth of Wit*, where he calls Shakespeare a 'tiger's heart wrapp'd in a play-er's hide' (which is based on York's insult to Margaret in *Part Three*) and moans that Shakespeare was an 'upstart crow ... beautified in our feathers'. No doubt Greene was annoyed that Shakespeare, an uneducated actor, was having more success than he; but perhaps Greene was also remembering Legge's Latin *Richardus Tertius* and criticising Shakespeare for trying to match that achievement with a three-part *Henry VI* written in English. For, if nothing else, Shakespeare brought to the London stage something that had been available before only to an educated university audience. It is surely more than a coincidence that Shakespeare chose as subject matter for his trilogy the events which led up to those Legge had already dramatised.

Whether or not the plays were written as a trilogy, from the beginning they have been unusually fit for adaptation. Their episodic structure can indeed be seen as a structure based on disorder and fragmentation, but this may be to put too modern a spin on them. In truth, Shakespeare was writing for a theatrical culture that demanded flexibility. The plays, like all of Shakespeare's, were performed only a few times (by our standards) to an audience that was relatively consistent and expected constant novelty. The repertory system familiar to us now did not exist then: plays were staged for one day and only revived if popular, and perhaps then on only a few occasions. Yet we know of – or rather, we can infer – at least one other kind of performance: context: that of the provincial tour.

There is no doubt that, at the very least, versions of *Part Two* and *Part Three* were toured during the mid-1590s, both probably by a company called Pembroke's Men. Some time in 1595, the company returned to London, exhausted and broke. To repair their finances, they sold their scripts to Thomas Millington, among them *The First Part of the Contention* and, in all likelihood, *Richard, Duke of York*. Although there are important differences between these plays and the ones published in Shakespeare's first Complete Works in 1623 (usually regarded as authoritative), they are clearly versions of the same plays: slimmed down perhaps, an earlier incarnation maybe, possibly texts written for the logistical realities of touring. Millington published little else in the drama area, but he made the most of his *Henry VI*s. The plays were reprinted several times over the next twenty-odd years, sometimes together to comprise a cycle.

From the plays' early printing history, account statements and contemporary allusions, we can infer one thing: the plays' texts were as malleable then, as open to adaptation, reduction and rewriting, as they have been ever since. We should bear in mind that the insistence on playing full or near-full texts of any Shakespeare play is a relatively modern one – even in the early twentieth century, it was still very common for companies to perform adaptations of many of his plays. But the *Henry VI* plays are the only ones to continue this tradition; in fact if anything, the practice has accelerated. There is no standard adaptation, no one model that solves the plays' logistical and (arguably) artistic problems. Instead, it is up to each director to assemble a text, to decide how much rewriting needs to be done, whether to conflate the plays to two, or to one, or even to inflate the cycle by adding *Richard III* to make a tetralogy. Neither theatre nor textual history clarifies whether the plays are understood best as a series of single works, or a trilogy, or a tetralogy. What this exercise shows is that, from the beginning, the texts have been unusually mobile, their episodic structure making them peculiarly open to reinvention, more so than any other Shakespeare play. Shakespeare wrote a theatre piece, not a work of literature, and he wrote it to be flexible and portable. They are single plays, they are a trilogy, they can be a duology, part of a heptalogy, all three plays can be done as one. Companies can choose the stories they want to tell, conceal others for economy, expand parts where appropriate, and add their own verse to help the story along. The *Henry VI* plays were written to be adapted.

Adapting *Henry VI*

What's in a name? Shakespeare does not seem to have given much thought to titles: for him they were functional and descriptive, and if they weren't, they said so from the outset: as you like it, what you will, much ado about nothing. Those plays which we now know by short if unexciting titles have been abbreviated over time, which has sensibly squeezed *The History of King Lear etc.* into the much more pithy *King Lear. Henry VI* breaks all the rules. Early editions do not agree on their titles at all: in 1592–95, they were *Harey the vj, The First part of the Contention* and *The true tragedie of Richard Duke of Yorke.* By 1623, these same plays (albeit with extra material and some minor editorial differences) were republished as *The First Part of King Henry the Sixth, The Second Part of King Henry the Sixth* and *The Third Part of King Henry the Sixth.* Upon their revival in the Restoration, they were billed as *The Miseries of Civil War* and *Henry VI* and then appeared intermittently, sometimes as *Humphrey, Duke of Glocester*, sometimes as *Richard, Duke of York.* A brief vogue for the Folio titles took hold towards the end of the nineteenth century and survived two world wars; but with the RSC's *The Wars of the Roses*, titles became once again fair game, and since then we have had variations on the Roses theme: *Wars of the Roses, The Red Rose and the White*, even *Rose Rage.*

Some titles have gone in the other direction and tried to create a Saturday morning, serial film feel, perhaps in homage to the often unacknowledged pleasure of watching episodic, cliff-hanger drama: hence we've had *The Battle for the Throne*, *The Wax King*, *Age of Kings*, *The Edged Sword*, *England's Fall*. On occasion, directors have tried to revive a true Shakespearean spirit and make the title as bland and informative as possible: *The Plantagenets*, *Talbot and Joan*, *Edward IV, His Death*. Few plays boast such a range of names, yet each one says curiously little about the plays themselves. Of these, perhaps only the irreverent *Rose Rage* and the reactionary *The Miseries of Civil War* describe a thematic idea that is central to the performance: the rest wish only to make more attractive plays which for most of their theatrical life have been unknown to both players and their audiences. Yet, in their departure from tradition, these newly minted titles advertise a kind of ownership over the *Henry VI* plays, which are open to reinvention with each performance. In many respects the story that this book tells is one of a constant negotiation between tradition and reinvention, between the iconicity of Shakespeare and the exuberant creativity that is not only permissible with *Henry VI* but apparently demanded of it by a legacy of textual uncertainty and theatrical opportunity.

Part One starts with the traditional ending for a tragedy (a funeral march, as in *Hamlet*) and closes with the traditional ending for a comedy, a wedding. This inversion is attractive to many critics but not so to the theatre, which has only infrequently revived it as a stand-alone play despite the *dramatis personae* including, as a central figure, the one historical character likely to be recognisable to modern audiences: Joan of Arc. Joan is even something of a liability, as Shakespeare seems to leave little doubt that Joan's real power does not derive from either a Holy Spirit or self-determination, but from the devils that desert her at the end of the play. Shakespeare adds a vicious end to her story by portraying Joan attempting to evade execution by claiming that she is not a holy maid but 'with child'. So horrified was George Bernard Shaw that he wrote his own version of the Joan of Arc story, and even in the early twentieth century directors such as Robert Atkins at the Old Vic felt compelled to rewrite Joan's part to introduce more ambiguity into her portrayal. More recently, an adaptation at Ashland in 2004 called *Talbot and Joan* began with a new scene depicting the moment that Joan became infused with divine fervour. For the rest of the production she was followed by a silent female figure dressed in blue, who was, it seemed, some sort of angel there to remind the audience that, whatever the text says, Joan is one of the good guys. A virtuous Joan is also an anaemic and theatrically dull Joan, at least in the play that Shakespeare wrote, so many directors have simply chosen to avoid this play altogether or to cherry-pick those scenes which are important to establish the key narratives of the next two plays: York and Somerset squabbling in the rose garden, Henry's weak attempt to control his feuding uncles in court, York's visit to Mortimer, Suffolk capturing Margaret on the battlefield. Adaptations often condense Talbot and Joan's story so that it has run its course by the first interval. Talbot can be a more interesting figure than Joan: his early bombast and derring-do battle scenes were a gift to Victorians and Edwardians who saw the play as nothing less than a patriotic romp. However, more recent and more sceptical productions have got a lot out of Talbot's sombre reflections on the value of heroism in his final scene which chime well with postwar sentiments about the horrors of war and post-Vietnam cynicism about the exploitation of war for political purposes.

Although often thought to be the best of the trilogy, *Part Two* is rarely seen on the stage these days. It suffers particularly in adaptations, which usually divide it at the end of Act III. The political intrigues surrounding the fall of Gloucester are made the final act of plays which are, in effect, extended versions of *Part One*, with battles conflated to make the running time shorter. The riots of Act IV and the Battle of St Albans in Act V are likewise made a prologue to an extended *Part Three*; Cade's scenes are reduced to one or two episodes and the Battle of St Albans is combined with the Battle of Tewkesbury (the first battle in *Part Three*). A typical sequence of events is that, following Cade's uprising, York immediately takes the throne, and there follows a long battle which includes the events of both St Albans and Tewkesbury, ending with York's death. Other key scenes frequently hit the cutting-room floor. Suffolk's death at the hands of pirates rarely gets staged even in full-text productions, coming as it does at an awkward place between the climactic death of Winchester and the start of the Cade scenes. Instead, Suffolk has met many different fates. Sometimes he has been ambushed by murderers at the edge of the stage or lynched by a mob of peasants. The pirate captain has been reinvented as both a swaggering naval aristocrat and the zombie of John Talbot. On occasion, the death has been cut altogether and one has learned of it only when Margaret cradles Suffolk's head in her lap. But it is the Duke of York who steals the play, literally, and in two-part adaptations he is often more obviously the central character of the trilogy.

Part Two is also a significant play because it is arguably the only one of the histories that gives a substantial voice to the presence of ordinary people in history and their ability to mobilise themselves in sufficient numbers – Shakespeare's stage directions actually call for 'infinite numbers' – to disrupt the conventional notion of history as the story of kings and nobles. The commoners first appear as petitioners, creeping through a gap in the fences of enclosed lands, almost as if stealing themselves into the pages of history. Suffolk and Margaret tear their petitions; but one, an apprentice, presents Suffolk with a political opportunity to undermine his rivals at court. The apprentice, Peter Thump, is a comic character, as can be surmised from his name, which would not be out of place in a Peter Quince production. The whole scene is set for comedy, yet it ends in a furious murder that visibly upsets the court, who quickly exit. Thump is often one of the first scenes to be cut from adaptations, but without it, the ensuing riot is little more than an unannounced episode of black comedy. From this point in the play, the lower orders become increasingly vocal, volatile and finally violent. They throng at the doors when Gloucester is killed, they are whipped up by York's stooge, the maverick Jack Cade, and they dominate the stage for an act in a bloody carnival of misrule before being finally shackled again. Whether Cade should be played as an out-and-out monster or a revolutionary who marshals genuine grievances has differed not only from production to production but from era to era. In the 1960s and 1970s, for example, a strong interest in countercultural politics cast Cade as almost a Che Guevara figure, his allegiances to York played down. In the 1980s, he was a neo-fascist, a football hooligan; in the millennium, he was a demonic comedian, an anarchist from hell.

Few companies will not be tempted to revel in and even embellish the comedy of the Cade scenes. Rarely cut is the knockabout violence of the scene in which Cade declares death to anyone who calls him Jack Cade. Just then, a messenger runs onstage calling for him, only to meet his death. Played right, the scene is funny, and of course it is funny only because, like all comedy, there is an implicit, knowing relation with the audience, as if the actor playing Cade were winking to them to say 'you know this is not real, it is only play'. The messenger's death is flippant. If staged with any realism, Cade's barbarity would be repulsive, but as comedy its effect is to diminish the importance of Cade and his band of rebels. The danger, and the accusation often levelled at Shakespeare, is that, by playing Cade in this way, he is reduced to a cartoonish, Tom-and-Jerry-like clown, the common people likewise treated as simpletons and fools. In the text, Cade is introduced as an indomitable soldier in York's Irish campaigns and, in lines often cut, he expresses his own sense of pity. Shakespeare's Cade is not inhuman, he is moved by Lord Saye's desperate attempts to plead for his life. When Cade is abandoned by his people and makes his way to an enclosed garden, much like the one in which the commoners first made their entrance, he loses his fight only through starvation. There is clearly room for a Cade who is complex, who is at once a violent butcher, a political manipulator and a hero. This Cade has rarely seen the stage.

Part Three opens with a striking theatrical image. The Yorkists break down the doors of Parliament and invade the stage. York avoids sitting on the throne for a while, but Warwick finally persuades him. Henry enters with his men to find the usurper already seated on the throne. What follows is a heated debate about historical legitimacy, but history fails to give one or the other the throne. It is difficult today to recapture the enormous symbolic power of the throne and, for an Elizabethan audience, the moment when York takes the throne is a momentous transgression. Ordinary Londoners entering the city were used to seeing the thirty-or-so heads of traitors displayed on pikes on the city walls. Even to think about usurpation was dangerous: government spies lurked in inns and playhouses, seeking out sedition. Religious fanatics, Catholic and Puritan, threatened the stability of the state. York was no religious zealot but, with his 'mad flaw', he was a fanatic. Many adaptations botch this moment, especially if, as discussed above, the end of *Part Two* and the beginning of *Part Three* are conflated. Often York is already on the throne, surrounded on both sides by his sons and his army. This is to miss the point. Shakespeare deliberately keeps York back, intentionally creates suspense over whether York will or will not take the final step, enact the decisive transgression, intervene in history and displace Henry. It is crucial that the Yorkists break on to the stage, and crucial too that York should dally, aware himself of the enormity of the act he is about to commit. It could lead to his death. It does.

York's death is an early climax. Theatrically, it is both bold and unforgettable. York, already exhausted, is caught on the edge of battle by Margaret and Clifford. Before killing him, the pair taunt him, punish him for his pretensions to the throne. Now no longer on the throne, York is placed on a molehill, elevated only to be mocked. Then Margaret makes a paper crown, puts it on his head, and finally wipes his face with a napkin dipped in the blood of young Rutland, York's son, killed by Clifford in a previous scene. The scene's emotive power derives from its different levels of humiliation: Margaret, the mother turned murderer; York, the father turned usurper. Each is mocked by the other. The scene made such an impression on Robert Greene that he quoted from it, using Shakespeare's own language to humiliate him. It also made an impression on Shakespeare, because he describes it three times in *Richard III*. Challenging Margaret, Richard says,

> The curse my noble father laid on thee,
> When thou didst crown his warlike brows with paper
> And with thy scorns drew'st rivers from his eyes,
> And then, to dry them, gav'st the duke a clout
> Steep'd in the faultless blood of pretty Rutland –
> His curses, then from bitterness of soul
> Denounced against thee, are all fall'n upon thee (I.iii.171–7)

Here, perhaps, are echoes of real performance which give us a taste of what was played at the Rose playhouse in 1592. If so, York began proud and 'warlike'; he was consumed by tears, 'rivers from his eyes', and then, in his final long invective, bitterly cursed Margaret. We do not often see such histrionics from York now. He is more restrained: he may catch a sob, but his final speech is steel, his passion gathered for one last blast. His 'rivers' are not the tears of a man reduced to nothing, unable to understand the nature of a woman-sadist. Richard alludes to the murder of his brother and father two more times in *Richard III*, as if Shakespeare was delib-erately invoking for audiences their favourite moment from the previous play. Today, directors are more likely to highlight fore-shadowings of *Richard III* in the *Henry VI* plays to engage audi-ence interest; but, when writing *Richard III*, Shakespeare needed to capitalise on his earlier success.

Apart from Margaret, York is the most interesting part, perhaps the reason that in its first printing the play was called *The True Tragedy of Richard, Duke of York*, even though the titular character dies so early. In the eighteenth century, Edmund Kean employed John Herman Merivale to write a play called *Richard, Duke of York* based on materials culled from the *Henry VI* plays, with this scene the climax. That it should come so early tells us something about Shakespeare's conception of the play: it is episodic, its actorly moments aria-like so that, though the tragedian playing York might complain about his lack of lines, he had his moment on the stage which, if played right, few in the audience would ever forget. The play is full of such arias. Warwick's change of allegiance and lonely death; Margaret's desperation after her son is murdered; Henry VI watching with horror as a soldier drags a body off the field to loot it and discovers it to be his son, and another does the same to find his father.

If the Duke of York is a short-lived character in his own play, this is possibly because Shakespeare had found another character who offered more opportunities to entertain and terrify audiences: this was Richard Gloucester, the son of York, and later Richard III. There are many for whom the *Henry VI* plays are of interest only as 'prequels' to *Richard III*; many more do not realise that the bunch-backed toad appeared in plays other than the one that bears his name. For generations of theatregoers, the last act of *Part Three* was included in *Richard III* because of its depiction of the regicidal Richard. Colly Cibber's adaptation of *Richard III*, written towards the end of the seventeenth century, decapitated *Part Three*, robbing it of its concluding Act and so making it virtually unplayable on stages where this newly minted Richard was fast becoming the dominant text. (Even recently Cibber's adaptation has haunted productions – both films starring Olivier and later Ian McKellen in the title role included materials from *Henry VI* as Cibber had done.) Colly's nephew, Theophilus Cibber, tried to rewrite *Part Three* with the final Act missing. But this attempt to create a new prequel failed and his text is unlikely to have been performed more than once. Modern productions of *Part Three* continue to feel the pull of *Richard III* – it is rare to see the last scene played without Richard starting to recite the first words of his famous soliloquy, 'Now is the winter of our discontent ...' Academics often cringe at such blatant attempts to underline to audiences what comes next. But it does at least serve to underscore the dramatic irony of the final scene, when Edward IV celebrates his 'lasting joy' (*Part Three* V.vii.46) by presenting to the court his child, whom we know will be murdered in the next play.

Richard is a devil from the old morality plays, Backbiter from *The Castle of Perseverance*, the Bad Angel from *Doctor Faustus*. He begins the play carrying the head of Somerset. He persuades his father to break his oath, arguing much like the Bad Angel. He ghoulishly mocks Clifford's body and later Warwick's, and he slaughters Henry as if the previous three plays had been little more than a childish game. Although a fierce soldier, a revenger who never lets up after news of his father's death, Richard ends the play with an extraordinary statement: 'I had no father, I am like no father' (V.vi.80). This is not the same Richard whose love for his father in Act II drives him into a seemingly suicidal battle rage. The play's final Act sees the murder of Prince Edward by York's three sons, each stabbing their prisoner. But what is, for Clarence and Edward, essentially a political act, a last step needed to secure their power base and bid 'farewell' to 'our annoy' (V.vii.45), is for Richard an intense moment of blood frenzy which can have only one sequel. Dashing off the stage, not even pausing to kill Margaret, he heads for a bloody supper in the Tower. Edward's remark, 'He's sudden if a thing comes in his head' (V.v.85), notes Richard's urgency, which goes beyond political need. In the penultimate scene, denying his father and his brothers openly to the audience, insisting 'I am myself alone' (V.vi.84), Richard rejects the basis of his father's rebellion. York appealed to history as his judge, to true lineage and past transgressions; Henry, in his defence, pointed to his ancestor's military achievements. Neither matters to Richard: his ambition is a pure desire for power which has no interest in the claims of past or present. This extraordinary character is modelled on the Marlovian overreacher, a Tamburlaine combined with Barabas. But, unlike those characters, Richard has a smack of modernity about him. For modern directors and actors, Richard is often a way to explore contemporary anxieties about a desire that is not anchored to any wider purpose. He has been a Thatcherite entrepreneur, a football hooligan, a Serbian war criminal: in each incarnation, he represents fear of excess, of unchecked ambition.

Henry VI in the Restoration

Despite their popularity in the 1590s, the *Henry VI* plays were not revived again for nearly a century when, twenty years after the Restoration of the monarchy, a playwright and eager courtier called John Crowne thought the plays' emphasis on civil war good

material for a strong social message about the dangers of insurrection and the evil of popery. In this final section of the chapter,
we will look more closely at these Restoration adaptations and
explore how *Henry VI*'s first adapters responded to Shakespeare's
text and refashioned it for their own ends. Any student of the
Restoration will know that Shakespeare's plays, which had been
offstage for years because of the Interregnum and the Civil War,
were frequently adapted, and even a cursory scan of the Cornmill
facsimiles in a decent library will reveal a surprising range of titles
for plays such as *Measure for Measure* and *Coriolanus* which had
no stage lives of their own, but survived by the oxygen of new
writing. *Henry VI* was no exception, but its first adaptations were
surprisingly political in their response to Shakespeare's texts.

The first known performance of the *Henry VI* plays after the
Restoration was in 1680, when John Crowne's adaptation of *Part
Two* and *Part Three*, titled *The Miseries of Civil War*, opened at
the Dorset Garden. The following year, Crowne returned with a
prequel, *Henry the Sixth, the First Part*. Both productions were
shaped by, and tried to intervene in, contemporaneous national
politics: in particular, the political instabilities that resulted when
the Papal plot and the exclusion crisis threatened to tip the nation
back into civil war. John Crowne can claim to be the first adapter
of the Folio texts – and indeed, he does make such a claim, both
in the prologue to *The Miseries of Civil War* and in the dedicatory
letter in the published edition of *Henry the Sixth, the First Part*. In
the prologue, Crowne announces to his audience that 'the Divine
Shakespeare did not lay one stone'. In the light of subsequent,
modern debates about the authorship of the plays, Crowne's statement can easily be misinterpreted as an early example of doubts
about the plays' qualities and authenticity. Here, however, Crowne's
intention is to lay claim to authorship of the *adaptation* and not
let Shakespeare take any of the credit for it, 'for by his [the Poet's]
feeble Skill 'tis built alone'. Crowne was anxious to be seen as the
principal author of the adaptation, and he had good reason. Both
plays were strongly royalist and strongly anti-Catholic.

Crowne effectively shaped two different pathways for the *Henry
VI* plays in the Restoration period. The story of York's rise and
fall, and the subsequent rise of Richard, became a cautionary
text against insurrection, while the feud between Gloucester and
Winchester was refigured as a celebration of a proto-Protestant
martyr. In both, Crowne sensationalised Shakespeare's language,

refashioning it as a 'rhetoric of massacre' that, like many Shakespearean adaptations from the period, invoked 'the horrors of civil war' (Wikander 341). Despite the clear reactionary strategies in these adaptorial choices, the political reception of these plays in the post-Restoration period was unexpectedly hostile. There is evidence that authorities twice tried to suppress adaptations of materials from the *Henry VI* plays. Crowne's *Henry the Sixth, the First Part* was 'stifled by command', as the author complained in his dedication to *The English Friar* (1689). A few years later, Colly Cibber's adaptation of *Richard III*, the first act of which is appropriated from the last act of *Part Three*, was performed with its first act missing, because (according to Cibber) it was feared that the weak, effeminate Henry called to mind the deposed James II.

The Miseries of Civil War preached the folly of civil war and dissention from the monarchy. Characters were altered to reinforce the point so that Edward, despite having usurped the throne himself, was horrified by Richard's 'bloody supper in the tower' but George, more worldy-wise, sermonised 'that's all a nation gets by civil war' (*Miseries* V.vii.30). Crowne's most substantial, and most remarkable, addition to the play was a scene involving soldiers who rob a 'couple of seditious rogues' (i.e. supporters of civil war) and rape their daughters. The scene was played in the same comic vein as the Simpcox scenes, except this time the punishment for civil disobedience was more extreme. Before hanging them, the soldiers gave the rogues a stern lesson on the consequences of rising up against the Crown. At this point, according to the stage directions, 'The Scene is drawn, and there appears Houses and Towns burning, Men and Women hang'd upon Trees, and Children on the tops of Pikes.' Here, the miseries of civil war were dramatically visualised to make an unashamedly political point, a graphic, visceral and gaudy emblematisation of the consequences of public insurrection. The scene was likely to have been three-dimensional, perhaps made out of papier mâché, and would probably have been the most expensive and the most spectacular part of the production. It was the image which centred and defined Crowne's interpretation of the civil war theme.

In 1720 Theophilus Cibber wrote *The Historical Tragedy of Henry VI* which, like Crowne's play, was an adaptation of *Part Two* and *Part Three*. *The Historical Tragedy* was clearly meant to be a prequel to his uncle Colly Cibber's *Richard III*, which had been republished in 1718 and was now played in full. Theophilus turned to those parts of the *Henry VI* plays which centred on Richard's story. The links between his and his uncle's adaptations were strengthened by developing the character of Lady Anne in *The Historical Tragedy*, who of course is only mentioned in passing in Shakespeare's plays. However, Cibber had a problem: his uncle had appropriated the death of Henry to the start of his play. As a consequence, the last scene of *The Historical Tragedy* dramatised the death of Prince Edward, which was crudely combined with the last scene of *Part Three* (skipping over Henry's murder entirely). Richard does exit to make his 'bloody supper in the tower', but audiences had to wait for *Richard III* to see it happen. It is an odd way to end: the play is deprived of its most powerful scene and struggles to justify its titular claim to be the *tragedy* of Henry VI.

Theophilus Cibber was guided not merely by the desire to capitalise on his forebear's work; there is evidence that he consulted and was influenced by Crowne's *The Miseries of Civil War*, from which he borrowed the line 'o piteous spectacle, o sad confusions' (Crowne, *Miseries* IV.i.46; Cibber III.iv.19). Cibber also shared Crowne's interest in exploring the nature of civil war. The prologue, spoken by Cibber himself, intoned 'England can never be, but by her Self Undone' while Cibber added a couplet to Edward's final speech, so that 'our lasting joy' continued with 'And may this Land, learn from our Houses Jars / Ever to dread th' Event of Civil Wars' (V.vi.114). Given this interest in the plays as cautionary texts against insurrection, it is strange that Cibber cuts entirely the characters of the father who has killed his son and the son who has killed his father; but they reappear instead as a speech by Henry, who tells the audience that 'Just now I met a Son bearing his Father / And an unhappy Father with his Son' (III.iv.14–15). By 1720, then, the potential for political controversy surrounding the figure of Henry himself seemed, on the face of it, to be diffused.

Crowne's *Henry VI* focused on Gloucester as a Protestant hero. His anti-clerical squabbles with Beaufort became, in the Restoration climate, a heroic and forward-thinking battle against Catholicism – Gloucester was not just the people's hero, he was the hero of the Protestant majority. In his preface, Crowne even chided Shakespeare for failing to seize the dramatic opportunities presented by the character: 'he has huddled up the Murder of Duke Humphrey, as if he had been guilty of it himself, and was afraid to show how it was done'. But, Crowne boasts, 'I have been more bold, to the great displeasure of some ...' *Henry VI* was a less considered adap-

[28]

tation than *Miseries* and lacked the latter's theatrical daring and vibrancy. It was, as Crowne says himself in the prologue, Shakespeare's *Part One* and *Part Two* reworked, with 'a little Vinegar against the Pope'. The stage directions hint at some vivid staging images, perhaps reflecting the influence of Betterton as annotator of the original manuscript. The witchcraft scene was bolstered with some Macbeth-like poetry: 'Our time is in the deep and Silent Night / The time when Cities are set on fire' (II.iii.24–5) and the stage direction, 'The Witch flings something on the Coales, and then the Conjurer immediately falls prostrate, makes a circle with his wand, then takes a Book and Reads'. The stage direction for the opening of Act III describes 'The Duke of York's House, long Scrolls lying on a table'. The scrolls, of course, would have been the records that York uses to demonstrate his claim to the throne, so visualising for the audience what was otherwise a difficult part of the story. This problem has confounded subsequent directors of the play, some of whom have come up with similar solutions. Michael Hayes used a strikingly similar set-up for the same scene in *An Age of Kings* (see Chapter V) and more recently Michael Boyd's actors used stones to map York's family tree (see Chapter IX). Crowne's main agenda was to make Gloucester the main character and his adaptation even opened with Gloucester lamenting the death of Henry V in a scene which conflated the opening of *Part One* with the opening of *Part Two*. To strengthen Gloucester's story, Crowne expanded Eleanor's (in this play renamed Elianor) role and stressed her innocence. Suffolk and Margaret became the instigators of the plot to entrap the Duchess, the Queen willingly giving power to Suffolk as Crowne shows us by reworking one of Suffolk's lines from *Part One* and giving it to Margaret: 'I'll govern that [England], and thou shalt govern me' (II.ii.327). Elianor's trial was the centrepiece of Act III, her fall and shame the emotional turning point for Gloucester, whose own trial covered Act IV. Crowne was true to his word, the murder of Gloucester was given full theatrical justice. The Cardinal stood in the wings watching the murderers and egging them on and preceded the scene with a pep talk in which he developed a murder plan in a wonderfully moustache-twirling, obsessively sinister way:

> Which way it shall please Heaven to inspire you.
> Stay, let me see! – Strangling I think were best,
> Ay strangling! Strangling! (IV.iii.47–9)

At this point, the curtain was drawn to reveal 'the Duke of Gloucester sitting and reading in his Night-Gown'. He was strangled, the Cardinal watching from the top of the stage, and left dead, propped up in his chair. The scene curtain was closed, and then drawn again when Henry came to visit him. In the next scene, the Cardinal was haunted by Gloucester's ghost. At this point, Crowne added a little more vinegar to the recipe with the two murderers, who entered to discover the Cardinal raving:

> *2 Mur.* He names the Duke of Gloucester
> *1 Mur.* Oh! Does he so?
> Is his Infallibility come to that? (IV.iv.39–41)

The death of the evil, Popish Cardinal, his clerical infallibility finally mocked and exposed, ended the play. Suffolk's death was only reported, along with news of Cade's rebellion (dovetailing neatly on to the first act of *The Miseries of Civil War*). Crowne's adaptation reduced Shakespeare's complex political drama to a one-sided, dogmatic Protestant revision of history; but it nevertheless preserved much of Shakespeare's own work, despite Crowne's apparent contempt for it, and preserved the basic structure of the narrative which Shakespeare composed out of the chronicle sources.

Ambrose Phillips's *Humphrey, Duke of Glocester* (1723) went (if it were possible) even further than Crowne in insisting upon Gloucester as a Protestant hero and in altering Shakespeare to suit his own vision. In his dedication, Phillips describes Gloucester as 'a man of Singular Goodness; a wise and upright Statesman; a great Opposer of the oppressive Usurpations of the See of *Rome*; a generous Favourer of the, then, poor and distressed Commons'. Remarkably, Phillips considered poverty a thing of the past; the eighteenth-century commons, it seemed, were no longer distressed, but were under threat of Papist oppression. The prologue, not written by Phillips, develops the theme:

> Our free-born Bard a free-born Hero draws
> But, sure Destruction is the patriot's Doom,
> When Kings are only Ministers of Rome.
> ... Britain, collect this Moral from our Tale:
> Should, once again, the Papal power prevail
> Again, Religious Fires would dreadful shine;
> And Inquisitions prove their Right Divine.

This Gloucester was not just a Protestant hero but a model statesman: Rome represented not just corruption and religious bankruptcy but political oppression. Phillips went further than Crowne in restructuring the play to emphasise these themes. York, being an enemy of the Cardinal, was thoroughly reconstructed as the hero of the play (an extraordinary switch for a future usurper), while, in Phillips's most remarkable alteration, Henry did not appear in the play at all. In many respects, Phillips follows the outline of Crowne's work closely, using the trial of Eleanor (conducted offstage), the trial and murder of the Duke and the final, harrowing death of the Cardinal as the main markers along the way. Though much of the part Shakespeare wrote was cut, in other respects Eleanor was developed even further, reflecting the progress of her reconstruction since 1680. Phillips's Eleanor was a victim of a Catholic plot. She was noble, pious and pure – all very much removed from Shakespeare's affronted schemer. We never get to see her dabble in magic; York and the rest are talking about her arrest at the start of the play, with York, bizarrely, playing her most staunch defender. Indeed, for Phillips, Eleanor was the victim, and there was no need to make her role in any way ambiguous. Her trial was also not staged, but delivered through report. However, neither Humphrey nor Eleanor appeared until Scene vii of Act I. Humphrey begins his part with railings against the Cardinal. Eleanor was more sanguine, a good Protestant wife bearing her misfortunes with dignity. At the end of the play, Beaufort, raving, asked for Eleanor's forgiveness, and she was brought out of exile to his bedside where, in a final, sentimental act of piety and pity, she forgave him. Henry was relegated to an offstage part: after all, he was a Catholic, and was hence edged out of his own story.

Though written across fifty years, these four adaptations show the dominant themes of the plays' reception in the post-Restoration period and the complexity of playing *Henry VI* in a political environment which was even more rigidly anti-Papist than Shakespeare's audiences were, and in which the memory of civil war was recent and vivid. That *Henry VI* should attract political controversy and suppression twice is remarkable. But by this point, the performance of a religious and weak king was clearly an uncomfortable idea to have in cultural circulation. The interpretation of Humphrey as proto-Protestant hero, the Cardinal as evil prelate and the plays as cautionary (to the point of obsession) tales against the perils of civil war not only recovered a *Henry VI* more suitable for the age, it also diffused some of the potentially troubling aspects of the plays. Henry's part was eroded to the point of extinction, while York's part (and Cade's) was played down with first his son Edward, then York himself becoming the very image of a strong, compassionate prince.

CHAPTER II

Rediscoveries: nation, war and Empire (1899–1953)

Caught up in a theatrical cycle of rediscovery and reburial since the nineteenth century, the *Henry VI* plays remain somehow perpetually beneath the surface of theatrical memory, very occasionally coming into view to excite audiences, then sinking once again. Never having generated much by the way of performance history or tradition, the trilogy has been approached by each subsequent production as essentially a new 'found object', directors and actors often describing their work in rehearsal and performance as a kind of 'rediscovery', an adventure for those who have never played them, never seen them before. This can be exciting, even spiritual for performers or viewers who believe that they can gain more understanding about Shakespeare by getting to know his 'apprentice works'. But discovery can also be unnerving. Actors and directors (as well as spectators) may know from experience what to expect when they start digging into *Hamlet*, but no one quite knows what they are going to find when they level their spades at *Henry VI*. In her study of the 1989 excavation of Henslowe's Rose playhouse (where one version of *Henry VI* was first staged), Peggy Phelan argues that the disinterment of the remains of the past is bound up with 'selective memory, anxiety and desire', for the ability to fascinate and horrify the present gives the object of excavation a subversive power. That's also true of textual and theatrical excavations. When the *Henry VI* plays are performed, and when the questions that haunt them are engaged with – 'Are they Shakespeare?'; 'Are they any good?' – theatre practitioners and audiences alike participate in a process of 'memory, anxiety and desire'. The possibility that new knowledge about Shakespeare might be uncovered is seductive, even addictive; but there is also a danger that what is found might challenge some of our deepest-held preconceptions about Shakespeare, his work and its relationship with the present.

In fact, the real danger, as Phelan notes in her 'psychoanalysis of excavation', is that what is uncovered may reveal things about *ourselves* that we would rather repress. Maybe this is why *Henry VI*'s rediscovery is often followed by its reburial.

In the nineteenth century, the few attempts made at staging *Henry VI* were indeed anxious rediscoveries by directors desperately trying to ignore Shakespeare's dissection of England's collapsing Empire. Productions by Edmund Kean, Charles Flower and Osmond Tearle manifested their concerns by rewriting the plays and cutting key characters. As British history declined from Empire in the nineteenth century through the waste of the First World War to the holocaust of the Second, *Henry VI*'s directors, among them Frank Benson, Robert Atkins and Nugent Monck, turned a blind eye to the increasingly relevant themes the plays explored, they being otherwise engaged, caught up in projects of showmanship: for them, the trilogy really only figured in their individual schemes to stage the Complete Works. However, after the Second World War something changed. Almost as soon as the British Empire came to its (unofficial) end, the *Henry VI* trilogy acquired a new urgency, and, with it, a new theatrical afterlife. In this chapter, two stories that present contrasting anxieties and fantasies about *Henry VI* and its rediscovery are told. One rehearses *Henry VI*'s intermittent theatrical afterlife before the Second World War; the other remembers the first modern production to engage with the plays' more difficult representations of nationhood.

Staging Empire

Because the *Henry VI* plays are also English history plays, they carry with them the potential to comment directly on contemporary politics, and they do so in ways that are hard to contain. They work best as *timely* plays. That is to say, their theatrical power resides chiefly in their ability to comment on the present. They need audiences who recognise something of their own situation in what they see; without that recognition, the plays are simply relics to be enjoyed at the level of historical curiosity. Although Shakespeare's other history plays can be equally trenchant in their portrayal of politics, they are more easily containable by patriotic interpretation – as we know from many such productions of *Henry V*. By contrast, *Henry VI* is the story of those who, as Shakespeare put it, made Henry V's 'England bleed'. The trilogy shows England in

1 *Part One* (1889). Mary Kingsley as Joan of Arc

defeat, losing its Empire, betraying its national identity. Usurpers triumph, the good guys are murdered and a peaceful empire is lost through infighting. This difference is highlighted early in *Part One* when, in the first scene, a messenger complains to the nobility that the English are losing the French wars because of 'want of men and money' (*Part One* I.i.74); later, York and Somerset's arrogant refusal to send Talbot aid is a powerful examination of the cruelty of factionalism.

Kean's *Richard, Duke of York* (adapted by J. H. Merivale, 1817) cut Talbot, provoking one reviewer to complain that, without him, seeing the play was 'like walking among the Elgin Marbles and seeing an empty place where the Theseus had reclined' (reprinted in Wells *Shakespeare in the Theatre* 52). Talbot is a great character for patriotic English theatre: Nashe remembered the tears of Talbot's first spectators as they watched him fight his last battles. By cutting the part, Merivale and Kean were making sure that their rediscovery did not invite topical reflection on England's most recent war with France, which had ended only two years earlier with the Battle of Waterloo (1815). There were plenty of candidates for present-day Talbots – and Yorks. Developing his Duke of York as a 'determined but increasingly isolated and doomed hero' (Martin 15), Kean may well have been unconsciously shaping the part around that other doomed hero, Napoleon Bonaparte, then languishing in exile. Be that as it may, Talbot's 1817 counterpart is much easier to identify, and this perhaps gives a clue to Merivale and Kean's reluctance to include him in the performance: Arthur Wellesley, the Duke of Wellington and the hero of Waterloo. Like Talbot, he embodied the aspirations of England in its war with France and, like Talbot, he was made a peer as a reward for his service. (Shakespeare shows Talbot being dubbed the first Earl of Shrewsbury in III.viii – but this, like all the other Talbot scenes, was cut from Merivale's script.) Neither Merivale nor Kean, it seems, had much appetite for playing Talbot, whose final defeat happens partly as a consequence of York's Napoleonic empire-building.

The handling of Talbot in Osmond Tearle's energetic 1889 version of *Part One* betrayed more fantasies than anxieties. The adaptation was written by the eminent Victorian philanthropist and brewer Charles Flower, who founded the Shakespeare Memorial Theatre Festival where *Part One* was staged. Between them, Flower and Tearle transformed the play into a rollicking imperial adventure that celebrated the exploits of the Empire abroad and muted the darker tones of Talbot's tragedy. The promptbooks describe in some detail a series of spectacular battles, most with Talbot as the hero. In one such scene, Talbot leapt on to a gun carriage, threw a sentry to the ground and then jumped over some battle-ments, leading an army of archers, gunmen and knights, all fully equipped with battle gear. Cannons breached the walls, archers shot arrows from behind the guns, and the din was made even more deafening by the cries of 'A Talbot!' His last stand was equally heroic: the promptbook includes notes on a series of fights between young John Talbot, Charles, Reignier and Talbot. In contrast to all this derring-do, Talbot's death scene was practically glossed over. Flower and Tearle cut most of the dialogue and turned the scene into a moonlit tableau of grieving soldiers. Flower was a *Henry VI* enthusiast, a true believer who spent years trying to convince his main Festival Director, Frank Benson, to stage all three plays as a cycle. Of course, what he discovered in the plays was his own fantasy about the adventure of Empire – a fantasy he could sustain only by suppressing aspects of the play that might challenge it.

Benson may have disagreed with Flower about staging *Henry VI*, but he was, like Flower, committed to culture and Empire, and when he finally *did* discover the plays (after Flower's death), his productions reflected these sympathies. Like Flower, Benson enjoyed the spectacle of war. As Gordon Crosse remembers, there were 'scaling ladders, battering rams and in general as much as he [Benson] could give us of the pomp and circumstances of medi-eval warfare' (Crosse 33). When Benson was not in Stratford (at this time, the Festival ran for only a few weeks every year), he was on tour with his company, which often took him across the Empire. Benson saw it as a patriotic duty to educate the people of the Empire with Shakespeare. We are accustomed now to accounts of Shakespeare's dissemination across the colonies and the impli-cations this had for post-colonial engagements with Shakespeare – but Benson was one of those who actually put ideology into prac-tice. His own notes to the *Henry VI* cycle he staged in 1906 at the Memorial Theatre suggest that he celebrated the liberal notion of the 'benign' Empire; he even tried to sell the plays as a story about that Empire's origins, for 'during the death and the ruin of so many nobles and gentry, the commons of England were growing in power and importance and laying the foundation of the English empire'. In other words, he was saying, don't just look at the politics in the foreground, look at what is happening in the background as well.

Is this comment bizarre, given that the 'Commons of England' spend much of *Part Two* running riot across the stage? Perhaps not. For in 1864, James Anderson had played a Cade who died 'like a courageous rebel of the true English type' (Salgado 88). If Cade could be a true Englishman, Benson's own conviction that *Part Two* could be a play about the 'Commons of England' makes sense. Of the three plays he was first drawn to *Part Two*, which he staged in a single performance at Stratford in 1899; in the audience was the poet W. B. Yeats, who remembered vividly 'insurgent crowds ... and ... people of the gutter' (quoted by Trewin 127). In 1906, after the final curtain fell on *Part Three*, Benson came down to the footlights, still in costume (he was playing Richard), and made a short speech 'apologising for any defects' in the plays and urging his audience to reflect instead on Shakespeare's 'philosophy of History and his patriotic desire to point out the evils of civil war' (quoted in Hattaway *Part Three* 39). Benson's focus on the role of the commons was, perhaps, a way of flattering his audience by emphasising that the trilogy told *their* story. Hardly disguised, however, is an interesting anxiety brought out by the juxtaposition of Benson's reference to the 'ruin of so many nobles' in his programme note and to the threat of 'the evils of civil war' in his curtain speech. Tilting *Henry VI* towards the English commons, Benson was perhaps also dimly aware of the faultlines in the oxymoronic ideal of a liberal empire. It may be significant that Benson's first production of this play was staged (as Foulkes points out) at the height of the Boer War (Foulkes 170), a disastrous conflict which led many to question the ideals of the British Empire. Not long after, of course, the aristocracy would face ruin again in the First World War.

If there was ever a time when the *Henry VI* plays had a strong meaning for a contemporary audience, it was surely in the wake of the 1914–18 conflict (known then as the Great War or 'the war to end all wars'). After 1918, many audiences and actors had a direct and, for many, personal experience of fighting a war in France. One reviewer of a production at the Old Vic commented that 'just now the historical value of the *Henry VI* trilogy has a special interest for us' (*The Sunday Times* 4 February 1923). This 'special interest', however, did not really emerge strongly in any of the three productions between 1914 and 1939, each of which noticeably avoided picking at the scabs of Britain's war wounds. None showed any appetite for remembering their own war as they dressed in military uniforms and recreated French battlefields. If anything, *Henry VI*'s various rediscoveries in this period were indebted to the same kind of patriotic enthusiasm that saw millions of men volunteer for the army in 1914. Each one was produced by a company that was determined to share (as Sir Barry Jackson later put it) the 'honour and duty of having given its public the whole Shakespearean canon' (Jackson 49).

Robert Atkins directed the plays for the Old Vic in 1923, but it might as well have been 1889, for the actor Ernest Meade, playing Talbot, roared his lines so stirringly that he roused one reviewer to praise 'the splendid English spirit that runs through the inspiring patriotism of [his] lines' which 'should make the blood of every true Englishman rush proudly through his veins' (*The Sunday Times* 4 February 1923). Atkins did nothing to give new life to the plays, which he cut down drastically (flouting the Old Vic's 'no cuts' approach to Shakespeare). And his production failed to excite reviewers: *The Observer* thought it 'very ragged' and sniffed: 'the players seemed to get tired long before the audience did' (18 February 1923). However, Atkins did make some important innovations, and one of them was textual, for he was the first British director to adapt the plays into two parts and then add *Richard III* to form a new trilogy, a practice that has since become the standard way of staging the plays as a cycle. In order to give a sense of the historical sweep of the narrative, Atkins recast the lead roles for the second play so that, for example, Henry was played by Guy Martineau as a boyish king in the first part and by the older John Garside in the next. Atkins exploited this further by casting Martineau as the 'son who has killed his father …' to add an extra level of irony to Henry's battlefield meditations on the state of the nation.

But perhaps Atkins's most significance revision was to do not with war but with gender, for he rewrote Joan's part to make her more sympathetic; in his own words, he 'thought fit to rob St Joan of Arc of all unpleasant lines' which, as *The Sunday Times* noted, brought 'her within a modern conception of the character' (4 February 1923). According to *The Observer*, Joan flashed through battle scenes with amazing power and personality (4 February 1923). *The Sunday Times* bristled at this early act of political correctness: 'I can see no justification at all for this. On this principle Mr. Atkins might as well convert all the Frenchmen to Germans.'

Interest in the *Henry VI* plays was also sustained by the readings of the British Empire Shakespeare Society (BESS), a semi-amateur organisation with academic, theatrical and clerical patrons that promoted the teaching and performance of Shakespeare's plays. BESS often gave one-off performances of plays in modern dress and in the 1920s performed all three *Henry VI* plays, each with a different cast and director. BESS had already read *Part One* in 1912 at the Haymarket. Between 1925 and 1926, BESS produced one-off dramatic readings of all three plays at either the Haymarket or the Lyric Hammersmith. The 1926 performance of *Part Three* was particularly distinguished: produced by Edith Craig (sister of Edward Gordon Craig), it starred Harcourt Williams as Henry and a young John Gielgud as Richard Crookback.

In 1933, the same year that Hitler took power with a brutality that reminded Brecht of Richard Gloucester, Nugent Monck staged a two-part adaptation in Norwich at the Maddermarket Theatre which, though an amateur theatre featuring amateur actors, produced work from Monck that was highly respected and drew the attention of Shaw, Yeats and Poel. The *Henry VI* cycle was an especially important event for Monck because, with it, the Maddermarket could boast that it had staged the Complete Works. Not far from Monck's mind, then, was a sense of achievement not unlike those other adventurers of the British Empire who endeavoured to scale Everest or reach the Earth's poles. Like Atkins, Monck made sweeping cuts, all with the aim of speeding the narrative drive. (Known for fast-paced theatre, Monck's *Henry VI* was breathless, running at breakneck speed.) The Maddermarket was (and remains) a small, intimate playing space with an apron stage at the front and a curtain across the centre of the playing area. This arrangement allowed Monck to alternate between 'front' scenes and large court scenes without pauses for scene changes. But it may have been that the memory of the Great War was still too sensitive to revive by theatrical recall, for Monck substantially cut the early French scenes and Talbot's death, which was reported, not staged. Monck shied away from some of the horrors of war by adapting the episode in which Henry watches a soldier drag the body of his enemy (whom he has just killed in battle) on to the stage only to discover that his victim is his father. In Monck's version, the soldier entered to find his father already dead, so absolving the son of patricide.[1]

Despite attracting curious audiences, none of these productions succeeded in awakening actors and audiences to the *Henry VI* plays' theatrical potential. On the contrary, silence followed each one – and most have since been completely forgotten. The only director in the interwar years even to consider staging the *Henry VI* plays in a way that would directly engage with the memory of war was Orson Welles, with a legendary history cycle, *Five Kings*, that set the second tetralogy on a revolving stage dressed to recall the First World War. Welles never realised his original ambition to complete his cycle with *Henry VI* – a double loss, since in Welles the *Henry VI* plays would have found what they needed, a director with more courage, vision and sheer audacity than Atkins, Benson, Flower or Tearle.

Fire and slaughter: the Birmingham Rep, 1951–53

In 1951, the plays finally met their match in Douglas Seale and Sir Barry Jackson, whose decade-long project to stage the entire cycle at the Birmingham Rep (starting out of sequence with *Part Two*) produced performances that revolutionised the way theatre and audiences thought about the *Henry VI* plays. Seale directed, and Jackson, the Rep's founder, wrote the scripts (leaving them largely uncut and free of interpolations). That their astonishing work has not been well remembered is partly the fault of Peter Hall who, when he was producing his own *Henry VI* cycle for the RSC in the 1960s, looked back on 'recent' productions – 'recent' productions could only be the Rep's – as staging 'a mess of angry and undifferentiated barons, thrashing about in a mass of diffuse narrative' (Hall and Barton vii). Hall's work heralded such a step-change from the past that the innovations at the Rep have suffered in comparison. Yet Hall himself was later repentant about his remarks and praised the muscularity of Seale's direction. In truth, the Rep inspired Hall.

In their otherwise excellent edition of *Part Three*, John D. Cox and Eric Rasmussen rather unfairly characterise Jackson (and, by association, his productions of *Henry VI*) as a 'product of the historicising movement of nineteenth-century criticism and performance' whose main idea was to 'recapture historical stage conditions' (Cox and Rasmussen 19). It is true that Jackson's *Henry VI*s were staged in period dress (as most productions are), but the 'period' was the reign of King Henry VI, not Elizabeth I; there is no evidence from photographs that either Jackson or Seale wanted to recreate an authentic Elizabethan experience for their audiences. On the contrary, even though he was in his seventies in 1951 (and thus old enough to have grown up a Victorian), Jackson was very much a man of the present, not the past. One of the pioneers of the British repertory movement, he had staged, in the early years of the Rep, many new plays that were then thought uncommercial, among them plays by Chekhov and several premieres of Shaw's work. During his brief tenure as Artistic Director of the Shakespeare Memorial Theatre, Jackson oversaw what would be remembered as a legendary Watteauesque production of *Love's Labour's Lost* directed by his protégé (and fellow Rep émigré) Peter Brook. In fact, far from being a crusty mock-Elizabethan, Jackson has often been credited as the first twentieth-century director regularly to stage Shakespeare in contemporary dress. Although he was in the last decade of his life when he started on *Henry VI* (he died in 1961), Jackson was still alive to the contemporary possibilities of theatre and still keen to experiment.

Jackson was conscious of the plays' relevance and their power to speak to recent trauma, not least because in Birmingham the Second World War was very much a live memory, the city still bearing war scars on its surface: the Rep had been bombed and parts of the city remained in ruins. In this milieu, a scene from *Part Three* stood out with a terrible clarity for Jackson, the scene in which a soldier brings onstage an enemy he has killed – the same scene whose tragic potency Monck had sought to defuse. Reflecting on the awful moment of the son's discovery, Jackson saw its double 'in our own lifetime', in the 'family cleavages of such a tragic nature' that had so recently 'occurred in Germany' (Jackson 51). Conventional critical opinion, led by Tillyard, thought this scene 'dull, primitive, and ingenuous' and mocked 'the utter artlessness of the language' (Tillyard 195), but Jackson saw in it a powerful and moving piece of theatre that 'threw more light on the horror of civil war than all the scenes of wasteful bloodshed': 'the still figures of the father and son speaking quietly and unemotionally, as though voicing the thoughts that strike the saintly, sad King's conscience, presented a moment of calm and terrible reflection' (Jackson 51).

This scene, framed by three brightly painted arches set far upstage that made living stained-glass windows out of the stories enacted under their embrace, was one of a number that developed a sense of disempowerment and sacrifice – both edgy issues for postwar Britain. It began with Henry asleep, surrounded by corpses from the battle; when he woke, the corpses came back to life, two of them playing the father and the son, the rest listening alongside Henry, the dead bearing witness to the sufferings of war. The King, 'saintly, sad', was an image of innocence and despair, like Walter Benjamin's 'angel of history' who stands gaping at the wreckage of human life, human misadventure piling up before it, its wings turned against the future. At the end of *Part Three* came another image of disempowerment and sacrifice: Henry's butchered body was pressed against the portcullis that now covered the central arch, his arms spread out in an image of the crucifixion, a death that faintly remembered Talbot's. (Earlier, set inside the sacramentalising frame of the central arch, the old warrior's death had put him at the centre of the story, cradling his son's body before laying it on top of a pile of corpses. That York and Somerset were stood in the arches flanking him only made the scene more painful and poignant: the relationship between their aristocratic indifference and Talbot's defeat was penetratingly clear.)

Putting Jackson's cycle into historical context sheds important light on the problematic reflections the plays cast on recent history and suggests why they struck contemporary British audiences with such force. 1951 was the year of the Festival of Britain, and Jackson's newly opened *Part Two* was clearly timed to coincide with the Festival's opening ceremonies in May. Although not designated an official Festival event, *Part Two* was exactly the kind of cultural occasion taking place all over the country that year on both professional and amateur stages, and, while the Festival's centrepiece was a major exhibition on London's South Bank, other local festivals and exhibitions took place all across the country, with many towns and villages mounting their own historical pageants to celebrate Festival year. As it turned out, however, the Rep's take on British history collided with the wider purpose of the Festival which, if anything, was meant to be about moving on from the trauma of war: Jackson and Seale's productions after 1951 would perform an increasingly dark version of festival, memory and history.

For, although on one level it was a commemoration of British history, on another the Festival was arguably an elaborate attempt to forget the recent past. The 1951 Festival was a significant event for Britain which left an impression on those who participated in it – and more or less everyone did. Assembling what the Festival souvenir programme called a 'national reassessment', the Festival organisers carefully avoided references to war, to the end of Empire and even to the class and gender struggles that had driven much recent social history. Instead, the Festival chose to remember

Britain's cultural achievements – which told the story of 'British contributions to world civilisation in the arts of peace'. On the face of it, the event was an unusually large, peculiarly national form of what Pierre Nora calls *lieux de mémoire*, usually translated as sites (or realms) of memory. However, by creating a sense of the past where certain memories were glossed over and others forgotten, the Festival avoided the essential interplay of memory and history that Nora, tracing these *lieux* in his monumental study of French culture, finds necessary for their interpretation. In fact, as a site of memory, the Festival was curiously amnesiac – a reminder perhaps that, as Nietzsche once argued, history is a type of forgetting. Still, the war was not wholly repressed; indeed, it returned in an unexpected place when King George VI opened the Festival by remembering how 'Britain's glory' had been swept away by 'fire and slaughter'. And it returned, too, in the Rep's uncomfortable reminders of a far-distant English past that bore disturbing resemblance to the English present.

With uncanny but appropriate prescience, *Part Two* began with a failed festival. The play's opening scene invites players and spectators to reflect on the tension between memory and forgetting, structured around a national ceremony – a royal wedding – that needs both to remember and forget. England has been at war with France, but now an English prince is marrying a French princess, pacifying hostilities, binding up brokenness, repairing loss in a ceremony of restoration, an incorporation of French Margaret into English history. The trouble is, the ceremony fails. Gloucester begins to play his part in the ritual, reading out the marriage treaty to the assembled court; but as the political reality becomes clear to him, his voice falters: the King's uncle, the Lord Protector, cannot carry on. He drops the treaty – a literalisation of a troubling idea, that the ceremonies and performances of the court no longer reflect political reality; that, rather, they are a vast distraction. In Seale's production, set on the Rep's small, crowded, ordered stage, when Gloucester dropped the treaty he triggered a different kind of history to the one being staged, just down the road from the Rep, that same year at the Memorial Theatre (which, unlike the Rep, was designated an official Festival venue). According to J. C. Trewin, the performance 'moved like an angry surge from its opening' (Trewin 149–50), which is a nicely prescient comment: while the 'angry young men' of John Osborne's invention would not arrive on the English stage for another five years, in Seale's production (and Trewin's review) they seem already massed in the wings. Seale's was a young company, and the energy of the first scene was sustained through all three productions, many reviewers noting the pace, clarity and energy of the acting. York, Somerset, Suffolk and even Gloucester were prototypical Jimmy Porters, railing at the betrayals of history; Joan and Margaret were forceful revelations, discovering for the first time a real urgency and a dangerous sexuality in these parts. Performed by a huge cast in a small theatre – at the time, the Rep seated fewer than five hundred people – *Henry VI* was explosive. And it was meant to be. History was angry. History was 'in-your-face'.

Lions and unicorns

One of the ways the Festival of Britain defined British culture was by appropriating the heraldic sign of the Lion and the Unicorn, the traditional icon of Great Britain. Original Folio and Quarto editions of Shakespeare's works were displayed in an exhibition on the South Bank, presided over by the heraldic animals who troped the dual nature of the British character: the Lion represented 'action', the Unicorn, 'imagination'. In this exhibition, culture and 'the arts of peace' were on prominent display while, as Alan Sinfield points out, 'warlike achievements were strictly excluded' (Sinfield 'The Government, the People and the Festival' 185). Yet references to war kept surfacing, almost like repressed memories. In fact, the tent was framed by symptoms of this repression. The heraldic symbol blazoned at the entrance to the exhibition would have been instantly recognisable to millions of men and women who had seen active service as the badge of the British Army uniform; and, at the exit, the final exhibit was a large display of the old (and unrelated) nursery rhyme about the Lion and the Unicorn 'fighting for the crown'.[2]

A similar tension between history and memory, between 'action' and 'imagination', structured the Rep productions, where young Henry was a unicorn (though of limited, specialised imagination) surrounded by ambitious lions. Jack May played him straight off the page as a weak and pious king unable to comprehend either the political or the sexual games his subjects were addicted to, games that jeopardised the future of England. He himself moved in the company of monks and nuns, desexualised proxies of the gender wars happening elsewhere who troped Henry's own nostalgia both for the moral certainties of religion and the innocence of pre-sexuality. But May's Henry was out of place in the postwar, post-imperial world of *Part Two*.

Out-facing the unicorn, Suffolk and York were lions, champing at the bit for power. The action was driven by two power-house performances from Richard Pasco as Suffolk and John Arnatt as York. Both were villains, and in some ways both were the most modern characters onstage: Pasco smouldered his way through most of his scenes as a romantic anti-hero, a Rhett Butler in medieval dress. Arnatt, Russian by birth, looked the part of a dissident outsider, an existentialist with no place in the dominant order of things. The main theme remained that of postwar politics, but Pasco and Arnatt voiced potential instabilities in the new national order. Both characters were brought into the opening pageants of *Part One*, anachronistically mourning Henry V. But it was the opening of *Part Two* which really defined their relationship, Suffolk at the centre of things, not only a substitute bridegroom but a substitute king as well, already dominating politics through his presentation of Margaret to the ineffectual King; York, skulking on the margins of political action, eyeing the ceremonies that should have been his, a self-excluded figure, biding his time.

An audience unfamiliar with the plays might have thought, at the outset of *Part Two*, that Richard Pasco was playing the king: he was fierce, handsome and swarthy, and he commanded the stage in a way that Jack May's shy Henry never could. Suffolk's public subservience to the King was coded and ironic: at St Albans he obediently knelt to Henry and then lounged, a man relaxed in his erotic self-assurance, with Margaret, openly flirting with her. Only Henry was unable to read the signs. Suffolk's love scenes with Margaret were pure Hollywood romance: one photograph shows Margaret resting her head against his manly chest, digging her nails into his arms, Suffolk gazing into the distance with an impassive expression. Such scenes mined clichés from films like *Gone with the Wind* and even seemed to remember wartime weepies like *Brief Encounter*. But Suffolk was clearly the villain of the piece. His agent Hume had remained onstage from the previous scene (with the Duchess of Gloucester); as Margaret berated the commoners who wanted to petition Gloucester, Suffolk signalled to Hume. From this point, spectators knew that Suffolk had set a trap for the Duchess.

After Gloucester's death, there was a rare moment when Henry broke out of the political frame which trapped him. Suffolk knelt once more to Henry, but the King said, distantly, 'Lay not thy hands on me.' It was a decisive moment: Suffolk's hold on the king was broken; the game was no longer being played by Suffolk's rules. In a nice non-naturalistic touch, he backed slowly into the darkness (the stage was lit only above the centre arch). Suffolk, who had begun as the central actor in a spectacle of national unity, was now powerless. In keeping with Hollywood melodrama, his final scene with Margaret was histrionic; but rather than directing Suffolk's exit, as scripted in Shakespeare's playtext, Seale kept him onstage to watch Margaret go. For a moment, the man who had commanded both the stage and the woman was alone – but only for a moment. Four pirates were waiting in the shadows at the edge of the stage to kill him.

The real Lion, though, was York, who moved from being an outsider in *Part One* to a brooding Machiavel in *Part Two* and a tragic father in *Part Three*. Twice in *Part One*, York's story was used as a lead-in to the interval (each Part having two intervals), the curtain for the first interval coming down on York unfolding his claim to Warwick in the Temple Garden, and for the second, on York picking up a white rose discarded by Henry. Since York is not a main player in *Part One*, these curtain scenes brought his story more into the foreground of the trilogy. Played by Alan Bridges in 1951–52, York was a clear-cut, even cartoonish villain whose 'mad flaw' made him, in effect, a prototype Richard III. Bridges (who would later abandon acting for a career as a director) was only in his early twenties and had to be heavily made-up to play the older York of *Part Three* (in fact, he was younger than Paul Daneman, who played his son Richard). But in 1953, Jackson and Seale gave the part to a tall, slender actor called John Arnatt who could play both a young and a mature York. Known for his golden voice, Arnatt recreated York as a man who is ambitious but 'nobly graced': in *Part One* and *Part Two* he skilfully navigated the politics of Henry's court, often watching with grim horror the ruin of the kingdom he claimed. But it was in his death scene in *Part Three* that Arnatt's interpretation came into its own. Where Bridges had intoned and declaimed his final speeches, Arnatt spoke them softly, with a 'quiet realism' which belied the interior tragedy of a man with no ambition left. This transformed the scene: in the earlier version, Margaret had put the paper crown on York's head while he was held down by sneering soldiers. In Arnatt's performance, York tried to pull away from Margaret as she came near him; but after he had spoken his final words, he stood up, quiet and resigned, and contemplated the stained handkerchief. Then, weeping, he removed the paper crown from his head and held it out to Margaret, transforming Bridges' simplistic, bombastic defiance into tragic pathos. As York offered the crown, which Margaret declined to take, the gesture acknowledged that these two players in history were linked, both un-childed parents, York's son already dead, Margaret's soon to follow.[3]

Playing across this scene, too, was a sense of it summoning ghosts that were elsewhere haunting the Festival, not least in the way it recalled and travestied the tradition of the player-king. No doubt, numbers of spectators had themselves played the king in one of the countless history pageants that were being staged locally across the country. Certainly, most would have seen such an event. Whether or not, while watching *Henry VI*, they related the performance of nationhood in the theatre to the celebration of the national history on the street, the recirculation of these images from triumphal communities to the lonely and wasted scene on the molehill made such a conjunction possible. But, perhaps to reinforce the point, Jackson and Seale made sure that York was the *second* player-king to wear the crown. The first was a boy, dressed as a jester, first seen playing in the background, wearing the paper crown, as hunchbacked Richard tried to persuade his father York to break his oath. (This boy – a curious and unexplained double of Rutland – was later slaughtered alongside York's youngest child by the 'pent-up lion', Clifford.) From its first sighting, the paper crown was an ironic counterpoint to York's failed desires. Later, poised silently between York and Margaret, it brought together history and festival in one ruined image.

But what of the British people in Festival Britain? Where were they in the *Henry VIs*? A clue comes in the posters for the 1951 *Part Two*, which aimed to sell the show on the strength of 'the wry humour of Saunders Simpcox' – despite the fact that Simpcox, whose miraculous cure Gloucester exposes as a fraud in Act III, has only one scene in the play. He is a poor man's Falstaff, his con trick a brief interlude whose main function as 'fall guy' is to presage Gloucester's fall from power. His prominence on the poster suggests a certain kind of play – history with gags – and a certain kind of audience – one that wants to see itself on stage – an advertising ploy that is both populist and popular, bringing the story of the ordinary people of Britain into view and promising a crowd-pleasing comic turn. And in this case, the ad-man got it right: the commoners' story stood literally at the centre of Jackson's script for *Part Two*, the whole of the middle act devoted to them, from Simpcox to Cade.

Jackson and Seale built on the banter between Gloucester and Simpcox to make a comic routine out of the charade, almost as if Gloucester and Simpcox were a double act, with the nobleman playing straight-man to the plebeian clown. This vaudeville pastiche continued in the Cade scenes. When *Part Two* was revived in 1953, Seale cast as Smith the Weaver the rising comedian Kenneth Williams, who would later make a name for himself in radio shows like *Round the Horne* and in *Carry On* films as a master of comic voice impressions and sexual *double entendre*. Here, he stole the show. Smith's part was developed, with lines culled from other commoners and extra non-Shakespearean routines thrown in. Much of the humour was slapstick, repeatedly playing on the gag line, 'Thou hast hit it!' But it moved on to more dangerous ground – territory Williams would explore and colonise in the later *Carry On* films – where sexual anxiety lurked: as he hustled a peasant girl offstage as his 'prize', the others raucously called after him, 'Tumble her, Smith, tumble her!'

All this humour was deeply fractured. Simpcox disappeared after only one scene; the carnival banter of Smith and Cade turned violent, decapitated heads serving as banners for their class uprising. So with whom on this stage should an audience have identified in Festival year? The patriarch Gloucester, who mocks the lower classes? Or Smith the Weaver, whose seaside postcard humour degenerates into anarchic violence? The simple answer was that, despite its initial promise, the Rep did not offer a vision of British identity that was compatible with that of Festival Britain. While the Festival was busy smoothing over class difference, memorialising a past that aimed to present the British people as a harmoniously unified race, the Rep, particularly in the competing claims made by those comic performances, was drawing attention to class tensions, class difference. What an audience finds funny, Seale's productions suggested, at some level betrays its members' own investment in a society that was still clearly structured along class lines.

Another instability that Britain in Festival year wanted wishfully to ignore but finally had to face was gender. Times were changing.

Even since Atkins's cycle, the roles of Joan and Margaret (and subsidiary characters such as Eleanor and Jourdain) had become both more important and more problematic. This was all part of a number of anxieties about 'the modern career woman' – a creature spawned in the 'all hands to the pump' war years when women discovered they could plough field and build aeroplanes. The consumer age was just beginning, and Britain, having coaxed war-industrious women back into their 'proper' place of work, the kitchen, was struggling to find a way to talk about them that acknowledged their independence and consumer power without overthrowing too many of the nice conventions – femininity, modesty, the 'double standard' – that organised gender relations. The Festival appeared to create a space where Britain could imagine what a world of gender equality might be like. Thus one futuristic Festival design laid out a 'bed-sitting room for the modern bachelor girl' – which depicted a young woman thoughtfully knitting in a room that included the latest sewing machine and a handmade sewing table. Advertisements in the Festival's souvenir programme were also geared to a particular view of a female future: one advertisement for a vacuum cleaner promised to save 'millions of housewives from hard, wearisome drudgery'; another, for Prestige housewares, promised consumer goods that would make light work of kitchen tasks 'long after the Festival of Britain has become a memory'. Stereotypes like these were confronted head-on when Joan la Pucelle stepped on to the Rep stage. Finding the Dauphin dallying with a peasant girl perched on his knee, Joan saw her off then challenged him to test his manhood on her – but almost immediately, the girl returned, threw herself into the fight and started scrapping with Joan, a bizarre twist to Shakespeare's scenario that manoeuvred Joan back into a more familiar gender role, a woman fighting with another woman for the man. Things got stranger still when, some time later, the peasant girl returned to the stage, this time as one of Joan's spirits. For spectators, the penny could finally drop: she had been, from the beginning, an aspect of Joan's transgressive power and part of the set-up.

That power was as much sexual as martial. The co-ordinates of Joan's character were established early on when, in an added scene that played out action only reported in *Part One*, Joan taunted Young Talbot (John Greenwood), 'Thou maiden youth, be vanquished by a maid.' He retorted that 'Young Talbot was not born to be the pillage of a giglot wench', before discovering, after

2 *Part One* (1953). Joan (Nancie Jackson) faces York (John Arnatt)

a flurry of action, that indeed he *was*. This exchange, then, positioned Joan as both maid and 'giglot' – that is, wanton – 'wench', able to move easily between roles. Finally, though, captured by English soldiers who circled her but stood way back, nervously pointing their spears at her, this audacious example of female careerism, this powerful modern woman, could be dealt with only by shackling her and finally incinerating her.

That same scene of capture was repeated for Margaret, but, where Joan was fierce and frightening, Margaret was a plaything; the scenario, sexual foreplay. This time, the spears were clearly phallic symbols wielded by soldiers toying with Reignier's daughter, blocking her way, then letting her go, only to block her way again. Now, the space was controlled entirely by macho display: the modern career woman, it seemed to suggest, would have to play a sexual game – and this is exactly what Margaret did in *Part Two*.

A thematic link between Joan's powers and the sexual politics

3 *Part Two* (1951). Eleanor (Hazel Hughes) and Hume (Max Brimmell) watch a witches' dance

of *Part Two* was also established by casting Eleanor Bryan (the peasant girl and Joan's demon in *Part One*) as Eleanor, who is, of course, the most careerist woman in the play and one who, like Joan, seeks her career advancement through magic. Jourdain's incantations were suitably spooky: Seale and Jackson added to the stage a whole witches' coven who performed a 'witches' dance' (elaborately choreographed in the promptbook) to give the scene a smack of *Macbeth*-style supernaturalism. Eleanor stood in the shadows at the back of the stage, half-horrified, half-seduced by the spectacle of the witches gathered around a pool of light. Along with Simpcox's humour and the banter that livened up the Cade scenes, here was one more 'festival' added to the play for Festival year.

The Rep histories did not commemorate national identity, nor were they a theatrical equivalent to the Festival of Britain. Rather, they traded on the irresolution and fracture of a country traumatised by war and victimised by the appalling destructiveness of power politics. If the Festival set out to show the Britons 'to themselves' in a celebratory mood, the Rep offered, as a contrast, a darker, more introspective engagement with recent history. It performed the nation through, as *The Times* put it, a 'cumulative disorder' in which the violence of the recent past was not elided but revived. Seale's company surprised reviewers by not ending the cycle with *Richard III*. Instead, the end came with Edward's optimistic hope for 'lasting joy'. The bells rang out, and the people cheered, just as they had on VE Day, just as they would on Elizabeth II's coronation day in 1953. But this exultant mood was broken by a voice – it was Richard's – cutting through the celebrations with a speech that began, 'Now is the winter of our discontent ...' The bells eventually drowned out the words, but the point had been made: try as he might to declare a 'festival for Britain', Edward, at the end, could deliver no happy ending.

CHAPTER III

The Wars of the Roses: the RSC's *Henry VI* and *Edward IV* (1963–64)

The year 1963 was, as Philip Larkin observed, an 'Annus Mirabilis' that transformed the cultural face of Britain, and the institutions of authority that composed it, almost beyond recognition. Irreverence, even anarchy, defined the new anti-Establishment and cockily adolescent national self-image – a portrait by Hockney or Warhol fly-posted over the Godfrey Kneller. That year, the Beatles topped the charts with 'She Loves You' and 'I Want to Hold Your Hand'; the mini skirt became ubiquitous along the King's Road and Carnaby Street; Mary Quant's designs went into mass production; *Oh! What a Lovely War* opened at Stratford East and, at the cinema, Stanley Kubrick's *Dr Strangelove*; the Profumo scandal broke – spilling the beans on ministerial high jinks, Russian spies and a call-girl willing to pass on government secrets she'd learned in bed; the Reynolds gang pulled off the Great Train Robbery, a heist that staggered the popular imagination (and made folk heroes of what the media hyped as latter-day Robin Hoods) as much for the snook it cocked at Britain's 'sacred' institutions (the Bank of England, the Royal Mail) as for the million-pound haul; Philby defected to Moscow; Kennedy was assassinated; fifty thousand Campaign for Nuclear Disarmament (CND) protesters marched on London; the BBC ended its official ban on mentioning royalty, religion, sex and politics in its comedy shows; and, of course, as Larkin noticed, 'Sexual intercourse began'.

Meanwhile, in Stratford-upon-Avon, the Royal Shakespeare Company was enjoying its own 'year of wonders'. Building on transformations initiated three seasons earlier by the newly appointed (and, at twenty-nine, barely post-adolescent) Artistic Director, Peter Hall, the company was revolutionising its image. It had a new company structure, replacing the old hierarchic star system with the beginnings of a permanent, democratic ensemble. It had a new name, chosen to project a new youthful dynamism – and, paradoxically, a new populism. As in-house press releases stated, the point of making the RSC 'royal' was to signal that the company 'virtually belongs to the Nation' (Addenbrooke 48). It had a new stage, equipped with a rake and a fourteen–foot thrust, declaring in architectural terms the company's commitment to 'modern' Shakespeare performance. (It replaced an actor-trap notorious for stranding productions on the far side of an obsolete orchestra pit behind a proscenium arch, a legacy of Victorian theatre design, which was both too low and too narrow, prompting one actor, Balliol Halloway, to observe that, standing downstage 'on a clear day', he 'could just about see the boiled shirts in the first row' of the stalls: it was 'like acting to Calais from the cliffs of Dover' (quoted in Beauman 113).) The year 1963 took the revolution further. That year the RSC won the battle for public subsidy, received its first Arts Council grant, discovered Brecht as a model for theatrical aesthetic – and settled into the image that would define its visual house style for the rest of the decade. But most notably, that year, the RSC discovered 'political Shakespeare': finding, in *The Wars of the Roses* – a trilogy adapted from the three parts of *Henry VI* and *Richard III* – a Shakespeare who articulated 'the pressure of now' (a phrase Hall used a lot in interviews at this time), who anatomised power (institutional, oppositional, personal, renegade), and so anticipated the concerns – and rhetoric – of the militant 1960s; a Shakespeare fully implicated in popular culture's project of re-imagining England. For Bernard Levin in the *Daily Mail*, *The Wars of the Roses* was a 'landmark and beacon in the postwar English theatre' (18 July 1963). Harold Hobson doubted that 'anything as valuable has ever been done for Shakespeare in the whole previous history of the world's stage' (*The Sunday Times*). Emerging from this 'unforgettable production' (T. C. Worsley *The Financial Times*) was 'a view of history that restores the connexion between political tactics and the basic human passions' (*The Times*), a view that required 'little imagination' to 'apply ... to all history anywhere' (*Tribune*). Indeed, the production offered to teach spectators to read their own history: in the troubled pacifist Henry VI they could see 'the archetype of every honest CND demonstrator who ever sat down in Trafalgar Square' (B. A. Young *Punch*). Almost immediately the stuff of theatrical legend, *Wars* would come, retrospectively, to serve Hall's new-model RSC as the founding text in a creation myth of its own 1960s socialist-activist origins.

Like most myths-of-our-time, of course, this one has undergone revisionist scrutiny, Alan Sinfield and Robert Shaughnessy (among others) exposing the RSC's institutional politics as less radical than was claimed, more confused and, anyway, constructed *post hoc* – English liberal-socialism at its conservative woolliest (Sinfield 'Royal Shakespeare' 158–81; Shaughnessy 11–33). It is just as well, then, to pause here and remember just where the status quo stood in July 1963, as *Wars* prepared to open.

The season in Stratford was not going well. Colin Blatchley's *Julius Caesar* was 'smaller than life': 'all snaffle and bit, and no bloody horse', Tynan complained in *The Observer* (14 April 1963). *The Tempest* – co-directed by Clifford Williams and Peter Brook – was 'prosaic'. On an island 'transported into outer space' Prospero wore 'a dilapidated dressing gown' and Caliban looked 'like a malevolent Man Friday, strayed from a pantomime about Robinson Crusoe' (*The Morning Advertiser* 7 May 1963). The only bright spot in the repertoire was the revival of the previous season's surprise hit, *The Comedy of Errors*, directed by Williams. Reviewing *Caesar* in *The Sunday Times* a dispirited Harold Hobson – the same who'd saved Peter Hall's theatrical bacon in 1955 (when others saw him for the chop) with a thrilled review of *Waiting for Godot* – cast a lacklustre eye over Hall's third season: 'Our great Captain's resolution to turn the Stratford theatre into a place which conventional playgoers can stay away from with pleasure strengthens apace' (14 April 1963).

Who were Hobson's 'conventional playgoers'? Collectively, they were 'Edna' – that fictitious 'Aunt' (from somewhere ordinary but terribly well-bred in the English home counties) invented by the playwright Terence Rattigan a decade earlier to be the barometer of middle-class 'shock', whom Hobson invokes in his review to address as his confidante of shared assumptions. Edna, Hobson felt, would *surely* find Stratford shocking. 'The curtain', he reported darkly, 'still has not returned.' (An early act of subversion by Peter Hall in Brechtian mode had been to remove, ostensibly for cleaning, the theatre's velvet stage drapes: for many spectators, their rise at 'curtain up' in a dust cloud heavy not just with anticipation but with the distilled odours of every past production, to reveal the 'real' world behind, troped the authentic experience of theatregoing.) Without the curtain the stage was – well, a *stage*, naked of illusion. 'Spectators, as soon as they enter the theatre, can see scenery which would once have been concealed until the play began, and which wouldn't have been worth looking at even then.' Other changes were worse – like the new demographics. There were no tiaras or boiled shirts on view in the stalls, no evening dress among the first night audience watching *Caesar*. 'According to my observation on Tuesday night,' Hobson told Edna, 'play-goers need no longer bring their collar and tie with them; I doubt if skirts are necessary, either.' This new Shakespeare audience was 'popular', even plebeian, and, as Hobson expressed with wide-eyed mock irony, mobilising the decade's conventional racism, it affronted every 'normal' code validating high culture's exclusivity: 'I saw leotards and a gentleman in a crumpled high-necked jumper. (Of course I know he was a gentleman, Edna: he was a Negro.) A white-faced boy brought bottles of pop into the auditorium for his pa and ma to refresh themselves with during the interval.' There might, Hobson concluded, still be 'a long way to go' before 'The Theatre Royal, Stratford-upon-Avon, ... looks on a first night like Bramall Lane on August Bank Holiday'. 'But it progresses, lads, it progresses' (*The Sunday Times* 14 April 1963).

The background noise we hear in Hobson's review is the unmistakable sound of the tectonic plates of cultural change sliding uneasily across each other, one still-dominant cultural formation moving into the space of the residual, displaced by the emergent – terms Raymond Williams was making familiar. The audience Hobson expected to see at the RSC in the summer of 1963 was the one familiar to him, the 'right' Shakespeare audience, the one he'd been rubbing elbows with for thirty years, an audience of elitist consensus, the corporate guarantor of conservative (and exclusive) English middle-class values. The one he started to pick out like sore thumbs from among his highbrow Ednas was the audience Peter Hall saw as the future – the future of an RSC wanting to extend the cultural franchise to consumers of 'pop'. Sceptics of Hall's radical politics – Sinfield et al. – need to remember that, in terms of 1963, Hall did not need to move very far left of the right-aligned status quo to be called revolutionary. Equally, the revolution he managed in the auditorium was undoubtedly more seismic than anything he put on the stage. As it happened, however, in *Wars* unwitting Edna would herself emerge as a target of what Hall took to be the trilogy's fundamental project of political scrutiny: he wanted the plays to expose and interrogate

[57]

the unexamined 'sanctions' – 'God', 'the king', 'the Church' – that
politicians mobilised as universally shared assumptions, as idealised permissions to legitimate and justify their own self-interested
actions and opinions. What was Hobson's Edna if not a cultural
version of the political 'sanction'?

A mass of diffuse narrative

For Peter Hall, *The Wars of the Roses* was, first, a project about
constructing an acting text, an ambitious, even daring project that
needed also to be economically viable. Hall envisaged the RSC
staging a full English history cycle to celebrate Shakespeare's
quatercentenary in 1964: the first tetralogy in 1963 would be the
advance party. But calculating that the box office would not sustain
three unknown plays – the *Henry VIs* – in one season, he assigned
his old Cambridge colleague and recently appointed RSC Associate Director, John Barton, the job of adapting them, squaring
his conscience with what he called the 'ultimate literary heresy:
Shakespeare cut, rewritten, and rearranged' by arguing that the
Henry VIs weren't really Shakespeare – not Shakespeare the way
King Lear and *Hamlet* were Shakespeare. These plays, Hall argued,
were probably early collaborations – which would explain the ham
fists he saw in the writing; at best, uneven apprentice work or 'Elizabethan hackwork' that bore the botched signs of contemporary
revision. By this reading, Barton would be merely a *subsequent*
adapter, offering 'a further revision' to 'only partly revised origi-
nals' (Hall and Barton xxiv).

By any measure, Barton's adaptation was radical. He reshaped
the three parts of *Henry VI* into two new plays, titled *Henry VI*
and *Edward IV*, making deep cuts that reduced the 9500 or so
lines of Shakespeare's trilogy by more than half. Of the 4800 lines
contained in Barton's final playing version, 3600 were from original texts – largely from Quarto and Folio versions of the *Henry*
plays, but with interpolations also from Edward Hall's *Chronicles*, *Gorboduc* and *Edward III*. The remaining 1200 lines were
pastiche Shakespeare written by Barton. In the revision process,
entire scenes were dropped, rearranged or relocated; speeches
dismantled, reconstructed, reassigned; new scenes and speeches
supplied; dozens of characters cut, parts conflated, 'alarums and
excursions' conflated and curtailed. The object was to tidy the trilogy's (perceived) clutter and, by rewriting, to clarify the narrative

line by directing it to the political point – as Peter Hall defined it. For if one of the convictions that licensed Barton's adaptation was Hall's attitude toward 'authentic' Shakespeare, another was his interpretation of *political* Shakespeare, of Shakespeare writing political history, and writing political history that was as relevant to the age of Elizabeth II as Elizabeth I.

Trained on E. M. W. Tillyard (whom no one so far had much contested), Hall understood Shakespeare's politics to be historically constituted, grounded in the conservative Elizabethan concept of 'the world picture': the idea 'that there was a natural order in nature, starting with the lowest forms of life and moving up through the beasts to man and to God'. 'Order' was the key to Elizabethan politics ideologically but also discursively, providing it with a language of self-representation and legitimation that functioned at not just an institutional but a personal level. 'All Shakespeare's thinking, whether religious, political or moral', was 'based on a complete acceptance of this concept of order' (Hall and Barton x). *Dis*-order, then, was 'chaos', 'sin'. 'Revolution' – in individuals, families, states – led inevitably 'to destructive anarchy' and, just as inevitably, to the 'punishment' that must follow (Hall and Barton x). For Hall, the histories revealed 'an intricate pattern of retribution, of paying for sins, misjudgements, misgovernments'; in them, Shakespeare 'says that history is a constant tragic pressure on all human beings, and unless they govern themselves and their institutions pragmatically there is a natural tendency to return to chaos' (*Henry VI* Programme note).

This Shakespeare who spoke to 'all human beings' was, of course, not the Elizabethan playwright. He was, rather, the universal Bard – whose politics, uncannily topical, belonged to the present and diagnosed 'now'. This Shakespeare was the audience's contemporary. And tutored by Jan Kott (whose book, *Shakespeare Our Contemporary*, he read in proof on the train en route to *Wars* rehearsals in Stratford), Hall was able to see in the *Henry VI*s a *contemporary* political landscape he recognised, one that everywhere presented 'an ironic revelation of the time-honoured practices of politicians'. He realised 'that the mechanism of power had not changed in centuries' (Hall and Barton xi). The same political justifications or 'sanctions' the barons used to bully Henry and brawl among themselves – 'God', 'Duty', 'Lancaster', 'York', 'Allegiance', 'the Commons', 'the Crown' – survived (with minor updates) in 1960s Whitehall. But no matter what legitimating fictions politicians used to mask their naked ambitions, power was their object. And history narrated the processes of power. (All of these were insights that Hall conveyed to his audience in another of his innovations for the RSC, the glossy extended programme that, in 1963, replaced the old-format cast list).

Barton's adaptation cut Shakespeare to fit Hall's political cloth. He followed instructions to register the curse on the House of Lancaster from the beginning: in a voiceover Prologue (a speech Barton borrowed from Edward Hall's *Chronicles*) the dead Henry V, whose body lay coffined on the stage, delivered his legacy *ex cathedra*, a series of commands that took the force of sanctions as he tried to pass on, detoxified, the contaminated inheritance of his own usurping father. Barton then kept the curse in view, rewriting individual acts of savagery – the assassination of Gloucester, the mob murder of Suffolk, the agonised death of Beaufort – to make them pattern out the larger workings of guilt and retributive justice. Those treacherous 'sanctions' that Hall found implicit in Shakespeare – though not in Shakespeare's text: 'sanction' isn't a word known in Shakespeare – Barton made explicit. He wrote a deliciously mordant soliloquy for the double-crossing secret agent John Hume, whom he made to muse ironically on those 'lofty traitors', his employers, who, Hume said, swore oxymoronically that they did 'their treasons on the King's behalf' – an equivocal kind of loyalty. They 'swear 'tis so; should I suspect their oaths?' Hume wondered, deadpan (*Henry VI* Scene 18). But irony deserted him, the traitors' traitor, when, in lines added to his next scene, Barton had him arrested with the others – for treason.

Barton's boldest stroke came in answer to Hall's worries that, as they stood, the *Henry VI*s were unplayable because unintelligible, 'a mess of angry and undifferentiated barons, thrashing about in a mass of diffuse narrative' (Hall and Barton vii). They lacked a central character; they lacked a linear narrative, the kind of plot that throws a noose around the throat of a play then tightens it. Dynamically, they seemed to work 'like a pendulum' swinging 'between two principles, one patriotic and constructive, but *misguided*, the other destructive and selfish' (Hall and Barton xx) – or, in another formulation, 'between man the animal in action, murdering to protect, or lying to save' and 'moral men trying to rule by a developed human ethic' (*Henry VI* Programme). Barton's response? If the plays lacked a focus, he – the play-'wrighter' – would construct one.

His fine inspiration was to fix it on neither narrative nor character. Barton's focus was theatrical. He invented a material point of scenic return that set up characters – and spectators – for sequential *déjà vu*, revisiting and reanimating redundant histories as if *replaying* them under new conditions that turned out always to be the same, a focus trained on that most basic of theatre props, a table. In a long addition to Scene 6, at the beginning of *Henry VI*, Barton had Gloucester, the young king's uncle and Lord Protector, institute 'the council-board', a functional meeting place, but also a metonym of political discourse, a 'practic [*sic*] of proceeding', as Gloucester called it, which he intended should curb Henry's fractious barons and 'check that canker emulation / Which doth deface our flower of government'. Seated at the table, where he was flanked by Gloucester and Winchester, and facing Warwick, Somerset, Suffolk and Exeter, Barton's King Henry listened to Gloucester's proposed 'practic':

> When we are met upon some troubled question,
> Let us resolve it by our general voice:
> And when the matter hath been given vent,
> Let the opinion of the greater part
> Be straight upheld, and those that are outvoic'd
> Yield their intents unto the general.

Warwick responds, 'it is a pleasing policy'; 'I gladly cleave to it.' The King approves 'with all my heart', and the truculent barons, miraculously docile, fall into line. 'One thing more,' adds Gloucester. They are to remember that every man 'gives his voice not on his own behalf, / But on the King's'. So that,

> If it should chance at some unlook'd-for time
> That what we do propose mislikes his highness,
> Then should we yield to his opinion.

This amazingly anachronistic interpolation was daft history, but smart theatre – a mock-Tudor ideological catch-22. The council table would be the place where co-operation – 'moral men, trying to rule' – would take a stand against self-seeking individualism – 'man the animal in action'. It established, on the one hand, consensus government, a kind of medieval kitchen cabinet where the cutlery would be laid aside so that carnage could be avoided, and where 'voices' were going to count like votes in a democratic election: the majority would rule, and the outvoted sweetly yield. But on the other hand, it proposed monarchical absolutism: the

4 *Edward IV* (1963). Henry (David Warner) and Queen Margaret (Peggy Ashcroft) at the council table

King's authority was supreme (registered here as a type of veto), and the King had an absolute duty to rule absolutely. When Henry worried (in lines written for him by Barton), 'Alas, that I should have so great a voice!', his uncle chivvied him, 'My lord, you must … assert your sovereign *will*.' Thus, as a formulation of practical politics, Barton's additions put maximum – and equal – pressure both on the individual and on the group, excusing no one from the failure of politics that would divide the kingdom in civil war and fill London's municipal conduits to overflowing not with wine, as in Jack Cade's utopian fantasy, but with blood. The barons had a corporate duty to resolve their disputes, to 'subscribe in silence' to the common good; the King had a singular duty to be decisive, to direct and dispose. When Henry objected of his 'sovereign will' that 'Self-will is sin', Gloucester neatly detached the King's personal piety from his public duty by retorting, 'A subject's vice may be a sovereign's virtue.' The 'council-board', then, troped these ideas. Around it was staged the wrangling interplay between subject and sovereign, virtuous and vicious self-will. The table was a peace-maker. It brought men together in a kind of circle. But only uneasily – its disproportioned, jagged, five-sided shape made it look like some kind of monstrous primitive weapon. And indeed, the council table would eventually prove the instrument to destroy the very politician – Gloucester – who designed it.

As implausible as Barton's additions to Scene 6 look retro-spectively, at the time, they passed unnoticed. These plays, never performed before in Stratford, were strangers to reviewers and spectators who could mouth the words to *Hamlet* but couldn't tell Barton's *Henry* from Shakespeare's – either poetically *or* ideologically, not yet having acquired what they would possess consciously by the end of the decade, habits of political scepticism and anti-authoritarianism that would make them instantly alert to rhetoric like Gloucester's.[1] (Habits, significantly, that *Wars* would play a part in promoting.) Besides, attention was focused else-where – on the powerful spectacle presented on the stage, where John Bury had designed for the plays not a set but as a world in steel, a natural habitat for 'man the animal in action'.

Another thirty-something young turk like Hall and Barton, Bury came to the *Wars* in Stratford hotfoot from a very different *War* in another Stratford, Stratford East, where shoestring budgets had taught him to design productions out of junk salvaged off construction sites and builders' skips, made over into sets and props. Winding up his ten-year apprenticeship under Joan Little-wood at Theatre Workshop, his 'graduation piece' was a triumph, the design for the just-opened *Oh! What a Lovely War*, Littlewood's satire on militarism, masculinity and the Establishment which rendered the Great War as end-of-pier entertainment, its charac-ters cast from the ranks of music hall – chinless wonders, comic Krauts, frou-frou crinolines. Peter Hall's warriors were a different breed entirely, heavyweight thugs, dinosaurs to Littlewood's gadflies. Bury put them in a black box, a steel-clad cage, its floors flagged in stretched-metal mesh, its walls lined in steel, its furni-ture apparently forged by a smith, its occupants plated: men and women were fashioned in metal – chain mail, armour, helmets, swords. A massive armoured wall set with double doors – 'like gigantically magnified doors to the vaults of the Bank of England' (*The Sunday Telegraph* 21 July 1963) – was swung into positions that changed the physical geography of this world – and the interior mental spaces it troped. For battle scenes, the entire set was swung off, leaving the vast, metal flagged floor bare except for steel-clad bodies. In this world, even the roses were forced up iron trellises, and all human exchange was noisy, every step, every touch a clang or clash. By turns set centre stage, the throne (shunted forward and back) and the council table (manhandled into place) vied for political and imaginative precedence. Neither offered comfortable seating, both being built of ugly angles, brutalism inscribed on pointed, polished surfaces. Behind this political world, spectating upon it or perhaps haunting the court, stood a stone effigy, its eroded outlines making just visible the face of a medieval king – or a martyred saint. Later, the court of the lecherous *Edward IV* offered a momentary blaze of fevered splendour, the final scene backed with gold, sun-covered drapes before the flame was extinguished by the dark night of *Richard III* settling in. Boldly conceptual, Bury's design was strikingly modern in its use of materials to simulate the dull gorgeousness, the heavy textures of a primitive world, not just steel, but liquid latex (or as Bury called the stuff he introduced to Stratford, 'gunk'): painted over costumes, it produced the weighted effect of medieval couched needlework.[2] But over and above its powerful visual effect, the design was practical, 'a sounding board', as Bury said, 'for the actor's imagination, to supply him with the basic imagery that he needs' (Addenbrooke 110), and also a platform, space for actors to play out the physical manoeuvres that put muscle and sinew on their characters' political ambitions, a performance space for power plays.

A mess of angry barons

The big story this production wanted to tell was political: the crisis of the aristocracy that split the Plantagenets into rival houses and those houses into factions, and England into civil war; a crisis provoked by the premature death of Henry V. It's a story Shakespeare sets up from the first entrance in *Part One*, 'Enter the Funerall of King Henry the Fift' (Folio stage direction). Nicely paradoxical, this beginning (which is also an ending) defines the political moment as an absence hedged in by too much presence, a family portrait of male power relations that presents (almost) all the players and lays out what is at stake for the future. The dead king – whose fame is going to hang over his son's reign like a dazzling but nagging planet, always in view – is attended by too much family for his heir's subsequent good (brothers and uncles, legitimate and bastard; silent 'cousins' who will step forward later, hired gunslingers in the future wars). His coffin registers the power vacuum which they rush in to fill, they being also, of course, his officers of state in a household regulated by intramural rivalry: Lord Protector, Regent of France, Bishop of Winchester. Presenting an image of the ordered state metonymised in the ordered ceremony of the state funeral, this opening scene proceeds to dismantle the idea, destabilising Harry's obsequies with unseemly interruption then, almost comically, routing them as mourners peel off one by one, leaving an ignominious shambles – the pattern of things to come.

Solving the problems of Shakespeare's opening scene in the theatre was clearly going to be critical to the success of the whole *Wars* project, and Hall and Barton went about it by pointing the political argument, first axing more than half of Shakespeare's play-text (but adding Suffolk to the tableau to establish him as a main player from the beginning – William Squires, square-jawed, aloof, equal parts aristocratic hauteur and dangerous sexuality[3]). Next, they supplied the 'back-story'. Lying in arms, his empty throne conspicuous in the background, Henry V spoke from beyond the grave, commanding his family-subjects, 'as touching the estate of my realm', 'to render your allegiance unto my son', 'to love and join together' in 'one unfeigned amity', not least against the upstart 'Charles, calling himself Dauphin' pretender in 'our Realm of France' (Hall and Barton 3) – an 'estate' which would shortly lie in ruins. Most important, as became clear when the barons' opening salvoes began cross-firing over the corpse, Hall and Barton sharpened the debate by making Shakespeare *sound* different. One of the things to emerge from the company's rehearsal period was a new RSC house style of verse speaking: cool, rational, analytical; Shakespeare spoken the way F. R. Leavis (one of Hall's academic tutors at Cambridge) read him, an acoustic register that drained language of emotion and scaled down the text's Tamburlaine-sized rhetoric to the calculated discourse of a boardroom. This was verse speaking as management technique. When Gloucester set about Winchester ('None do you like but an effeminate Prince') and Winchester hit back ('whate'er we like, thou art Protector'), or when Talbot's Captain entered with disastrous news from France ('Awake, awake, English nobility! / … Cropp'd are the flower-de-luces in your arms') their speeches were like reportage, delivered in voices produced from the back of the throat, not through flared nostrils. Acoustically, this England was not so much a bear pit as a slightly chilled anatomy theatre, the barons heavyweight political scientists coolly, if crudely, dissecting the body of state.

This story's protagonist was Gloucester. The old order was dead – or on its last geriatric legs, like Bedford, whose collapse in Scene 5 was surely emblematic: he was unable, finally, to lift a sword after threatening France in 'high astounding terms'. Bedford represented a redundant feudalism, bred – like that other antique warhorse, Talbot – to a class that privileged brutalism as honour and managed domestic politics by busying giddy minds with foreign wars. The new men were self-promoters; chief among them, Nicholas Selby's Winchester, a secular priest in a jewel-crusted cope (with a mouth like a salamander's) who personified empty spirituality, 'God' reduced to 'sanction', and who gave himself away by only just remembering to make the sign of the cross over King Henry's corpse before gathering his canonical skirts up and bustling off. Silent in the background stood a watchful Warwick, a mountain of a man as played by Brewster Mason, whose bemused spectatorship, watching the cracks appearing in the façade of family solidarity, was registered with precise delicacy: eyebrows raised ironically, he aimed sideways glances at Suffolk.

These roles emerged in performance as case studies in political opportunism. Among the peers, Gloucester was the only moderate – but even he had a short fuse, and Winchester knew just when to apply the touch paper. Patiently schooling the young King ('Conclude the peace ... / Recall the jangling peers, and take a wife'), but testy when Henry balked at his instruction ('What signifies thy *liking*? Thou art King; / Seek not what likes thee, but what likes thy kingdom' (Scene 13)), Paul Hardwick's Gloucester, uniquely, saw England solving England's problems not with piety or French blood but with English speaking, with rational debate around the council or conference table.[4] His miscalculation was double: that Henry could be groomed to 'become a King' modelled to his specifications, and that the peers would act as disinterestedly as he.

His impeachment in Scene 22 was *Henry VI*'s crisis, a test the young King Henry failed. Arrested on trumped-up charges, Gloucester sat at the council table answering each of the increasingly ludicrous and malicious accusations calmly, smiling briefly when the King reached across to take his hand; but when Suffolk ended his interrogation by announcing 'mightier crimes' and throwing open the walled doors at the back of the chamber, summoning the guards, Gloucester became urgent. He was giving his last tutorial as schoolmaster to the King, and he didn't have much time left. Addressing Henry eye to eye, he analysed the 'plotted tragedy' being staged around them, himself merely 'the prologue to their play', and named the players by the signs that gave them away: 'Beaufort's red sparkling eyes', Suffolk's 'cloudy brow', Warwick's 'policies', Margaret's 'stirr'd up' enmity, and 'dogged York, that reaches at the moon' (Scene 22). But now Suffolk, arrogantly confident, played his ace. 'I challenge law,' he said, the very law Gloucester had introduced in Scene 6, and, producing his dagger, laid it on the council table, signalling himself 'content to abide the general voice'. Other daggers clanged down. After a pause, silently, Exeter added his. And the reluctant King, 'since all approve', required himself to 'abide it, too'. Now, though, Gloucester had his own ace to play, reminding the peers of the 'further article', 'the right reserv'd unto the King' to 'void and oversway' what 'offends his princely conscience'. Gloucester faced the King, his 'appeal unto your majesty: / Dost thou in conscience cleave to their consent?', adding *sotto voce*, 'As thou art King, now answer like a King.' In the long silence, Henry, who shortly would see Gloucester as a calf led away to slaughter and himself as the cow, 'lowing up and down', 'wail[ing] her darling's loss', wildly scanned the faces of the butchers who held him at bay – then capitulated: 'The Council's will shall be our conscience.' Gloucester, exhausted, walked through the double doors; Margaret's hand fluttered excitedly to her mouth as a squeal of pleasure escaped; Henry laid his head upon the council table and wept.

What he consented to was Gloucester's trial; what he unwittingly sanctioned was his assassination. So like his grandfather, Bolingbroke, whose 'original sin' was his complicity in King Richard's death, Henry too was guilty of 'original sin'. Retribution was immediate. Taught in Scene 23 (by an unlikely tutor, Warwick) to read the signs of murder upon the corpse of Gloucester when it was produced for ghastly public inspection, Henry banished Suffolk – who walked through the same double doors, straight into the hands of the clamouring commons who answered his arrogance – 'Obscure and lousy swains … Out of my way' – with mob violence, knocking him down, then hacking at his head until it came off, using it as a pulped battering ram to thud at the palace gates for the King's attention before dumping it for 'the Queen his mistress' to collect. Meanwhile, another anti-Gloucester conspirator lay sweating in his fur-heaped bed, hallucinating mad bargains with Death – 'I'll give thee England's treasure ... / So thou wilt let me live, and feel no pain.' Winchester (now Cardinal) implicated himself in Gloucester's death by what his guilty conscience fantasised – 'Comb down his hair; look, look! it stands upright' – but implicated Henry, too, making him, in lines written by Barton, confront again the appalling image of his delinquency: 'Thou might'st have sav'd him: but in holy cowardice / Thou durst not do it.' This was the closing scene of Hall and Barton's *Henry VI*. With Gloucester dead, and moderation dead, the political world was left to improvisations of power – and to anarchy, the Warwick–York faction emerging from authority's ruin as the inverted double of Gloucester–Henry.

More single-mindedly than Shakespeare and from early on, Barton established Warwick, the 'king-maker', as the director of *de facto* improvisations, already prepping York for power in Scene 3, the Temple Garden scene (promoted from II.iv in Shakespeare's playtext), where the plucking of the roses was the metaphoric prelude to the despoiling of England. A burly but deeply meditative Machiavel, Brewster Mason's Warwick was the perfect foil to Donald Sinden's choleric York, who seemed always to be speaking through a cud he was chewing of stinging nettles. When York raged ('How I am brav'd ...!'), Warwick soothed ('be patient til the rest go down'; 'contain thee'). While York claimed a 'brain more busy than the labouring spider' weaving 'tedious snares to trap mine enemies', Warwick was the true arachnid, hardly moving from the centre of the web, masterminding the double bluff around Gloucester's death, and, from the opening of *Edward IV* (Barton's Scene 26), playing faction against faction so deftly that he appeared to stand on both sides at once, proclaiming York king in Scene 31 and in Scene 33 defending (restored) King Henry against the hard-liners when the compromise between York and Lancaster gave Henry back the crown. But like Winchester (via the 'effeminate prince'), Suffolk (via Margaret), and even potentially Gloucester (as Protector) before him, Warwick, as he coolly informed the audience, gazing straight at them, had in mind a puppet-government where he would pull the strings, where York – or Lancaster – might be king, but 'I shall bear the sway' (Scene 26).

As if proleptically imagining this 'puppet' world, Warwick produced its hyperbolised simulation: in Barton's *Wars* it is he, not York, who mobilises Jack Cade – played by Clive Swift as a bearded ruffian munchkin with a twinkling, murderous stare and a way of turning lines into laughter, a black joker at the head of a mob out of Brueghel, backed by a crude banner with a cartoon rose slap-stitched on to it.[5] Marching through Blackheath, Cade's rout was the carnivalised twin of Westminster's 'mess of angry barons'. In the same instant that he enacted the overthrow of order by usurping a title, Cade lampooned the pretensions constituting that order, mocking courtly ritual in his skewed performance of it. So, to outface Stafford 'with a man as good as himself', he dubbed *himself* a knight, instantly promoting himself from the ranks of the plebs to an elevated aristocrat. But then, having grabbed a common billhook from one of his followers to use for the dubbing, he satirically converted that same billhook into a a different category of prop, to demonstrate the metaphor of state he wanted to impress upon his hearers – a metaphor he might have borrowed from his aristocratic antitype. England, he said, was a garden, and he and his followers 'a sort of gardeners to the commonweal', their intent 'no greater harm than weeding' (Scene 27). Stepping down from his political speech and his Mother Courage cart, Cade with a curt motion stopped Stafford in his tracks by bringing in tight around him the crowd, the slack-jawed 'filth and scum of Kent', as Stafford had just called them. But how dangerously obsolete that arrogance sounded in this 'popular' world. Laughing, Cade showed Stafford the point of the billhook, his 'weeding' tool, then lowered it between his legs. Stafford's eyes widened as he felt the hook inserted, and he screamed as it was drawn up his torso, laying him open like a bullock to a butcher while the mob-on-holiday shouted triumph. Cade's mad manifesto ('Burn all the records of the realm: my mouth shall be the parliament of England'), his carnival violence ('The first thing we do, let's kill all the lawyers'), his parodic procession, a dance of death 'Up Fish Street! down Saint Magnus' Corner!' (Scenes 27, 29) materialised, disseminated and made 'common' the anarchy let loose earlier at Gloucester's demise.

Ultimately, however, this was footling stuff that rapidly ran out of steam, like a funfair balloon deflating, the mob mindlessly capitulating to order as instantly as they had capitulated to anarchy, merely buzzing annoyingly before being slapped down by the jewel-handled fly-swatter of state. And yet, how prophetic these scenes of urban guerrilla street-fighting would look, retrospectively, five, six, seven years on, when The Weathermen, Baader-Meinhof, Black

Panthers, the Angry Brigade were in the headlines and authority worldwide was under siege by youth culture's Jack Cades. For now, though, the real threat to Establishment order came from within the aristocracy, in the cultured youth it was training up to its own elite brand of terrorism – the York boys, Edward (Roy Dotrice), George (Charles Kay) and 'Dicky', that 'valiant crook-back prodigy' (Ian Holm). When they were introduced in *Edward IV* (Scene 34), they were occupied, in that time of truce negotiated between their father and King Henry, with 'mockeries', with displacement activity. They were rough-housing around a vaulting horse, trying to snatch a paper crown off their little brother Rutland's head (a crown that he still wore when he was ambushed and murdered by Clifford in Scene 35; a crown that found its way into Margaret's hands and finished up on their father York's agonised head moments before it was chopped off in the following scene). At play, these boys staged fake violence that looked strangely, comically, like Cade's carnival violence. Their laughter was an uncanny echo of his. But where Cade's grotesque disorder served to validate the order it inverted, the York sons, solipsistic amoralists, occupied a space outside order. The terrifying products of the older generation's opportunism and self-interest, these children were like black holes – their centre, a void collapsing every human value into 'naught'. Sexuality was debased in a lecherously exhibitionist Edward who sprawled on his new-won throne intent on seduction, exposing his 'meaning' to Widow Grey between his splayed legs; loyalty, in a fickle, pretty-boy George whose changes of mind – and side – were framed as 'legitimate' changes of a too-tender heart. But it was Holm's baby-faced Richard, a Puck with a buckled back, a delinquent cherub with eyes deadened into psychopathic impassivity, who expressed the absolute nullity of this annulled generation. Symptomatically, he was the outcome of Henry's lenity. It was entirely appropriate that these two should emerge as the new twins of political reckoning, the one so exquisitely sensitive that his voice spoke prophecy, the other insensate, ending prophecy with the thrust of a dagger that was as dead to feeling as the hand that grasped it. They would recognise each other, as in a mirror, the king and the killer, when they met in the Tower.

'A school-boy' and 'effeminate prince'

For reviewers, David Warner – Henry – was 'the find of the decade' (Bernard Levin *Daily Mail* 18 July 1963). For spectators, this unknown twenty-two-year-old, fresh out of **RADA** (the Royal Academy of Dramatic Art), in his first professional theatre job, discovered in Shakespeare's virtually unknown king one of his great parts. Tall, gangling, walking 'with the slouching gait of a clumsy scholar or farm-hand' (Harold Hobson *The Sunday Times* 21 July 1963) and dressed like a holy fool out of Dostoevsky in a rough, low-belted smock and round-toed peasant boots, he was awkwardly, sweetly boyish, a tow-haired fringe falling across his forehead. But his habitual posture sitting on his throne, bony shoulders hunched, knees tight together, hands clasped around them, securing to his body the tiny breviary he carried, open, with him everywhere, made him seem prematurely old, a walking embodiment of the monumental stone effigy that stood as the background presence to his court, or a funerary *transi*, a skeleton-in-waiting.

John Barton's early verdict on King Henry, communicated to Peter Hall in a letter while they were still working on the script, that 'his saintliness' was 'only a label', 'his weakness an uninteresting fact'; that he was 'not complex, merely wet' (Hall and Barton xviii), reckoned without David Warner. Warner made Henry a contemplative in a world that scorned contemplation, that celebrated action then brutalised it, that glamorised power then degraded it by the atrocities – the killings, the humiliations, the tortures and betrayals – that so fleetingly secured it. In this context, Warner's study of weakness was fascinating. Where, in his textual additions (most notably to Scenes 22, 25 and 39, Gloucester's impeachment, Beaufort's death and the molehill scene), Barton aimed to make Henry responsible, Warner did something much greater, making Henry *aware*. He was no absolutist. How could he be, knowing that he himself, a king, was subject to a much greater king? But only absolutism would awe the bully-boys who shook his throne. Ironically, then, it seemed his reign was one long, sometimes wry, sometimes grief-stricken rumination on the rhetorical question Richard Plantagenet had long ago posed, 'Subjected thus, / How can you say to me I am a king?' (*Richard II* III.ii.172–3).

Much of what David Warner elaborated for this part was cued by an early speech (indeed, in Shakespeare's text, Henry's opening speech). Appealing to his warring uncles pointedly as 'the special watchmen of our English weal', Henry attempted mediation: 'I would prevail, if prayers might prevail, / To join your hearts in love and amity.' Already, 'my tender years can tell', he said, 'Civil dissension is a viperous worm / That gnaws the bowels of the commonwealth' (Scene 6). The voice was mild, and also childishly over-earnest; the political point, hardly more than elementary, sounded like something the schoolboy king had been swatting up with a tutor, the sensationalist trope – the 'worm' that is both satanic and parasitic – connecting political abstraction via the metaphor of the body politic to morbid pathology. A youth nervous of authority was revealed in the tentativeness of his utterance ('I would'; 'if'); yet 'prevail' – twice – suggested a different kind of man. 'Prayers' – both 'prayers' and 'pray-ers', as the iambic pentameter requires – was the operative word here, for its reference effectively translated political discourse into a different realm, a different metaphysical space. This man's saintliness was no mere label; and, given the eternal scale of his reckoning, Henry's thoughtfulness trained the audience to hear as madness the petty, costly and parochial dynastic bickering that turned secular existence into brutishness.

This was a king whose crown didn't fit, who had to reach up, at his coronation, to steady his over-large inheritance (Scene 8) – and who afterwards never wore it, though his queen and son wore theirs like extensions of their flesh; a king tractable to correction, believing of Gloucester that he 'chideth me from love, / From love to England and unto myself' (Scene 6); a king who skipped up the steps to his throne, delighted, anticipating his bride, but failed to notice her disappointment at the kiss he gave her – chastely on the cheek; a pious man who knelt, wondering, before the sight-restored peasant at St Albans but who knew before anyone else where Gloucester's interrogations were going, the miracle-revealed-as-a-fraud cruelly disarming his faith before the next assaults upon it rushed in. As a result, the arrest of Eleanor and the trumped-up accusations against the Lord Protector (Scene 21) registered not as what they were, crises of rule engineered by court Machiavels, but crises of faith, heard in Henry's anguished question, 'O God, seest / Thou this, and bearest so long?'

Visibly aged, Henry in *Edward IV* served England as her unheard conscience. While Clifford crowed, Henry gazed, stricken, at York's head impaled on York gate (Scene 38) then, curtly dismissed from the battle ('The Queen hath best success when you are absent'), wandered across the field, settling hunched on a molehill – wishing himself dead. Tears from his haunted eyes ran slowly down his grimed, unshaved cheeks as he fantasised a quiet life, a shepherd's life, a fantasy – 'how sweet! how lovely!' – mocked by the appearance out of the gloom behind him, as if they were materialising his meditations, first of the son who has killed his father, then the father who has killed his son. Antiphonal voices spoke like a chorus of doom across this scene while Warner's Henry seemed to absorb into himself all pain, becoming a wretched icon of sorrow that was, strangely, as he said, 'like civil war', his heart, his eyes, like the very heart and eyes of state, being broken with grief and blinded with tears (Scene 39).

From here on, Warner made Henry's journey into political awareness a journey into black comedy. The Keepers ('subjects sworn in all allegiance') whom he quizzed in Scene 42 ('But did you never swear, and break an oath?'; 'Where did you dwell when I was King of England?') were like a double act out of Beckett: 'You are the King King Edward hath depos'd'; 'we were subjects but while you were King.' Released from the Tower in Scene 48 by, absurdly, Warwick ('new-revolted' back to Lancaster), Henry made a brief tour of freedom, a lap around the green sward as it were, then sanely re-admitted himself *to the Tower* – not a prison but a 'sanctuary', an asylum from the madness outside. The final comic twist for this old man who had seen too much, and who wore that 'too much' inscribed in gaunt lines on his face, was looking up from quiet study in his cell into the empty eyes of the blackest joker in the York family brat-pack. Instinctively, Henry shoved the rude crucifix that stood on his table between himself and Richard, a gesture that amused them both. Henry knew that 'Roscius' had arrived 'to act' his latest 'scene of death'. But as Ian Holm's Richard sat, relaxed, like an off-duty *putto*, his sword cradled in his folded arms, the killer who felt nothing, bandying line for line with the king who felt everything and whose voice seemed to come from beyond the grave, the farthest extremes of political performance were brought into intimate proximity. England's past and future here came face to face, and redundant Henry became prophetic. Leaning toward Richard and urging the future upon him as he, the father, mourned the son whom the monster had so lately murdered, Warner's Henry moved beyond grief, finally to achieve a voice that matched his father's in authority and to resolve the legacy, the history of difference between them, the 'school-boy' prince and the 'dragon' king. Henry unrolled the future as Richard listened:

> ... many a thousand,
> Which now mistrust no parcel of my fear,
> And many an old man's sigh and many a widow's,
> And many an orphan's water-standing eye,
> Men for their sons, wives for their husbands,
> Shall rue the hour that ever thou wast born. (Scene 52)

Richard smiled as Henry called him 'an indigested and deformed lump', born with teeth, 'To signify thou cam'st to bite the world.' But at the next revelation, 'Thou cam'st –', Richard suddenly stood, and, in a bizarre travesty of an embrace from behind, clamped his hand across Henry's mouth. Only when he released him, silent, did the audience hear the sound of Richard's sword entering the King's body, then the awful gurgling of the King's blood in his throat as he found his last words, 'slaughter', 'sins', 'pardon'. Henry's final gesture was to grasp Richard in his arms and to kiss him. But the kiss that condemned Richard's evil by forgiving it didn't end things, for the King wasn't dead yet. Stronger dying than living, he grappled with Richard who, recoiling, twisted, threw off the embrace, then stared at the audience as he stabbed – and stabbed.

'O tiger's heart wrapp'd in a woman's hide'

While Warner was inventing a role even his directors didn't quite know was there, Peggy Ashcroft was recovering a part notorious in the theatre from its original performance: Robert Greene, bitterly mocking Shakespeare as the 'upstart crow' in *A Groatsworth of Wit* (1592), was remembering Queen Margaret – and knew his readers would remember her, too, his satire depending on it – when he parodied York's line and fixed it on his rival: 'O tiger's heart wrapp'd in a player's hide' (see p. 16). In the move from Shakespeare's *Henrys* to Barton's *Wars* the women's parts mostly fell victim to the adapter's blue pencil, cut (the Countess of Auvergne), radically edited (Eleanor, Duchess of Gloucester), or reduced to bit parts and walk-ons (Simpcox's wife and Cade's busty doxy). But in Margaret and Joan la Pucelle, Hall and Barton saw roles that refocused, *re-gendered* their analysis of political power struggle, roles that could be recruited to their project of showing the state as, on the one hand, a machine driven by the powerful; on the other, a

[74]

metaphysical apparatus, a divine contract disastrously violated. One woman was, from her first entrance, a politician, an assured player at sexual politics who would manage to insinuate herself a place at the council table where she would throw as many spanners in the works as any of York's cronies but who, increasingly frustrated, would grow into 'an Amazon' (Hall and Barton xx) dressed in battle gear, heading the King's army. The other woman was a witch. Embodying the 'fatalistic' (Hall and Barton xx) and trafficking with 'familiar spirits' 'cull'd' out of the evil anti-empire placed 'in the powerful regions under earth' (Scene 14), she was the one who would translate the curse on the House of Lancaster into an actual body count. Both of them, usefully (for English chauvinism), were Frenchwomen who embodied a threat more dangerous than an army's.

Janet Suzman's Joan la Pucelle, lithe, athletic, dressed for combat in chain mail and, with her dark hair cropped short like a boy's, certainly more virile than the effete, brocaded Dauphin, got his attention by kicking over the chessboard where he sat, in his tent, playing at war instead of waging it (Scene 2). Barton marked la Pucelle's metaphysical agency from the beginning – a 'prophet' whose 'all-potent and infallible' 'spirits' swore 'That fate' had 'put a curse on England's house' (Scene 2). Triumphant when straddling the gates of Orleans, seductive when persuading Burgundy to desert the English: was it her spirits or *spirit* that worked such magic? Or was her power to 'raise' the French merely lewd, the 'holy maid' a trull? Scene 14 provided the final answer: left alone on a field swirling with the smoke of battle (this was the season the RSC discovered dry ice as a scenic effect), exposed by the latest craven French retreat, la Pucelle knelt, held out her hand like an offering – and drew across it her sword, cutting deep into her flesh. Her spirits were demons whom she fed on her blood and to whom she now promised her body, offering herself as, prostrated, she rolled on to her back, exposed her neck and breasts and smeared them with blood. Abandoned even by hell, she was indomitably back on her feet when York came upon her. He mocked her – 'Fell banning hag', 'ugly witch' – but had to kick her unconscious in the stomach to capture her, her body carried off by soldiers, doubled over a pike.

This sequence is written so that, in the theatre, as one femme fatale exits to be burnt as a witch, another appears, her double, who practises, it turns out, even more potent witchcraft. Entering (improbably, across the battlefield; but scenic, not narrative, logic is operating here) as Suffolk's captive, Margaret instantly captivates him. Here, the actor in the role doubled the effect of the magic in the narrative, for the fifty-five-year-old Peggy Ashcroft's transformation into the girl-Margaret was astonishing. Delicate but arch, skittish and with a natural hauteur that showed Suffolk he'd met his match, she held her hands in a gesture of defence that was also an invitation, and her body, flirtatiously, as if every nerve were alert. Her head was held high, but her eyes were lowered between looks that looked with the boldness of a man's looking. Long hair cascaded down her back, held in place by a gold circlet. When she spoke, she sounded like she looked, sixteen – and French: Ashcroft raised her vocal register half an octave in these early scenes and gave Margaret a Gallic accent that would permanently mark her out in the English court as Other – and enemy. (As she aged, her rolled r's would deepen into a growl.) When she pulled away from the kiss Suffolk urged as a 'loving token to his majesty', and laughed in his face, 'That for thyself! I will not presume / To send such peevish tokens to a king' (Scene 15), spectators saw Margaret in a dangerous replay of la Pucelle's first meeting with the Dauphin – and a replay of what he so hungrily wanted, seduction. They saw, too, that politics for women in these plays promised to be body politics, their power inscribed within the erotic. It followed that sexual politics troped a politics of transgression: nowhere could women be powerful without being defamed and demonised – an ideological formation, original to Shakespeare in the *Henrys*, which he continued to deploy and to interrogate for the rest of his career, in *Antony and Cleopatra*, *King Lear* and, most sensationally, *The Winter's Tale*.

Ashcroft's savvy Margaret had the appetite her politically anorexic husband altogether lacked. She dismissed English insults – over the matter of her dowry, for example – with the merest of Gallic shrugs. Moreover, she deflected Gloucester's humiliations with the silkiest of sarcasms. When, for example, he attempted to bar her place in council with the marginalising put-down, 'Madam, the King is old enough himself / To give his censure; these are no women's matters', she ignored the personal insult to exploit the weakness Gloucester had unwittingly exposed, wondering sweetly, 'If he be old enough, what needs your grace / To be protector of his excellence?' (Scene 19). Once the peers were off the premises, she circled the council table like a malign Lady

Fortune inspecting her wheel, counting the cogs she could jam or snap off – 'Warwick, Somerset ... grumbling York'. But scene by scene she lost patience with Henry's piety, mocking moderation as impotence, her frustrated ambitions turning her into Medusa, or rather, Medusa's victim. For Ashcroft's face hardened, aged, it seemed, overnight. She stopped playing politics when she learned that even knocking his prop – Gloucester – out from under him wouldn't make her husband stand on his own feet. When Suffolk's head was returned to her, pulped, she took up the men's new game, brutalism. But where men committing violence in these plays became somehow more themselves, more manly, violence serving to authenticate masculinity (so that Henry's pacifism made him a 'boy', 'effeminate'), Margaret's violence denatured her and made her monstrous. She entered Scene 36 a travesty of a woman, the silhouette still female, but made over into masculinity, for she was dressed head to toe in chain mail, her crown jammed down on her metal hood like steel strapping. Taken captive before her, tied to crossed pikes that made him look crucified and dragged to the dizzying heights of a molehill that, 'elevating' him, mocked his ambitions, York called her 'She-wolf of France', a 'tiger's heart wrapp'd in a woman's hide'. But she was worse than that. She was a harpy that, taunting him with his 'mess of sons', 'wanton Edward, ... lusty George ... that valiant crook-back prodigy, Dicky your boy', suddenly asked, sweetly savage, 'where is your darling Rutland?' Producing the napkin soaked in the child's still-wet blood as York howled 'No!', she slapped him across the face with it – and bloodied her own face. Crazed with hate, laughing, pressing, and snarling against his sweat-soaked agony, she produced the paper crown Rutland was playing with when he was surprised and killed and thrust it on to York's head: this was the man who 'raught at mountains with outstretched arms / Yet parted but the shadow with his hand'. She spat in his face. 'Off with the crown; and with the crown, his head.' Then, as York began, 'She-wolf ... adder ... Amazonian trull', she swayed like a savage around him, a cannibal feeding on grief, her mad hands working spasmodically in gestures that seemed to be pulling his words out of him like ropes of intestines. But the hysterical cackle died. When York asked, dumbly bewildered, 'How couldst thou drain the life-blood of the child?', Ashcroft's Margaret was stunned, her lip starting to tremble. Exeter wept, but Clifford stepped forward and stabbed, and Margaret, crying out ecstatically, lunged at him with her own

[77]

5 *Edward IV* (1963). Queen Margaret (Peggy Ashcroft) gets
ready for battle

sword. Instructing that York's head be set 'on York gates' was a
triumphalist joke: 'So York may overlook the town of York!' But
saying so, Margaret wiped her mailed hand across her sweaty face
– and left her mouth a bloody gash.

This scene produced its savage twin. Bleak but stunningly theatrical at Tewksbury, Margaret stood in the wailing, snow-swirling
wind, rousing her troops, exhausted, but mechanically holding her
posture erect (Scene 51). This time, it was her turn to be brought
in captive, to watch her own son taunted. Her protective embrace
only served to hold the prince upright as the York boys joked,
'Can so young a thorn begin to prick?' – and thrust into him like a

straw-filled sack. For an impossible moment the murdered prince stood, then fell in one crash. His mother's weeping was an animal's shrieks. Margaret staggered from butcher to butcher, showing the blood from her son on her hands, deeply serious when she exposed her throat and craved 'dispatch'. But George turned away disgusted, and Edward recoiled from her curse: 'So come to you and yours, as to this Prince.'

And Richard? Where was Richard, 'that devil's butcher', when Margaret wanted him? Already on his way to the Tower – to Henry. Even the atrocity committed there, however, wouldn't end the cycle of violence. Margaret's curse was already upon Edward and upon his progeny. (And Edward helplessly acknowledged as much, gazing momentarily into the dead face of Margaret's Edward before exiting 'to London' to a newborn son – another Edward.) Already, too, as Richard made his way first to the Tower then to his brother's court, 'chaos' was heading 'home', its object to deracinate affinity. Richard had gloated in Scene 52 that he was 'like no father', 'like no brother'; that he was 'myself alone'. But he was wrong. The 'mess of angry barons' might have been weeded out from these *Wars*, but 'man the animal in action, murdering to protect' and 'lying to save' was merely taking a breather. In the sequel, Henry VI's remaindered queen would take on the 'hunchback prodigy'.

CHAPTER IV

A true trilogy: the RSC's *Henry VI* (1977–79)

An anecdote from his late adolescence can perhaps be read as situating the 'originary moment' behind Terry Hands's *Henry VI* trilogy. Eighteen years of age, on his way to university, and already regulating his life by those uncompromising habits of self-discipline that would later earn him the title 'Gauleiter Hands' from actors (he's half German), he had set himself the task that summer of reading his way through the *Complete Works of William Shakespeare*. He was in Germany. It was hot. And when he came to the *Henrys* he was lying on a balcony, the book propped up against the ironwork. He remembers being completely 'gob-smacked' by the plays. They were like newsreels spooling out incident upon incident, news flash upon news flash, a seemingly endless line of characters caught in momentary flares of publicity – like photography, in sequences of quick-shot, high-definition frames. Absorbed, sweaty, mindless of the heat, Hands couldn't turn the pages fast enough. *What was going to happen next?* But the reading was interrupted – by something falling on the youth's half-naked body. Looking up he saw on the balcony above a woman of a certain age. She was throwing down upon him a leisurely volley of fat black grapes (Terry Hands in conversation 1978).

That slightly comic, quasi-erotic scene with the grapes – their ripe flesh splitting as they hit ripening flesh – is suggestive. Hall and Barton's *The Wars of the Roses* in 1963–64 saw men as political machines, as Terry Hands remembered very clearly, looking back at them in 1977, when he began rehearsals for his own RSC production of the *Henrys*. Hall's *Wars* was 'a study of power politics', but an incomplete study, the younger director thought, because 'Shakespeare goes far beyond politics. Politics is a very shallow science.' Politics, 'like the swelling associated with dropsy, is a fat and watery exterior to the real problem, which is a disease of the heart' (Shaughnessy 63). By contrast, Hands's *Henry*s would investigate the human heart, and they would get there by thinking through the flesh. Where Hall's players were cool, calculating, cerebral, rational, Hands's would be impetuous, hot-blooded, spontaneous, sensual, sensational, fleshy. As Hands read the *Henry*s, their central issue was a disastrous love affair, a failed marriage. Clustering around it were a dozen other grief-struck stories of failed desire and loss, and emerging from these bitter ashes was the story of a king making himself through trial – and more trial. Hall and Barton's *Wars* was directed as political tutorial; Hands directed the three *Henry*s as England's family tragedy. And like all Shakespeare's family tragedies from *Titus* to *Lear*, this one was shot through with laughter.

Masterminding his three-part invention was one 'shaping fantasy', Hands's non-negotiable *idée fixe*: he intended to direct the three plays uncut, in their entirety, in sequence, and to open them on consecutive nights, billing them as modern-day world premieres, the first performances of the unadapted texts since Shakespeare's lifetime.[1] It was a harebrained idea. Indeed, when Hands first proposed it to higher-ups in the RSC directorate in 1975 he was turned down flat. So instead, that season he directed a placebo history cycle, the two parts of *Henry IV* and a *Henry V* that broke RSC box office records, took London by storm, packed houses on tour in Britain, Europe and America, wiped out the RSC's deficit, and earned him the right to risk following his original theatrical instincts two years later, adjusting them only in so far as he made a strategic decision to revive his triumphant *Henry V* as the prequel to *Henry VI*. In this, Hands was clearly hedging his bets and throwing a rich sop to the company's grateful accountants, a calculated conservative gesture. But artistically and theatrically, he was doing something audacious, even radical, certainly unprecedented: he was devising a brand new tetralogy that offered across the four plays a very different reading of 'this England' by constructing a cycle arranged to show not a triumphant but a troubled history, a history culminating not in Agincourt but, post-Agincourt, in defeat, uncertainty, indirection, anarchy. In 1977, this was a history the times could tolerate: post-Empire, post-Vietnam, post-student activism, post-male supremacism, post-authoritarianism. (Some of this troubled consciousness was picked up in the publicity material. The production poster, designed in red, white and black, had splattered across its surface a rough-edged blob that might have been a blood-stain. Dissected three ways, it looked like a peace protester's CND badge.) In 1977, British politics had become decentralised, dispersed into issue politics, personal politics, things that mattered to particular human hearts. But in 1977, too, the idea of England, framed in the national symbolism of the monarchy, was on most people's minds: this was the year of the Queen's silver jubilee.

Hands's project was massively endowed by two crucial strokes of casting: he persuaded Alan Howard, his charismatic Hal and Harry, to return in the *Henry VI*s and double as his own son, the irresolute child king Henry. And he persuaded most of his *Henry V* company to sign on for another RSC season, to take on these unknown plays and their un-pedigreed roles, and to take them on at full cry. A true company who exemplified and vindicated Peter Hall's vision for the RSC from 1963, this ragged-arsed scrum of jobbing actors didn't count a star or prima donna among them. More importantly, having been through the wars together in 1975, they shared a common rehearsal vocabulary and knew what to expect of each other on the stage, which meant they could take short-cuts in rehearsals – which was just as well, really, for as Sally Beauman has observed with devastating understatement, 'There was not enough time' to do what Hands wanted done.[2] He came into rehearsals with a promptbook signalling as much. It forgot about 'parts' and 'acts'. Instead, it treated the trilogy like a single master-play, its scenes dauntingly numbered from one to seventy-nine.[3]

As it happened, re-citing the trilogy in this way, exposing its scenic axis – the almost breathless 'and then, and then, and then' quality of the writing – and acting on the 'naive' assumption that the trilogy wasn't textually corrupt, that Shakespeare was no ham-fisted apprentice in these plays but actually knew what he was doing, that, therefore, every scene 'belonged' and that their business was to find out *how*, forced serious readjustments at every level of production. The plays were clearly episodic. The sheer number of scenes (most of them short) and roles they introduced (many of them single-scene cameos) told actors that story, not character, was driving the narrative. In a theatre of such urgency, meanings were going to be located as much in structure as in characterisation – in, that is, the order of the storytelling and the pace of its telling; in the ways scenes were composed, juxtaposed and replayed; in continuities and discontinuities, anticipations and inversions; in sudden moves between macro- and microcosm, bluster and whisper; in repetitions of actions, gestures, rituals, utterances, signs, stillnesses; in the immediate and cumulative visual design. As Hands observed, 'None of the actors is given much time – often only four or five minutes – to get a hold on a scene.' Was that deliberate? Was Shakespeare, as Hands thought, inventing something new for the theatre in the *Henrys*, a poetry of 'dramatic juxtaposition'? That is, was he learning to write 'a different kind of poetry – not of the lyric line but of a person and a face and an emotion and an idea', a more-than-literary poetry, a poetry whose grammar was space and light and the 'sudden change from grandeur to simplicity', from the 'high rhetoric about Joan down to a soldier in the rain and cold' or, in the opposite aesthetic direction, 'from simplicity to grandeur' (quoted in Swander 149)? The company would find out in rehearsal.

For actors, rethinking what they'd taken to be the standard rela-tionship between plot and character in Shakespeare meant seeing themselves in the *Henry VI*s the way Peter Quince's company does in *Pyramus and Thisbe*, as, literally, *parts*, their business to serve the story. Utterance in these plays is extrovert, and actors found that the rhetorical size of speech Shakespeare writes required an acting style that was full-frontal, presentational, theatrical, external, an acting style that privileged the performative, not interiority. Solil-oquy was not overheard meditation or anxious contemplation; rather, it was instant revelation of what was just being thought, immediate communication that actors learned to deliver straight to the audience, in direct address. Here, characters spoke iambic pentameter not because it was poetic but because it was the fastest way of communicating. If actors had any experience of this kind of robust 'in your face' performance, it was from pantomime or the club circuit. This was storytelling acting that instructed the actor, 'you are what you speak'.

For Terry Hands, too, a 'standard relationship' needed rethink-ing, the one he was proposing between himself, as director, and Shakespeare, because to hypothesise the integrity of Shakespeare's playtext – all seventy-nine scenes of it – meant submitting himself to a logic that seemingly made the modern director redundant (and certainly made his own authoritarian habits ridiculously over-determining). It meant relinquishing the notion of the director as *auteur*, bringing to the trilogy no 'concept', no 'image', no 'inter-pretation'. Whatever the play 'meant', Hands insisted, would be discovered by actors putting it – *all* of it – on its feet in rehearsal, and would not finally be released until the production met spectators in the theatre. The approach was naive – Hands said so himself – and, given the time pressures, absurdly empirical (Terry Hands in conversation 1978). But committed to rehearsing the play beat by beat, scene by scene, he nevertheless had a feel for the trilogy's big architecture, what he later called its 'double structure', three 'inner plays' set inside a 'super-play'. Talbot in *Part One*, Jack Cade in *Part Two* and the York sons in *Part Three* epitomised and localised the large-scale disorder framed in the bigger picture where Henry, Margaret, York and Warwick occupied the foreground with Gloucester, Winchester and Suffolk just behind. One consequence of taking on the full text was rediscovering the part the commons played in the story of 'this England', a part all but cut from Hall and Barton's *Wars*. Theirs had been a Tory reading of history: great men, troublesome women, ambition, huge folly, power the discourse of the elite. Restoring scenes and roles, Hands's version was decidedly Whiggish: the common soldier, the French peasant, the armourer's apprentice, the gunner's son, masses of poor petitioners and liveried servants voiced a plebeian history. Admittedly, it was a marginal and interstitial one, for ultimately the plebs were bit players in a history *subject* to the aristocracy. Still, whenever they took the stage, their rowdy contestations of the powerful and privileged were uninhibited, their class actions demonstrating the symbiosis in the commonwealth between high and low which, if diacritical, was also, like physiology, constitutive. Dissension at the head, they demonstrated, dispersed dissension through the whole body politic: arms rebellious to command, rumblings from the belly, the big toe disabling English virility with a kick to the groin. It infected like a disease, an idea that also registered in the production poster: one of its segments figured England as nobles posed in a medieval tapestry; the next dispersed the population as bacteria on a microscope slide.

These bit parts (or so they seemed in the playtext) were transformed in performance, connected into powerful through-lines, the happy but surprise effect of solving a production problem. Even with a forty-eight-strong company Hands had too few actors to cover parts that seemed to spring up like dragon's teeth in Shakespeare's writing. Hands had to adopt Elizabethan stage practice, not just doubling parts but doubling the doubling. The results were revelatory. Soldiers returned as citizens returned as rebels-in-arms; the Dauphin returned as Cade; Talbot's Captain as Dick the Butcher; the Countess of Auvergne as Lady Eleanor; Simpcox's abject wife, blood-smeared, as one of the Kentish rabble. The messengers' parts, dozens of them, were strung into one. By the end of *Part Three* he appeared like the angel of doom. Double and triple casting invited spectators to see history as continuity fashioned from difference, to observe terrible and ironic patterns, the appalling durability of particular ideas whose consequences for humanity were always, and evidently, fatal. The political view that emerged was neither providentially Tillyardian nor bleakly Kottian, but Erasmian: 'this England' was a ship of fools, anchored, as we will see, by Alan Howard's profound reading of the wise fool, King Henry.

Terry Hands's regularly quoted and frequently pilloried claim to be producing the 'full text' of Shakespeare's *Henrys* needs to be revisited. As a sound bite, it was the kind of thing reviewers and spin doctors adored, even then, long before bite and spin were the journalist's *lingua franca*. But for Hands the 'full text' never meant simply the playtext – that is, the words. It included the visual performance text, what was going to be put on the stage for spectators to view and make sense of. To discover a way of trans-lating Shakespeare's early modern performance text into a contem-porary idiom, Hands turned to Robert Fludd's seventeenth-century theories of mnemonic space and the compositional techniques of, for example, Queen Elizabeth's Armada portrait, a painting that represents the Spanish threat and its defeat *simultaneously* as scenes viewed through windows set behind the gorgeously resplendent figure of the monarch. Hands wanted the immediacy of Shakespeare's language to be matched by this sort of imme-diacy of presentation, by continuous play, so that spectators could observe the developing patterns-in-action spatially, and could see too where Shakespeare was cutting so quickly from scene to scene, from location to location, that simultaneous staging was the only way to perform this dramaturgy. Farrah, who had worked with Hands on *Henry V*, designed just such a performance space: a black, raked platform that thrust forward into the audience and stretched backward to the theatre's back wall, the biggest stage Stratford had ever seen, a vast, open space to perform what Michael Billington called 'Shakespeare's dance to the broken music of time' (quoted in Beauman 341).

There were no sets and few props: a coffin, the throne, a siege gun, a clutch of decapitated heads, an armoury's worth of swords, and the crown, plucked from the deposed, tossed into the grasp of the next 'wannabe king', degraded into a fashion accessory for aspiration. In *Part One*, a massive bridge was flown in mid-stage for the walls of Orleans and Rouen; in *Part Two*, the stage was covered with a grass-green carpet that was stripped out as Cade advanced on London.

Starving the spectator's eye of 'stuff' was entirely calculated. Hands as a director does not offer to construct on the stage through design a 'whole' world, a world dense in visual detail that, by conceit, simulates or approximates 'reality'. His signature is austerity, and his most stunning visual effects are achieved formally, almost architecturally, by locating bodies in space and writing physical compositions in what Barbara Hodgdon terms a 'spatial poetry'.[4] His spectacular images, as in poetry, serve the particular moment, but then are reiterated – rhymed, even – with later images that remember them. Where other directors design in 'stuff', Hands designs in light. He had invented for *Henry V* something he called a 'light curtain', originally constructed from fifty automobile headlights packed inside a box, used as a beaming system. Massively developed for *Henry VI* (now with some 150 proper theatre lamps), its effect was to stand in for scenery, to bring down (literally) curtains of light to isolate space on the stage, cutting off the forestage, or illuminating the far distant upstage while plunging the rest of the huge stage into impenetrable darkness, or focusing bars of intense light on one area or another. The entire stage could be flooded with light or three distinct grounds on the playing field of the stage could be lit (foreground, mid-ground, background). In effect, Hands had three stages to play with, and he could set up scenes on each of them, constructing effects using depth of field by superimposing one scenic image upon another – like the Armada portrait staged. The spectator's eye, travelling through the scene, registered separate stories simultaneously, reading their allusiveness, their coincidence, their ironies as a kind of spatial intertextuality. Hands was finding a way of playing in the theatre what he read in Shakespeare's playtext, a 'poetry in juxtaposition': not just, that is, Shakespeare's 'literary poetry' but his physical poetry, composed, said Hands, of 'the space and the light and the face' (Swander 149).

Part One: the loss of Empire

To begin with, space was cramped, and faces hidden. The stage at the opening of *Part One* was set as an icon remembering the old order. Down centre, hemmed in by funeral blacks, the unattended coffin of Henry V lay draped in the royal standard; on it, a pair of now-hollow signifiers, his empty helmet and the axe-headed mace that hung from his wrist, in life, like an extra arm. A dead march, scored for oboes, brought on a double file of six mourners, hooded, in black. Only their heraldic badges fixed to their arms identified them. They stood, bowed, flanking the coffin, then in turn lifted their heads to address the audience: 'Hung be the heavens with black! Yield day to night'; 'England ne'er had a king until his time'; 'We mourn in black; why mourn we not in blood?' (I.i.1, 8, 17, Scene I). This high rhetorical poetry boomed like timpani, each speaker making over the dead king in his own, appropriating imagery. All the issues that would trouble the future were loaded into these speeches – and into their speaking, for eulogy, it seemed, worked like a verbal form of gelignite exploding animosity. Gloucester (Graham Crowden) growled from deep inside the cavern of his hood, 'The Church?', a jibe that made Winchester (John Rhys-Davies) yank his hood back and lunge across the coffin, pounding its lid. So the violent process started, literally, of uncovering history, revealing faces, discovering bits of costume.

This was a world of instant emotion, immediate utterance, explosive relationship, and shocking fragmentation. Just as Bedford managed to pull the ritual back together ('Cease, cease these jars'), the messengers appeared, like bizarre postmen from a different world delivering dispatch upon dispatch. In mud-crusted battle fatigues, their red George Crosses just visible under the filth, they entered hotfoot from routs in France to interrupt the funeral and arraign Harry's brothers of slackness ('Let not sloth dim your honours new begot'). So family dispute metastasised into civil dissension. Before all eyes, a common solider rebuked the nobility ('Amongst the soldiers this is mutterèd'), instructing them in a world radically changed, where chivalry, like Harry, was dead, signalled by the stab in the back Talbot took from a *mercenary*.

Just as each sweating entrance urged the pace of this opening scene, so a stunning *volte face* reversed its energies, emptying the stage as swiftly as it filled. Stung by the soldier's rebuke, Bedford tugged off 'these disgraceful wailing robes'. Beneath, his 'steelèd coat' showed him already (always?) dressed for war, and his exit tripped a switch setting off a chain reaction. The Captain (who had stood throughout gazing bewildered at the coffin) ran after him. Gloucester with Somerset in tow bustled off 'to the Tower' to 'proclaim young Henry king'; Exeter (with Warwick) made for 'Eltham' where 'the young King is'. Only Winchester stayed behind. He stood in a box of hot light and fumed, a 'jack out of office' wanting work, and framing that work as mischief. He was no deep-contemplative Machiavel but a knotted up mass of exposed nerve fibres groping spasmodically toward a coup. When he stepped outside the light, he triggered the scene change (I.ii, Scene 2). The black funeral drapes flew out, the scenic aperture zoomimg wide to reveal the full stage as, through smoke and braying trumpets, four massive field guns trundled down toward the audience. The French, gorgeous in blue fleur-de-lys, swaggered before them. Light, noise, colour, movement hit all together, dazzling and deaf-ening spectators. When the smirking French, crowing contempt for the 'famished English' besieged in Orleans, turned upstage to 'rush on them', they instantly fell back in comic disarray, raising a huge laugh in response to their whining like thrashed schoolboys, 'I would ne'er have fled / But that they left me 'midst my enemies' (35).

In this action-packed twenty-minute opening sequence, Hands's production keyed in all the visual and rhetorical codes it would access across the following nine hours. This was a theatre of continuous play, of relentless narrative drive, where events were telescoped and characterisation delivered, not developed. Here, emotional switchbacks turned on caesuras in the middle of blank verse lines; everything was disconcertingly 'sudden' – the visual and acoustic non sequiturs, the jokes. Typically, dialogue played like Greek stichomythia. On the one hand, the script offered actors a densely allusive blank verse that worked rhetorically like bold brushstrokes to imagine the memory space of national nostalgia ('His arms spread wider than a dragon's wings'). On the other, it stripped poetry down to reportage: lines came like messages spewed out of a tickertape machine, punching out a cracking story at a break-neck pace ('The tenth of August last …'). Compared to Peter Hall's *Wars* company, the actors in Terry Hands's company were acrobats and daredevils who made it look as if 'a generation of high-wire walkers' had taken over the RSC stage 'from a team of superb civil engineers' (Beauman 342). For 'Terry's lads', *Part One* was 'cartoon strip Shakespeare'; for Irving Wardle in *The Times*, it was 'one damn thing after another' Shakespeare (13 July 1977). Perhaps better said, it was 'meanwhile' Shakespeare: 'meanwhile, in England'; 'meanwhile, in France'.

In France in I.ii (Scene 2), the Dauphin was first a boasting Mars, then a pouting Ajax. He needed a miracle. A miracle entered. Standing in a pool of clean, clear light, Charlotte Cornwell's Joan la Pucelle was radiant but also disturbing. She wore a rough linen tunic, low-belted around her hips, and peasant boots. Her hair, evidently cut round a pudding basin, was flame-coloured, and hanging from her neck, just visible, was a strange fetish (which somehow recalled those chivalric fetishes ornamenting King Harry's coffin). When her wide mouth broke into a grin she was no warrior woman or elected saint but a boyishly sexy, martial prick-tease who used erotic language to detail her divine commission and titillation to harden French manhood. She combined ferocity and guile: in hand-to-hand combat with James Laurenson's Dauphin, she parried sword blows – but stomped on his foot to bring him sprawling down, then, mounting, rode him hip to hip until he cried 'Stay!' But her best weapon was rhetorical assertion: 'Assigned am I to be the English scourge'; 'Expect Saint Martin's summer, halcyon's days' (129, 131). Standing centre stage, using her sword tip like a compass, she inscribed on the ground the limits of imperial triumph. 'Glory is like a circle in the water.' Now, 'With Henry's death, the English circle ends' (133, 136).

Meanwhile, holed up in Orleans (I.iv, Scene 4), David Swift's Talbot stood on the ramparts and considered England's chances. If spring-heeled Joan was the sign of France's future, this grizzled, hunched Talbot in animal skins, his shaggy head swinging like a bear's, troped England's obsolete past. One moment, Salisbury was standing next to him; the next, he was dead, blown up by a long-range cannon shot fired by a *boy*. Enraged, great Talbot, the terror of the French, stormed the main stage looking for revenge and turned to face – a girl. The bout he played with la Pucelle summarised difference (I.v, Scene 5). It pitched exhausted English stereotypes of virility against inspired – or cunning – female improvisiation: French Joan, unlike a 'proper' combatant, was never where Talbot aimed his blow. This production, then, kept the prophetess / sorceress binary alive. Calling Joan a 'witch', a 'strumpet', and laughing along with Burgundy's misogynistic sarcasm – 'Pray God she prove not masculine ere long' (II.i.22,

Scene 7) – Talbot located female power in the only categories dazed masculinity and anxious chauvinism knew, while at the same time marking the dangerous liaison between femininity, foreignness, eroticism and power that would find future representation in the Countess of Auvergne and Margaret of Anjou.

Meanwhile, in England, with the French cannon still in position, scenes that intercut with those in France played out the very scenarios which the disaffected soldiers in Scene 1 had 'mutterèd' (I.iii, Scene 3). Faction was literalised when, meeting in front of the Tower of London, Winchester's men (in red) set about Gloucester's men (in blue). Instantly, the masters themselves leaped into the fray, abusing each other with mouthfuls of insults: 'ambitious vizier'; 'peeled priest'. Crosier smashed against mace in a ludicrous show of unseemly street fisticuffs while, in the midst of the din, a dishevelled Lord Mayor read out the Riot Act on a single breath – then collapsed in a Monty-Pythonesque heap.

Meanwhile, another scene change (this one on a lighting cue that isolated the mid-stage in a shaft of light like late afternoon sun) took faction off the public streets of London and into the *hortus conclusus* of the Temple Garden, where altogether sleeker rats were starting to gnaw the cords of loyalty knitting the commonwealth (II.iv, Scene 10). Compared to Winchester's bully-boys, these nobles in black leather with their folded arms and relaxed hips looked like tut-tutting dandies splitting legalistic hairs. When *they* fell to insults they used words to mock and wound, not cudgels: 'Somer / summer-*set*'; 'yeo-*man*'. York (Emrys James), a little short-legged man who couldn't help mincing, wore a white silk scarf to remind him of his (stripped) title and a chip on both shoulders like imagined prosthetics to bulk himself out. Suffolk (Peter McEnery) was the languid playboy, keen Somerset (Oliver Ford Davies) the head boy's fag, Warwick (Julian Glover) as unreadable as a crocodile – and, immobile, as menacing. Downstage were set the 'rose bushes', metal barricades twined with dead-white and blood-red roses (earlier, at Orleans, they'd served as siege apparatus wrapped in barbed wire). The blocking of this scene worked simply to align faction. As York and the rest talked they took up positions that put the barricades between them, then plucked roses that colour-coded their animosity, divisions as obvious as Gloucester *v*. Winchester, England *v*. France.

These sequences show Shakespeare learning to manage his material, playing fast and loose with what he found in Hall and

Holinshed, reshaping historical narrative into theatrical meaning, inventing, for example, the roses as a way of condensing politics into resonant theatrical signifiers that absorb and animate conventional poetical tropes – sensuality, beauty, the rose as love token – but simultaneously pervert those tropes to the business of violent death. Over time, the real roses from the Temple Garden disappeared, replaced by roses hammered out of metal, a hardening that signified by registering faction now as institutionalised and constitutive: metal roses don't fade and don't go out of season. As signifying 'things', the artificial roses remembered their origins in the garden, but registered, too, the loss of origins. The children who were coming, the unborn heirs to the houses of York and Lancaster, would wear the insignia like dead metaphors. Ignorant of the original quarrel whose answer was roses, they would nevertheless slaughter each other in a war those forgotten roses named.

However daring Shakespeare shows himself to be in what he stages in these sequences, he proves himself even more daring in what he withholds, keeping offstage for over an hour of playing time what the opening scene promised and what, by now, spectators, taking in so much 'matter', have forgotten to expect – Henry V's heir. In Terry Hands's production, seeing Alan Howard's Harry return as his own son (III.i, Scene 12) was like looking through the wrong end of a telescope. Disconcertingly infantilised by shoulder-length hair under a pork-pie hat and in a rough black wool tunic belted around his hips, he looked shrunken. Spectators saw a twelve-year-old sitting on the throne – an astonishing performance helped by Farrah's design. (To trick perspective, Farrah built the throne slightly oversize and gave it a too-high footrest to make Howard sit with his knees hunched up like a child.) Henry's long-delayed first appearance was a premonition of things to come, for he was hardly on the stage before his presence was wrecked by his warring uncles. Gloucester presented a bill in Parliament, Winchester snatched and tore it – who was the child here? Silent Henry, like his dead father in the opening scene, was ignored as Protector and prelate hurled abuse over his head. 'Swivel-eyed', said *The Guardian*, Howard's Henry looked 'like a Wimbledon spectator watching Nastase play Nastase' (14 July 1977). When, after all, he spoke – seventy-five lines into the scene – and ventured political comment ('my tender years can tell / Civil dissension is a viperous worm …'), peace didn't suddenly break out, only more uproar. Goodwill was ineffectual, the child-king impotent. He stood there like a dry-docked swan, paralysed except for the nervous little treading of his feet. Every action he took for good was grudged by one side or the other. Astonishing even York by restoring to him not just his title but his inheritance, the king pacified York's faction – but alienated Somerset's. Ironically, however, not even Henry's *absence* achieved consensus. His exit from this scene left behind yet another uncle alone on the stage, Exeter, addressing the audience like a Chorus, his 'fatal prophecy' ('"Henry born at Monmouth … / … Henry born at Windsor"' (200–1)) an uncanny echo of other prophecies ('this brawl today … in the Temple Garden'; 'Assigned am I to be the English scourge').

In Shakespeare's playtext this ludicrously o'er parted and presumptively doomed child king looks utterly insignificant. But theatrically, in Hands's production things looked very different, for Alan Howard discovered in Henry what he took to be Shakespeare's true interest in the play: not plot, the accidents of events, but role, the growth of the self, the discovery of interiority. As Howard played it, *Part One* began a story that was about the education of the prince, a narrative Shakespeare would return to, rewriting in the later redraft this son's story in the adolescence of his father.

Howard explored these ideas about education and interiority in III.iv (Scene 15), the coronation scene (set in France and played continuously into IV.i (Scene 16)). This was the most spectacular scene of *Part One* – but even so, a huddled affair conducted in half-light upstage. More important was what was happening on the forestage, the cross-fire ricocheting off Vernon (his badge a white rose) and Basset (a red one) that ambushed the symbolism of the coronation even before it had a chance to be staged. Henry did not recognise Talbot when he gatecrashed the procession, a man in moth-eaten red wool looking poor against the courtiers' scarlet silk. Improvising an uncertain greeting ('When I was young – as yet I am not old – / I do remember how my father said …' (16–17)), Howard's Henry was making policy on the hoof, diffidently growing into monarchy in front of spectators' eyes. (Helpfully, he'd shed his childish curls, but now his pudding basin haircut made him, uncannily, a lookalike for la Pucelle.) Rewarding Talbot's service with an earldom with no prompting from his Uncle Gloucester was a good idea, a move, likewise, toward political maturity. But his naive reaction to news of Burgundy's revolt ('Is that the worst …?' (IV.i.66, Scene 16)) made his nobles' jaws drop, and his childish optimism ('Lord Talbot there shall talk with him' (68)) left Exeter dazed. Even worse, when Vernon and Basset, backed by York and Somerset, threw themselves at his feet, each demanding a combat to the death to revenge insults to 'this badge', 'the rose I wear' (31, 78), Henry, as with Burgundy's betrayal, couldn't take their rancour seriously. 'What madness rules in brainsick men?' (111), he wondered aloud as he handed his sceptre to York, his orb to Somerset. But when that show of impartiality failed and they threw down gauntlets, obdurately claiming the combat, Henry clutched at the diadem so recently set upon his head as if it were a band of heated iron, and prised it off. Howard's Henry didn't want power, he wanted peace. This English quarrel over English roses was 'a toy, a thing of no regard' (145) – to anyone, that is, who saw roses as roses, not tribal emblems. His agonised appeal – 'forget this quarrel'; 'remember where we are'; 'O, *think*' (136–7, 147) – was mature politics, a statement of common interest. In one sense, it explained what he did next; in another, not at all. He would, he said, 'be umpire in this doubtful strife' (151). But he failed to recognise the catch-22, that, if he made an umpire's choice, his choosing would cancel compromise. Ultimately, the logic of the child, not the adult, prevailed in the King. Gazing from peer to peer, Henry's eyes locked on the deep red blossom Basset proffered. As though mesmerised, he sighed, 'I see no reason, if I wear this rose ...' – and plucked the red rose from Basset's hand (152). Intending to efface difference and to say the roses meant nothing, Henry exaggerated difference, making them mean everything. Before, the red rose was Somerset's. Now it was Lancaster's, and Henry's exit from the scene figured England's fragmentation. Somerset, vindicated, went with him, but York stayed behind, Emrys James frantic with a rage unmollified by Warwick's phlegmatic 'Tush': 'sweet Prince, he thought no harm' (178). Their exit left Exeter alone to offer another baleful chorus. What was staggering for spectators, though, was to see displayed so graphically the imperative processes of absolute monarchy, the way 'fancy' translated into politics, inexperience into policy – call it, charitably, innocence; or worse, mind-boggling ineptitude. Whichever, the King speaks, and it is.

After this, *Part One* exhausts itself in 'alarums and excursions' that map England's imperial collapse. Burgundy was persuaded back to France by Joan who, seductive, standing on tiptoe, almost a fiend at his ear willing him to 'Look on fertile France' (III.iii.44,

Scene 14), suggested patriotism as erotic voyeurism. Talbot stayed dug-in at Bordeaux where his fresh-faced son (Ian Gelder) arrived just in time to embrace his father, war with him across couplets that rhyme 'flight' with 'fight', then die cradled in his father's dying arms, 'Icarus' fallen. This sequence from IV.ii to IV.vii (Scenes 17–22), where Talbot and young John, announcing all the fathers and sons to come, communicate in love poetry, was wonderfully staged. On paper the sequence looks crudely artificial; in the theatre, its rhetoric choreographs a poignant dance of death. As Talbot stood downstage threatening Bordeaux in a speech Shakespeare would later rewrite for Henry V at Harfleur, he caught the sound of the French drums, like tom-toms, and knew he was surrounded. Behind him, mid-stage, in half-dark, his Captain built a redoubt, sandbagging the barricades – the metal rose bushes, pressed back into military service. Against the Captain's weary slow motion, on the forestage, caught in a tight band of harsh lights, first York then Somerset postured and prated and, to spite the other, denied the aid that would save Talbot's life. The simultaneous staging here superimposed stage pictures whose coincidence was unbearable.

When the great warrior finally lay dead, la Pucelle mocked him, 'stinking and flyblown', but nevertheless stood over him for a long moment of recognition before, her body sagging, she trudged off (IV.vii.76, Scene 22). He was her twin. When his glorious circle ended, so did hers. Her capture followed directly, York ambushing her at 'prayer' where, kneeling, she finally declared the master she worshipped, offering her fetish as an oblation and her body, arms spread wide, to 'the lordly monarch of the north' (V.iii.6, Scene 25). York used his scarf to gag her demonic laughter – and hauled her off bridled. Uncannily, though, as she went, the female space she vacated was immediately filled by a new female form, her double, growing out of war's smoke and rubble, materialising like an Aphrodite born not from the sea but from slaughter. In figure-hugging velvet Helen Mirren's Margaret wandered through the debris, testing the wreckage delicately with a toe before she, too, was ambushed, by Suffolk. Played here as a mercurial mating dance – Suffolk a peacock (and married), Margaret feline (and knowing) – the proxy wooing was both fascinated and funny. (Her father arrived with a laundry list of demands (V.iii.151, Scene 25).) And the smile she flashed at Suffolk as she exited lingered suggestively across *Part One*'s final sequence, an ending that Shakespeare cuts together in the text as if he were a film editor, from quick shots in tight focus. La Pucelle was humiliated, denounced by her father while fastidious York lounged in the background sniffing a white rose (V.iv, Scene 26). An ignominious peace was concluded, the French flaunting a flashy banner where, already, 'saint' Joan was elevated into a national icon (Scene 26). The marriage was agreed – a tableau that 'froze' the English court on the play's final line with Henry staring up as Margaret entered on the bridge, above, to gaze down on him. And Suffolk ended *Part One* with a final Machi-avellian flourish on the play's last line – 'I will rule both her, the King, and realm' (V.v.108, Scene 27). Bringing faction home again to England, locating it squarely in the English court, in domestic space, he was bringing home, too, in Margaret, the foreign femme fatale, naturalising the enemy without as the (feminised) enemy within.

Part Two: losing England

Part One set the trilogy's pace; *Part Two* concentrated its focus, picking out from the crowded historical pageant individuals for picking off in the serial killings to come. The opening of *Part Two* (I.i, Scene 28) was set as a royal entry, the King's marriage mirroring the King's funeral from *Part One* and transforming mourning into joy on a stage carpeted in green – fertile England. Restrained behind red cord barriers far upstage stood the commoners, the Dicks, Smiths and Georges who would fall into line behind Cade later on. (The little Clerk of Chatham sat cross-legged to one side, absorbed in his book.) This Rabelaisian mob in jerkins, hose, leather aprons and holiday humour, waving red and white roses, gaped and gossiped as they played 'spot-the-aristo', wildly cheering the King but nervously retreating when Warwick strode towards them. On the forestage, smooth Suffolk handed Henry his French bride, and the looks this odd couple exchanged registered them falling instantly in love, a 'fact' that would determine the compli-cated relationship Mirren and Howard played out between them across the next two plays. She was like luscious soft fruit. In a rich velvet gown, half yellow, half green, Margaret looked like spring ripening into summer. He was myopically owlish, pinched, a sensual anorexic discovering appetite in one blast of erotic craving. For him, their kiss was an ecstatic revelation; for her, it was a damp squib. But his wonder at her captured her devotion: she gazed into his eyes while the marriage articles were read and exited delighted at the prospect of her coronation. She, like Henry, was oblivious to the political crisis left in their wake. Gloucester, the Lord Protector, stood rooted. He hadn't been able to finish reading the treaty. His voice, the *only* voice still keeping the political idealism of the past acoustically alive in this diminished generation, the only voice that never tired of negotiating England's good, choked on the articles that traded Reignier's undowered daughter for Anjou and Maine. Once again, Henry had made policy on the trot then exited, leaving others to calculate its effects: France ceded, Suffolk created duke, York relieved of his regency, the commons taxed to pay Suffolk's costs. How did his peers react? York imploded with impotent rage, Suffolk cracked a supercilious smirk, and heart-struck Gloucester uttered his grief, an act of memory ('What, did my brother Henry spend his youth, / His valour, coin, and people in the wars?' (76–7)) that was also prophecy ('shameful is this league, / Fatal this marriage ... / Undoing all, as all had never been!' (96–100)). But, agile as a toad in a cistern, Winchester twisted this pained 'confession' into an attack on Gloucester, reanimating their old grudge with this new bickering. Framing Gloucester as too officious, alleging that the Protector was king, not Henry, Winchester made expedient allies of everyone from Mirren's Margaret (hungry to be queen) to James's York (even hungrier to be king). His object was Gloucester's death.

Every scene promoted that plot. At home in I.ii (Scene 29), the grass floor shadowed in patterns of light and dark like a parterre, a maturely voluptuous Eleanor (Yvonne Coulette) twined her arms around upright Gloucester and traded love chat with him. They told each other their morning's dreams: his was a gruesome vision of decapitated heads, hers a vision of her own head crowned. Because Coulette doubled the parts, Eleanor brought into focus something from much earlier, an uncanny memory of the Countess of Auvergne's comic but dangerous attempted seduction of Talbot (Scene 9). Here, another warped love scene, another fatal marriage, twisted tenderness into coercion, eroticised female power and troped sexuality with witchcraft. The traitor betrayed, this elegant Eleanor would shortly fall victim to her own inelegant ambitions in a ludicrously mystified conjuration scene (I.iv, Scene 31). In it, gap-toothed Bolingbroke, bald as a billiard ball, rolling Groucho Marx eyes under weirdly absent eyebrows, traded mumbo-jumbo with Margery Jourdain, a claw-handed bag-lady who cracked into life like Frankenstein's bride at the sound of thunder. It was all so transparently fake that only a willing dupe would have been fooled by it. Or so it seemed, until the witch's prophecies came true.

At St Albans (II.i, Scene 32) the hawking was a stunning theatrical metaphor for the real blood-sport afoot, the beauty of the live falcons shaking their bells showing up the ugliness of human beastliness. One moment Gloucester was up, the wise if severe Protector protecting the realm by exposing the Simpcox fraud, seeing through pretended blindness. The next, he was laid low, implicated in his wife's treason, unable to penetrate York's fraud. Utterly exposed, Crowden's Gloucester stood centre stage as Winchester, Margaret, and Suffolk swooped their accusations down upon him like kites baiting an eagle. Unbowed in II.iii (Scene 34), he watched his duchess sentenced then wept; and having given up his staff of office, first almost threatening Henry with it then laying it gently at his feet, he made his long exit, covering the vast stage distance from the apron to the back wall with Winchester barking at his heels. Sparing himself no sorrow, he stood in the open street in II.iv (Scene 35) and watched Eleanor's penance. She was barefoot on the sharp flints, and dressed only in a white shift with a placard around her neck that published her crime in capital letters. But what made this exile unbearable was his heart-stopping optimism, telling 'Nell', 'The world may laugh again' (83). Eleanor knew different. Like everyone in these plays, she had acquired the urgent voice of political prophecy just before stepping into extinction and could see Gloucester's future.

Scene III.i finished off what II.i had begun (Scenes 36, 32). Savaged, the grief-wounded, still erect old man finally turned on the conspirators, his long last speech a *tour de force* redoing the political lesson from St Albans, teaching the young King to *see*. It was a lesson Henry didn't learn until it was too late: when Gloucester, summoned to his last audience with the King, arrived, he was dead, a corpse (III.ii, Scene 37). And Warwick, like a patient schoolmaster introducing a difficult text to a stupid child, forced the King to read the body for signs of murder, Gloucester's face 'black and full of blood', his nostrils 'stretched with struggling' (168–71). This ghastly instructive object was a new kind of political text, and it turned Winchester, for one, to stone. He looked on, horribly fascinated, unable to turn his gaze away.

Alan Howard's Henry sat paralysed on his throne, a half smile on his lips as if, behind his blank eyes, his mind was searching wanly into the abyss of absurdity. He had taken to wearing a rough grey wool tunic that looked monastic, and a plain pilgrim's cross, and to going bareheaded like a penitent. Mostly, he had been a silent bystander at court, bewildered by his people, stumbling upon political decisions, but so surprised by his own voice that he stepped back from its sound in alarm. He had been at first dazzled by Margaret, but increasingly disconcerted by her childish petulance (when she slapped his aunt, Eleanor), her cruel laughter (when she mocked poor petitioners), her hysterical bloody-mindedness (when she savaged Gloucester). He had stopped caring about York and Somerset's rivalry ('all's one to me'), and was deeply weary of Winchester's malice. But worst, he'd grown uncertain how to compute the moral arithmetic of the world. He had known, once, how things added up. After St Albans, nothing figured. Once, he'd depended on 'God' to 'defend the right' and on 'Justice', 'Whose beam stands sure, whose rightful cause prevails' – these were lines Howard paused over, freighting them with meaning as he mimed Justice's invisible scales (II.i.199–200, Scene 32). But the fraudulent miracle taught him scepticism: 'O God, seest thou this, and bear'st so long?' (150), he asked. God didn't answer. But Simpcox's anguished wife did. Kneeling face-to-face before her king in her ragged skirt and grubby smock that made her wretched poverty felt, she cried, 'Alas, sir we did it for pure *need*' (153). Henry, stunned, listened – the others just laughed. For an intense moment, the very top and bottom of the kingdom were locked in each other's gaze. Human *need* was uttering a claim for consideration, unprecedented in this political economy, laugh-ably a 'commonwealth', where instead, the exclusive politics of the aristocratic self and self-promotion marginalised all 'common' concerns. The look held between the King and the beggar woman: this was a radical moment, a moment of profound recognition. But Henry did nothing. Just as he did nothing to save Gloucester.

And now the uncle he'd imagined as an innocent calf, hauled to the 'bloody slaughter house' by a butcher who 'binds the wretch and beats it when it strains', indeed lay butchered. In the crazed distraction of that extraordinary speech in Scene 36 (III.i), Henry had figured himself as 'the dam', the frantic cow that ran 'lowing up and down / Looking the way her harmless young one went' (210–16). Now, though, looking past Gloucester's corpse, his face bloated with unshed tears and his eyes as hard as a basil-isk's, Henry was not distracted but intensely focused, and seeing his court as if for the first time. Banishing Suffolk, the terrible voice that roared 'IT IS IRREVOCABLE!' might have been his father's (III.ii.294, Scene 37). But the voice he achieved in the *next* scene was at last the authentic voice of his *own* monarchy. When Winchester, seized epileptically by killing guilt, stumbled across the stage, toppled Henry's throne and died self-damned beside it, and Warwick, looking on, prissily observed, 'So bad a death argues a monstrous life', Alan Howard's Henry howled, 'FORBEAR TO JUDGE!', then added in wry *sotto voce*: 'For we are sinners all' (III. iii.31, Scene 38).

This was the revelation Henry needed at St Albans. Now, it was too late. The commons, who had recently clamoured at the door for Suffolk's arrest, were 'up', a mob mobilised. Since the opening of *Part Two*, the band of hempen homespuns who kept turning up in scene after scene like history's extras had become increasingly disillusioned spectators on greatness. Removed to a distance upstage behind the red ropes, they'd cheered the royal marriage – but stopped when they heard they'd be paying for it. They'd handed their precious petitions to the wrong man – and stood impotent when Suffolk ripped them up and threw them in their faces. They'd danced attendance on Simpcox, the gullible among them still shouting 'miracle!' when the 'lame' man ran, the shrewder realising they'd become sport for nobs. They'd set up the Parliament benches at Bury St Edmunds (one of them even perching cheekily – symbolically? – on the throne) and watched, from behind the red ropes, their betters plot treason. They'd been both abused and dangerously empowered by II.iii (50–105, Scene 34), the 'trial by combat', a scene that started as farce but, shockingly, turned brutal. Set up by the aristocrats as a parody of the chivalric protocols which a trial by combat mobilises among the elite, the certainty that 'right makes might', this 'trial' simultaneously inverted the very aristocratic authority those protocols depended upon: the combatants, after all, were plebs, and the terrified little apprentice (Richard Derrington) triumphed over his swaggering master (Desmond Stokes) not because he was 'right' but because his master was drunk. Mob culture gained essential learning here. At first the boy, utterly inhibited from lifting a hand against his master, sparred only tentatively. But then, roused, violence overwhelmed him, a frenzy that did not exhaust itself even when the master was dead, for the boy went on battering him, pulping the corpse. Looking on at this brutal sight of social order inverted and

6 *Part Two* (1977). Jack Cade (James Laurenson) and Dick the Butcher (Barry Rutter) ponder the rebellion

violated, the mob were learning rebellion – not as a political theory but practically, as a demonstration in, and on, the flesh.

In IV.ii (Scene 40), the commons joined Cade because they'd had enough. They tore down the red ropes, the whole stage now their 'common' property, a violent playground where anarchy staged itself as physical mayhem: the next seven scenes ran together in one continuous riot. Set in terrifying gloom, these scenes were like nightmares; lit from below, faces in the mob emerged in grotesque cartoon outline. James Laurenson's Cade was a blend of Charlie Manson, Che Guevara and any number of strung-out long-haired student protesters, his political theory ('I will make it a felony to drink small beer; all the realm shall be in common'; 'there shall be no money' (63, 68)) uttered with the kind of surreal blend of utopian idealism and pig-headed extremism that one-time student activists in the audience no doubt recognised from their own recent experience of anti-war, anti-capitalist protest ('No, no, we won't go!'). Was this 'miserable ignorance' or enlightened radicalism, to laugh at or weep over? Laurenson's Cade made it both, bringing the commons' history into collision with the history of its spectators. In this production, the fall of France uneasily troped Vietnam. And neither commons (the one milling about on stage, the other watching from the stalls and galleries in the theatre auditorium) cared any longer to be conned by the Establishment. Cade-the-leveller was hyperactive with reforming zeal: like York, he couldn't stand still. But by the time he reached London Bridge (IV.vi, Scene 44) the people's revolutionary was wearing a filthy strip of royal ermine draped across his shoulders, and the fantastic anti-structure he was now proposing to his wide-eyed 'fellow-kings' who couldn't wait to 'pull down the Savoy' was sounding suspiciously like the official structure they wanted violently dismantled, only turned on its head.

His sidekick, Dick the Butcher (a goggle-eyed Barrie Rutter, a craftsman in slaughter usefully equipped with an ox-sized cleaver), had ideas of his own: 'The first thing we do, let's kill all the lawyers' got a huge laugh at every performance (IV.ii.71, Scene 40). The weaver, the clothier, the housewife and the other dozen citizens who, unlike the Butcher, were amateurs in killing, made a mess of the little Clerk of Chatham, strangling him ineptly with a noose improvised from the straps of his portable desk. (Why did they kill him? Because he could read and write – and so was clearly a nob.) The Butcher made mess art. Turning upstage over the half-dead body, he raised his cleaver. When he turned around to face spectators again he was a full-length painting in blood. Hearts stopped, then raced as the mob, snorting the stench of blood like a drug, fell in behind the Butcher in a carnival of killing, the entire stage an abattoir. Only when the heads of Lord Saye and his son were brought in, stuck on poles so tall the motion of carrying them made them judder sickeningly to life, did the rebels themselves sicken (IV.vii, Scene 45). It was, predictably, the Butcher who turned on Cade first when Buckingham (Charles Dance) promised 'reward', throwing into the exhausted crowd a few paltry groats that turned them into animals, grovelling and snatching, while he calmly roped them like cattle and sardonically invited, 'Follow me – *soldiers*!' (IV.viii.66, Scene 46).

Moving across this riot-littered stage, Alan Howard's Henry surveyed his kingdom's wreckage and silently knelt to bless a corpse (IV.iv, Scene 42). He was no holy fool out of Dostoevsky but an absurdist out of Beckett; Simpcox's wife and Gloucester's murder had made him a radical pacifist, aged in pain and militant only in endurance. When the failed rebels, terrified, shuffled in, he gently untied them (IV.ix, Scene 47). They exited grateful – crossing paths with a messenger who was entering with news of York, just landed from Ireland to take up where Cade left off: Cade was, after all, merely York's stooge. So as one threat collapsed others sprang up, like dragon's teeth, mocking clemency. Henry laughed out loud – then wearily sat where Cade had proclaimed his monstrous regiment. 'Come wife,' he said simply, 'Let's in and learn to govern better' (49). But there was no time. Fresh alarums were already summoning fresh roll-calls of death. Popular insurrection had simply cleared the playground for altogether bloodier action. Margaret wrecked the truce, flaunting Somerset. York declared war. When the ancient warhorse Salisbury, with his son Warwick, lined up behind York, Henry stood appalled. 'Where is faith?' he asked. 'O where is loyalty?' What Salisbury intended was insane: 'Thou mad misleader of thy brainsick son! / What, wilt thou on thy deathbed play the ruffian / And seek for sorrow with thy spectacles? / ... dig a grave to find out war ...?' (V.i.164, 161–3, 167, Scene 49). Salisbury's answer resigned Henry to civil war: 'Call Buckingham,' he instructed hollowly, walking out of the scene. 'And bid him arm himself' (191). So Somerset fell. And old Clifford. And spectators became aware of a new generation of youthful killers lining up with their elders, sons wearing insignia roses incorporated structurally into their armour, boys 'dedicate to war' with hearts 'turned to stone'. Conspicuously, there was the stunted child, York's Richard, whom young Clifford had called a 'foul stigmatic'. After the Yorkists had won at St Albans, jubilant old Salisbury picked Richard up and swung him in the air, then dropped him on his gammy leg (V.ii, Scene 50). His twisted grimace was the face of the future.

Part Three: lost boys

History grew empty; England desolate. In *Part Three*, once the popular *grand opéra bouffe* of Cade's rebellion had collapsed, there were no more mass actions. Instead, people plotted and died alone, or in tight-knit conspiracies, or in deadly duets. Alone, 'stigmatic' Richard counted 'this world but hell' and determined to make his 'heaven' dreaming on the crown; alone, 'wind-changing' Warwick sweated blood and died; together, the York cubs hunted in a pack of three; together, two jittery soldiers on border patrol arrested the third man, who underneath a filthy tunic turned out to be their one-time king. (Ruefully smiling as he pushed aside the crossbow held to his chest, Howard's Henry picked a feather off one of the soldiers's uniforms, blew it into the air and watched its wayward progress on the wind – a demonstration of his people's constancy (III.i, Scene 62).) And the deadliest duo of all: Emrys James's York and Helen Mirren's Margaret finally locked on to the course that would put their parallel egos into head-on colli- sion. They were both frustrated dynasts and 'desiring machines', though built to different specifications. He had Tamburlaine-sized ambitions in a runt's body and so much hyperactive resentment of Henry's 'bookish rule' that he couldn't stand still on the stage. An episode in *Part Two* had been revelatory: telling spectators about his plot to suborn 'stubborn Cade', York said he'd seen Cade in Ireland fight until 'his thighs with darts / Were almost like a sharp-quilled porcupine'. Then he would 'caper upright like a wild Morisco, / Shaking the bloody darts as he his bells' (III.i.362–6, Scene 36). York demonstrated the grotesque caper – and made himself grotesque. At the same time, as he simulated Cade, his mimicry made spectators see York and his 'substitute' as uncanny doubles and their rebellions, one serious, the other ludicrous, as disturbing twins informing each other. Taking centre stage in his long soliloquies, James uttered York's grasping thoughts with such clarity of detail that it was like listening to an anatomy lecturer articulate the intricate bones of the hand.

Meanwhile Mirren's Margaret had grown from spoiled flirtatious brat, sitting on Suffolk's lap, wanting him to fix things at court, to naive political rooky crowing 'Free lords!' triumphantly when the King walked out of his Parliament, to frantic consort, terrified that he had died when Henry fainted at Gloucester's death (III.ii, Scene 37). She used all her seductiveness to revive him, to woo him back to her, circling the throne where he sat catatonic, bending her body over him, remembering, as erotic persuasion, her perilous voyage to England when, to appease the angry sea, she took a token from around her neck, a heart-shaped jewel, and threw it into the waves. She was a drama queen who raged at Suffolk's banishment – but then kissed him farewell almost absent-mindedly. And once he was dead, she played an astonishing, macabre love scene with Suffolk's decapitated head before her husband's eyes, cradling 'this lovely face' that 'Ruled like a wandering planet over me', madly wondering, 'But where's the body that I should embrace?' (IV.iv, Scene 42). But when Henry dryly observed that, had he been dead, 'Thou wouldest not have mourned so much for me', her answer was devoid of irony: 'I should not mourn, but die for thee.' For this woman, divorcing Henry from her bed was no mere formality but sexual punishment that would cost her, too (although already she had another man in her arms, her son Ned). She was as hungry for power as York – and as frustrated by Henry as he. So when they met at Wakefield, York the filthy captive, Margaret sadistic and exultant, their encounter was fuelled by all the desire that had been denied (I.iv, Scene 55). They needed to punish in each other their resentments against the King. Their revenge, then, was as much voluptuous and erotic as political. Margaret, her golden hair flowing down her back, wore a metal dress that reproduced her curves in iron. Thrust on to his knees on the molehill, York brought Margaret to *her* knees, to wipe his face with the napkin soaked in his child-son's blood. As she smeared York's face they were so close to each other that they might have kissed. But then, quietly savage, York folded Margaret's savagery back upon her, making her sexuality monstrous. She was the 'She-wolf of France', the 'tiger's heart wrapp'd in a woman's hide' (111, 137); he, the bereft father whose tears, uncannily, made his child's blood flow again, this time down the father's face. Almost contemptuous as he handed back to her the paper crown, York suddenly made the giving a taking, a final violent clutching at life, grabbing Margaret, forcing her down under him, her legs apart. His climax was a curse. Clifford sprang forward, thrusting into him his sword. And Margaret, in a parody almost of phallic superiority, reached for a weapon, pushed it voluptuously into York, and, as he fell into her lap, stretched up her body as in orgasm before rolling away, disgusted, exhausted; then she recovered to command, brutally indifferent, 'Off with his head and set it on York gates' (179).

Almost immediately following, a differently keyed duet played on a different molehill, at Towton – a debate between a prince and a shepherd, the King himself arguing both sides. Henry had been sitting silently, cross-legged, beneath York's head, impaled on a high pole, as 'alarums and excursions' swept the battle for the city around him (II.ii, Scene 57). In II.v (Scene 60) he moved centre stage, sat like something in stone, and contemplated a life regulated by a shepherd's calendar, carving 'out dials quaintly, point by point' to 'see the minutes how they run'. The object? To determine that those minutes, hours, days, years would be 'Passed over to the *end they were created*' (39). For Howard's Henry, who spoke simply to the audience in a voice flat with grief, to divide time was to understand time properly as *time to live*. Here then, in the regimen of the *vita contemplativa*, was the life-saving response to the death-wish inscribed in his kingdom's *vita activa*. Finishing with the image of the shepherd's untroubled sleep 'under a fresh tree's shade' set against the prince's insomnia, 'couched in a curious bed / When care, mistrust, and treason waits on him' (53–4), Howard removed his crown and stared through its empty hole, a nihilistic visionary. But that wasn't all: for now, the debate he was voicing with his own conscience was externalised, personalised and enacted by other voices, set in choric counterpoint. From opposite upstage entrances came a father and a son, carrying bodies they had just killed in battle, bodies they would discover to be those of their own son and father. Set as a stylised tableau of civil war upstage behind the anguished king, this scene, played with utter simplicity, remembered and reanimated the death poetry of the trilogy's original Daedalus and Icarus, the Talbots, father and son. In remembering them, the scene found a trope for war's perverse creativity, for the 'nothings' war makes. Once again, the stage image reified loss: fathers lost, lost boys.

The latest Icarus was, of course, York's crippled son, not like his 'dogged' father 'reach[ing] for the moon' but instead reaching for the sun. Anton Lesser made Richard 'a little yelping crookbacked kid, constantly in pain, constantly itching to inflict it' (Beauman 342). He was ready to oblige Margaret, who, in V.v (Scene 77), with her own son's blood on her hands, stumbled, haggard, a demented old woman, from one York boy to the next urging them to kill her. Richard was willing, but Edward tackled him and shoved his sword aside. So Richard, cheeky, a voice like a metal-cutter slicing tin, put in train other ideas that his doltish big brother had trouble taking in: 'The Tower,' Richard hissed at uncomprehending Edward. 'The Tower!'

As Terry Hands directed it, Henry's death scene bizarrely remembered his father's scene of glory – reversing its imagery. In *Henry V* before Harfleur the raked forestage split and reared up so that spectators were looking at a steep black ramp. Over it, shouting, Harry's routed army suddenly swarmed, sliding down the front, the King appearing amid them, hanging on, rousing them 'Once more unto the breach … once more' – and, roused, they roared

7 *Part Three* (1977). Henry VI (Alan Howard) and Richard Gloucester (Anton Lesser)

and flung themselves back over the top, into victory. In *Henry VI* (V.vi, Scene 78) the forestage again reared up, but this time, hinged at the back, slowly opened like a jaw, letting spectators see inside the hell-mouth. The King, in a filthy once-white rough wool garment, his hair matted and his body streaked in dirt, squatted on a metal grille floor, his wrists chained to the grille above. Flooded with white light from below that produced in the metal bars an architecture of brutalism, this was an image both hellish and apocalyptic. Hunchbacked Richard appeared up through a little hatch in the grille and, like a stunted gargoyle, perched beside the King. There was nothing redemptive about what happened. Like so many before him, Henry acquired the prophetic voice as he looked at death. He was a father grieving for his son in a voice that rattled like dry bones. But then he was suddenly the king. In one of those vocal gear changes that Alan Howard alone among actors of his generation can produce, Howard 'voiced' Henry into a different dimension, on to a different plane of knowledge and expression – and power, for now Henry was seeing not his own but *England's* future; and like his father before Harfleur, he inventoried apocalypse, delivering seven lines of iambic pentameter on a single breath like a last powerful exhalation of everything on his heart and mind, relishing the sardonic absurdity of it all: 'And thus I prophesy: … many an old man's sigh, and many a widow's, / And many an orphan's … / Men … sons … wives … husbands … orphans … parents … / Shall rue the hour that ever thou wast born' (37–43). Richard reeled away from the words. He was the killer – but Henry was his tormentor, and when Richard drew his dagger, in self-defence it seemed, the King thrust himself forward on to it, a death that felt like both murder and suicide, willing and making certain Richard's damnation. As Richard pulled away, the red wound spreading across the dying King's body showed a 'side-piercing sight' (*King Lear* IV.vi.85). The corpse, sagging into death, hung from the chains, crucified. Richard sat on his haunches, cool, preoccupied with his next moves. He tapped his dagger against the metal grille, a mnemonic tattoo that drummed the murders to come into mind. Now, with all of Lancaster dead, assassination could start on York. Richard would make murder a family activity, ironically a method of instantiating his family-denying solipsism: 'I have no brother, I am like no brother / … I am myself alone' (80, 83). As Henry's death-trap slowly closed, Richard rolled out from under it and suddenly was standing in his brother's court, where Edward was holding in his arms a baby son (V.vii, Scene 79). Edward called for music. But when the trumpets brayed, the men instinctively sprang into defensive positions, pulling swords. Edward tried again. This time stately music played, music for dancing. The new queen came forward, Edward took her hand. Other couples joined them. They attempted the moves to the dance. But they faltered, wrong-footed. No one could remember the steps.

At the end, Hands's trilogy remembered its beginning. In its final moments it staged another family gathering and another broken ritual producing another infant to grow up into another lost boy with another Uncle Gloucester. *And how many ghosts?* As the lights went down, Richard stared out at the spectators who had watched the stage close over and hide the hell he had made, the hell the new regime didn't know was under their feet, waiting to break through, as they comically stumbled into position in a dance of death. Henry's prophecies hung in the air. The future was ready to begin.

CHAPTER V

Henry VI and the BBC
(1960 and 1981–83)

With the exception of the RSC, few theatre companies have produced the *Henry VI* plays more than once – but the BBC has televised them three times. In the 1960s, the plays were first adapted for the series *An Age of Kings* (1960), then Michael Hayes filmed the RSC's *The Wars of the Roses* (1965). This chapter, however, focuses on the only version to employ the full texts: directed by Jane Howell for the BBC/Time-Life Shakespeare series, these *Henry VI*s were broadcast over three Sunday nights early in 1983 and were followed by *Richard III* to complete the tetralogy. Howell translated Shakespeare successfully into television and in so doing raised a number of questions about the cultural politics of televising his work.

Initially reluctant to film the plays, Jane Howell was converted when she started to recognise their affinity with entertainments such as carnivals, pantomimes and fairgrounds. *Henry VI*, it seemed, belonged more to the world of popular traditions than it did to high culture and, in a sense, televising them created an opportunity for Howell to explore the relationship between the theatrical culture of the common people in the early modern period with its nearest modern equivalent, television. On television, *Henry VI* competed with game shows, soap operas, documentaries, period dramas and children's programmes. However, rather than use Shakespeare to elevate television above all this, as the Shakespeare series in general tried to do, Howell's achievement was to film a *Henry VI* trilogy that was completely at home in this environment.

Of Shakespeare's works, the *Henry VI* plays seem most fit for television – each play is episodic, spectacular and constantly varied. The main characters are simply drawn but have riveting story arcs which twist and turn just as they do in modern television serials.

Who would think that the young princess found on the battlefield would become the general of *Part Three*, or that the fiercely loyal son of the Duke of York would develop into a bloody murderer? Jane Howell was perceptive when she called the plays a 'medieval *Dallas*' (Fenwick *Part One* 22), referring to the gaudy Texas-based soap opera then dominating television schedules. In a way, Howell was right; the *Henry VI* plays were supreme products of the pulp-fiction theatre of the 1590s. Both television and the playhouses of the 1590s had broad-based audiences with an appetite for novelty, and both focused popular opinion; equally, both were relatively new forms, and those who produced drama for them were at their best when being experimental and when grappling with limited resources. In an illuminating study, Graham Holderness celebrates Howell's insight that television and Elizabethan theatre have much in common. He cites her work to support his contention that television offers 'unique opportunities for a democratic recovery of Shakespeare', although he also observes that 'where academics envisage television as a means of reconstituting the Elizabethan theatre, producers think more in terms of translating theatre into the discourse of television itself' ('Radical Potentiality' 216).

The point is often made that the chronicle structure of plays like *Henry VI* resembles the scheduled structure of modern television. This argument holds true if we look back to the pioneering work of Raymond Williams, who was one of the first critics to explore television theoretically. Television, he observed, is different from novels and the theatre because it is typically composed of discrete segments scheduled in a sequence. John Ellis, elaborating this point, argues that 'the form that tends to be adopted by TV fiction … is the same as TV news, with a continuous updating on the latest concatenation of events rather than a final ending or explanation', and notes that 'each scene is coherent in itself, delivering a particular meaning, an event, a relation between characters' (Ellis 120–1). Ellis could almost be describing the *Henry VI* plays here. News reports are even an important part of the story: the first scene of *Part One*, for example, is marked by three news flashes that interrupt the 'broadcast' of Henry V's funeral. Arguably, the *Henry VI* plays resemble more closely the structure of television news than they do the modern novel, or even Shakespeare's later works. Michael Hattaway describes their 'non-Aristotelian' stories as little more than 'a series of characters presented successively to the audience' (*Part One* 8–9) with no unified plot as such; rather, they consist of a series of segments, just like the news. Indeed, the plays are neither unified nor end-directed – in fact, the final scenes in each part look forward to the next play, reminding us that, as in a soap opera, history never ends; there is always another story to tell.

Williams's most useful insight was that television meaning or 'broadcast message' is constructed not through each segment but through the way they are put together. In the case of Howell's *Henry VI–Richard III* tetralogy, all sorts of ironic juxtapositions were created by a half-time live news broadcast, included because the BBC felt that the plays were too long. *Part One* broke at Talbot's death after a series of comic battle scenes; the headlines included the death of the popular comedian Dick Emery. For *Part Two*, the main headline was Margaret Thatcher's victory visit to the Falkland Islands, a story which rhymes with *Part Two*'s initial atmosphere of restored peace and triumph. The news for *Part Three* was as bleak as the play itself, as it related the story of a man who had been shot by police in a case of mistaken identity.

These news broadcasts were chance associations; the BBC used other strategies to secure the way it wanted the series to be received. Each episode was framed by a generic BBC title sequence which reinforced the series's ruling values. This began with a shot of Shakespeare's portrait from the first edition of the Complete Works, the 1623 'First Folio', a gesture perhaps to the cultural significance of the series' claim to be the first Complete *Televisual* Works. The camera then passed through Shakespeare's face, giving the sense of actually entering the book, to arrive at the title of the series and the play. These titles were in red script on a light brown background, mimicking the typeface and layout of the First Folio, as if we were indeed about to read the authentic Shakespearean text. To add to the general air of solemnity and seriousness, the series was credited to the grandly de-acronymed institution 'The British Broadcasting Corporation'. These titles worked to predetermine responses to the work before Howell's interpretation could properly begin. This is an example of what Williams called 'close-range' analysis, which studies a television programme as chains of segments which construct sequences and flows; Williams maintained that 'it is only as we come really close to the substance of what is spoken and shown that we see the real character of television flow' (Williams 115). Although television studies has made great strides forward since Williams's path-breaking work, his insights are very useful in exploring the institutional tensions evident in these broadcasts.

The place of the BBC's *Henry VI*s in the schedules tied the works into the fabric of the institution's other cultural products – as Williams puts it, 'flows of meaning' were constructed across the schedule, as viewers watched *Henry VI*, then watched other programmes such as the news, sitcoms and even advertisements. The institutional context of these *Henry VI*s was quite different from that surrounding those produced by the RSC because the BBC itself was already implicated in the spectacle of power. Since the 1920s, when the King's voice was first broadcast on radio, the BBC has occupied a unique role in British culture, bringing the rituals of power within reach of everybody with a radio or television set. Royal weddings, coronations, state funerals and jubilee celebrations are as much a part of the BBC's institutional identity as the making of drama. Its broadcast of Elizabeth II's coronation in 1953 was not only a definitive cultural moment, it also brought television into the mainstream of family life for the first time. By supplying a narrative voice for the processions, the BBC had become a mediator between the people and the ceremonial events in which British national identity is rehearsed and displayed. On the face of it, this role was congruent with producing Shakespearean television plays, which are sometimes held up as cultural equivalents of public pageantry. Yet each of the *Henry VI* plays began with an interrupted political spectacle (a funeral, a wedding and a coup), and in Howell's productions, each of these ceremonies was later revisited; in the return, layered with visual remembering, each of them made explicit the bitter divisions the spectacles were designed to conceal. Howell demanded viewers who were much more critically aware than those who watched royal pageantry. If television could unlock Shakespeare's radical potential, her productions also sounded Shakespeare's power to find the radical potential of television.

An Age of Kings

An early precursor to Howell's work was the 1960 BBC serial *An Age of Kings*, directed by Michael Hayes (who later filmed the RSC's *Wars* for television). In this fifteen-part series, the BBC's first production of the *Henry VI*s, Shakespeare's history plays were adapted by Peter Dews into hour-length episodes, five of them based on the *Henry VI* plays. The series exploited the suitability of the history plays for television but also encountered 'conservative drag': the hour-long format was deliberately reminiscent of the Sunday-afternoon period dramas that the BBC regularly produced at this time. Shakespeare's history plays were turned into a television soap opera, and each episode ended with a foreshadowing of the next: one closed on the Duke of York frantically writing a letter addressed to Jack Cade, another with Richard Crookback thoughtfully contemplating a malmsey butt (the same one that his goons would use to murder Clarence in *Richard III*).

An Age of Kings's grand title disclosed a different cultural agenda, for the BBC was, in effect, the modern-day king-maker – it had broadcast the coronation of both George VI and Elizabeth II, thus legitimating the monarchy for the modern age. *An Age of Kings* was a late product of the Festival of Britain spirit, and many of its actors had performed in the history play cycles staged at the Birmingham Rep and in Stratford-upon-Avon nearly a decade earlier. Their work belonged to that cultural moment, one that was subsequently commemorated by the funeral of Winston Churchill in 1966, an event that marked, as everyone from the Prime Minister to the tabloid newspapers insisted, the end of an era. In the pageantry that accompanied the funeral, broadcast by the BBC, *The Times* thought it could see 'centuries of British history woven into a living, moving tapestry', an effect produced visually as troops from all services, regiments and ranks marched with Churchill's coffin. A more recent historian said of the same event that 'British (not just English) history seemed to reconstitute itself in an immense assembly of mourning and memory' (Schama 402). Schama's comment could equally apply to the grand scale of *An Age of Kings* – it, too, was an 'immense assembly of mourning and memory' in that it marked off the past as the territory of nostalgia. Both the BBC's coverage of Churchill's funeral and its *An Age of Kings* serial revealed a shared vision of history, one shaped by the politics of the postwar years of mourning and reconstruction.

Michael Hayes discovered, however, that there are limitations as well as potential in televising Shakespearean history. As Shakespeare was not constrained by his theatre's ability to represent location physically, he wrote plays which range across England and France. Hayes was restricted by the resources available to him. Although *An Age of Kings* was born out of the nostalgia for the past inaugurated by the 1953 coronation and completed by

Churchill's funeral, it did not have a budget to match its ambitions. Sets were recycled to denote different places, and often a new setting was marked only by a curtain or a different prop. Nevertheless, Hayes took advantage of these limitations to create a sense of interiority. A visual pattern developed which linked certain kinds of scenes thematically across the five episodes: the same courtyard, for example, was the scene of the Temple Garden dispute, Margaret's capture by Suffolk, Cade's defeat and Edward's final celebrations. The Dauphin looked out of a castle window at the massing English army, the same window from which Henry later saw Cade's army, and later still, from which York and Rutland watched musicians in the street below. Through such repetition, Hayes hinted at an underlying unity often overlooked amidst the fragmentation of the civil wars fought in the last episodes. There were psychological interiors, too: soliloquies were spoken softly to the camera in close-up, as if characters were whispering confessions to the audience. Stretching the resources he had available, Hayes made adventurous use of televisual effects to create vivid, sometimes hallucinatory images: demons danced in the reflection of Joan's iris, the dying Warwick was shrouded in thick mist, the image of a burning barn was superimposed on battle scenes.

One episode did attempt to look beyond the nostalgia for a pastoral England. *The Morning's War*, based on the first three acts of *Part Three*, was the most ambitious of the adaptations. More than any of the other episodes, this was about England, whose rural landscapes were recreated in the studio and then subjected to the devastation of the civil wars. The episode began indoors, with sombre drums and a shot of Henry and Margaret's thrones hidden under a white sheet, as if ready for the cleaners, the colour also foreshadowing the snow that fell thickly later in the episode.

Nostalgia was explored critically in the Battle of Towton scenes, which took place beneath a derelict windmill covered in snow. The camera panned upwards, past two ragged sails, to a broken window at which, from the shadows within, Henry appeared, looking out over 'the morning's war' (*Part Three* II.v.1). Remaining outside looking in, the shot distanced the viewer from Henry as he drew a circle on the frosted window-pane in which he marked out the time of the shepherd's day; and, as he said softly 'how many makes the hour full complete' (26), each hand slowly closed the circle until it was opaque. Ironically, this, the most nostalgic speech in the play, was the least nostalgic part of the production, for, by looking at Henry from the outside, through a cracked, frosted window, Hayes acknowledged that both mourning and memory are limited in their capacity to engage us with the problems of history.

Hayes proved that the *Henry VI* plays can translate effectively to television. Their episodic structure easily adapted to television's serial format, and Hayes successfully created a sense of epic scope and the passage of time by showing the surviving characters visibly ageing each week. He negotiated the demands of the story with the limitations of live studio work by using what were then innovative televisual techniques such as montages and overlays, which lent to the plays a haunting and, in places, surreal quality that stage productions have seldom matched. Innovative as it was, however, *An Age of Kings* left some questions unanswered. Could the *Henry VI* plays work as television if each was allowed its full three-hour playing time? What else was to be learned from exploring televisual solutions to the theatrical challenges of the text? And how far could the political dissonance between the BBC's role as royal broadcaster and Shakespeare's depiction of national disintegration be pushed? Twenty years later, Jane Howell's remarkable productions for the BBC's Complete Works series offered some intriguing answers.

The BBC/Time-Life Shakespeare and Henry VI

The BBC/Time-Life Shakespeare Complete Works series has been widely criticised for its insistence on traditional performance values and tends today to be rather mocked for this, even though some of its episodes (including the *Henry VI*s) were finely done. At its worst, the series exemplified the horrors of approaching Shakespeare with a preconceived sense of cultural value and reverence for stereotypes of classical performance. In her definitive history of the series (which to some extent is also both a defence and an apology), Susan Willis locates its cultural impetus in the 'charge of the light brigade' determination 'that built the British Empire'. She suggests a hint of pigheadedness in those who commissioned the programmes without any real knowledge of what they were doing, beyond the conviction that the series should be 'gloriously British and gloriously BBC' (Willis 5). This is only half the story, for the Complete Works were put on a very sound commercial footing via the BBC's partnership with Time-Life. From the outset, the real market was an export one, notably the American education market. The BBC has rarely (if ever) repeated the series on British television and only a handful of the programmes have since been released on commercial video in the UK, although a box set was released in 2005, but the entire series is available in America on VHS and DVD. Mindful of its consumers, Time-Life apparently instigated clauses in its contract with the BBC that forbade modern interpretation, narrowing the artistic possibilities for directors.

The *Henry VI* episodes managed to navigate these strict rules and yet still produce innovative and politically challenging television. Howell is not a director who reveres Shakespeare uncritically; in 1973 she directed the first production of Edward Bond's *Bingo*, which depicts Shakespeare as a middle-aged capitalist siding with landowners against the working classes (there is a nice dedication to Howell from Edward Bond in the published edition of the play). With this behind her, Howell was never going to approach Shakespeare without interrogating and even distancing herself from a conservative interpretation of the text. Indeed, Howell was extremely committed to the kinds of popular theatre that the plays were written for and did not in fact appreciate the full theatrical potential of the plays until she recognised in them echoes of medieval drama (Fenwick *Part One* 21). Her own experience with medieval drama was recent, for in 1976 she had directed the York mystery plays with a cast of local actors at St Mary's Abbey in York. Influenced by a pageant-wagon production of the same cycle in Leeds, Howell dressed her actors as medieval artisans and used the production to explore the social interaction between community and performance in the mystery plays. Her *Henry VI*s were a secular version of the medieval plays: dramas not about people but about a society.

By approaching the plays through popular theatrical traditions, Howell was able to develop a distinct look and feel for the series that complied with the BBC/Time-Life contract without compromising her commitment to political drama. Howell deftly exploited both the theatrical potential of the plays and the possibilities offered by television in order to stay one step ahead of her audience (and the BBC) and to challenge preconceived notions of how Shakespeare should be televised. The scenography was Elizabethan and modern, contained and yet mysteriously uncontainable, naturalistic *and* stylised.

In all three parts, the acting was naturalistic, and costumes – all medieval – were beautifully designed recreations of fifteenth-century dress. However, for the setting, Howell looked back to the original staging conventions of the Shakespearean playhouse and to other forms of popular theatre for inspiration. Scenes were performed on nearly bare stages, with minimal props to suggest different locations. There was no verisimilitude in the depiction of place – a fake tree represented Iden's garden, a tent indicated France, and battles were fought across a wooden playground. Howell could not be accused of being inauthentic – on the contrary, by returning to sixteenth-century staging practices, she was being utterly true to the text. In practice, however, the merging of Elizabethan theatre and modern television created an iconoclastic work with a strong political subtext.

Fortunately, the 'house style' of the series had been revised following the appointment of Jonathan Miller as producer. Cedric Messina, Miller's predecessor and the main visionary behind the series, had explicitly forbidden directorial interpretation and insisted, perhaps naively, that the plays should 'speak for themselves'. Directors were further advised to 'keep the audience unaware of theatrical conventions' and play Shakespeare as naturalistically as possible (Bulman 572). Miller, a veteran director and a graduate of the 1960s review *Beyond the Fringe* (which, among other things, lampooned the *Henry VI* plays), was much more sensitive to the role of interpretation in performance. However, bound by the BBC/Time-Life's instruction to 'stage conservatively' and be 'orthodox', he could not give his directors much more freedom than Messina had. As a way round these restrictions, Miller briefed directors to stage the plays 'as Elizabethans would have understood them' (572), which meant that directors like Howell had much more freedom to explore explicitly theatrical techniques. James C. Bulman sees this as a fundamental shift in the series's house style. He quotes Alvin Rakoff (a friend of Messina's and director of the BBC's *Romeo and Juliet*) insisting that 'the most real medium in the world is television'; thus, audiences who had seen 'real blood and real violence' on the news would be alienated by any stylisation or 'pretend violence' when switching over to Shakespeare (578). Messina and Rakoff's anxieties about theatricality and audience expectations were misplaced concerns, however, for, as we have seen, the whole notion that news reporting is 'naturalistic' is a highly questionable one. By contrast, Bulman points out, Howell argued that 'television is *not* a realistic medium' (574). Her *Henry VI*s were full of artifice, both televisual and theatrical.[1]

The single, permanent set used for all three productions gave the series a theatrical feel, but unlike the dreary, stagy sets in some other episodes in the series, this one was dressed and shot in innovative ways and became, in effect, a character in its own right. In *Part One*, it was painted in bright primary colours; in successive episodes, the paintwork was progressively distressed to represent the eclipse of social values over time, until, in *Part Three*, a blanket of snow (recalling *An Age of Kings*) transformed the set into a blank white space not unlike a television studio.[2] Designed by Oliver Bayldon, the set was simultaneously a past and present space that evoked the timbered stages of the Elizabethan playhouses and the urban playgrounds of modern London. Although medieval in appearance, the set was actually based upon a playground that Howell and Bayldon found in Fulham (Fenwick *Part One* 24). The impression on screen was of a climbing frame modelled after a medieval fort: there were large swing doors for grand entrances and smaller ones for more intimate scenes, in addition to an upper level which actors ascended via long, rickety staircases.[3]

Beginning with medieval theatre and ending with modern television, the set's development mirrored the progress of the plays from the chivalric heroism of Henry V and Talbot to the contemporary, thuggish ambition of Richard Crookback. Performance styles followed a similar trajectory. *Part One* contained moments of pure artifice, such as Gloucester and Winchester riding brightly coloured hobbyhorses in a Parliament made of cushions, or the French charging around the stage like schoolboys, a clever fusion of pantomime with the visual language of children's television. Over the next two parts, the performance vocabulary was extended to include reportage, fairground con tricks, political spectacle and war reporting. Televisual devices interrupted any easy assumptions about the superiority of theatre as a medium for Shakespeare. Montages, split screens and mirrors wrought transformations into nightmarish visions of riots and battles. The set itself had only the illusion of being permanent: in practice, the walls could be reconfigured to form different kinds of playing spaces. Doors moved from one end of the studio to the other to create the illusion of different places, and for some scenes the walls were removed altogether to create haunted nights and snow-storms. When York left his uncle Mortimer in the dungeons, he walked through the cell door, and the camera cut to him walking straight into Parliament – a trick impossible to do in a theatre.

In the light of modern digital effects, such techniques can look dated and amateurish, but the videos of Howell's productions are still worth watching. Howell not only managed an exemplary marriage of Shakespeare and television, she also directed strong productions of the *Henry VI* plays, with relatively minor cuts, that remain amongst the most convincing and vibrant interpretations in recent memory. Despite the insistence of the BBC on traditional performance values, Howell took Shakespeare's exploration of political factions and their impact on society and made out of them a contemporary parable that continues to strike a chord. Taken together, the productions depict a world in the grip of dizzying social change, fuelled by violence and in-fighting. Howell was absolutely committed to seeing echoes of the present in the past: in her first address to the cast, she drew analogies between the plays and contemporary situations in Northern Ireland, Beirut and South Africa (Fenwick *Part One* 24), persuading a sceptical Bernard Hill (who played York) of the plays' 'continuing validity' to 'crucial modern problems and concerns' (Fenwick *Part Three* 26–7). Howell was also very interested in British society: as she told Harry Fenwick, 'everything is changing, people are not certain of what is coming'; society had the potential to swing sharply either to the left or to the right (Fenwick *Part One* 21). Margaret Thatcher's Conservative Party had been elected in 1979, only two years before Howell began work on the *Henry VI* plays, and the new Prime Minister's radical economic policy was already reshaping social debate.

In Howell's *Henry VI* plays, extreme violence emerged out of fractures in a social structure polarised by ambition and cruel exploitation. The heroic nature of war was commemorated by the funeral of Henry V, but then the violence of conflict was explored through increasingly graphic depictions of fighting and death. Violence was explicit and bloody, so much so that, when first broadcast in the United States, battle scenes were cut substantially in order to make the series more palatable.[4] Howell's aim was to begin with a naive sense of chivalric heroism and then to interrogate it progressively. Audiences who enjoyed the knockabout humour of the wars in *Part One* were confronted with increasingly harrowing depictions of war across the cycle. In *Part Two*, the chivalric world was finally buried in York's fight with Clifford, when the pair charged around a set already burnt by Cade's mob and now torn to pieces by their desperate battle; in *Part Three*, Henry's society was in ruins, held together only by ambition and grief. The remaining sections of this chapter will look at each part in turn, focusing on Howell's representation of history and violence and the various ways in which her work summons (or is haunted by) other forms of televisual historiography.

Part One: the flower of knighthood

Each part began with an elaborate opening: *Part One* with Henry V's funeral, *Part Two* with the wedding of Henry and Margaret and *Part Three* with York's *coup d'état*. These set pieces were more than just curtain-raisers, for they established key dynamics which were then picked apart over the course of the play. The national unity of the funeral, which celebrated the warrior king, was soon shattered by scenes of actual warfare – Talbot's story really began here, his name invoked over the coffin of Henry V, and ended with another lament when he held the body of his son in his arms. Henry and Margaret's wedding showed an outward display of national unity, but this, too, was quickly fragmented as political factions huddled on the stage, and the commoners who cheered Margaret jeered at Eleanor and eventually revolted against their masters. The third part opened with division and descended wearily into a horrific, even apocalyptic depiction of society at the edge of destruction.

The funeral of Henry V was a keynote for the whole series, linking society to rituals of death and mourning. Nothing was hurried – three minutes passed before the first words of the play were spoken. The event began in darkness, with a lament sung off-screen, the camera slowly fading to the face of the singer, a soldier played by Peter Benson (who also played Henry VI). His song was to the 'blessed king' Henry V, the 'flower of knighthood ne'er defiled'; behind him, hooded men gathered, holding candles, singing chants and beating drums. Howell filled in more details as the camera drew back: the darkness gave way to the first sight of the set, then to the whole company gathered for a state funeral. Henry V's cortège marched slowly through double doors, headed by soldiers carrying the crown and other symbols of the state. The coffin followed, a simple wooden box, adorned only with a skeleton sketched in chalk – a *memento mori* that keyed the production to the rites of the dead.

Joseph Roach points out that funerals (like theatrical performances) are 'rich in revealing contradictions' because 'they make publicly visible through symbolic action both the tangible exist-ence of social boundaries and, at the same time, the contingency of those boundaries on fictions of identity, their shoddy construc-tion out of inchoate otherness, and, consequently, their anxiety-inducing instability' (Roach 39). Roach's analysis depends on the inherent continuity between performance and social ritual; but, if we apply this theory to a state funeral, the 'fictions of identity' and their consequent 'anxiety-inducing instability' have much wider ramifications, for the subject of the funeral is not simply a person but the state itself. Howell's production was ghosted by a recent state funeral, that of Earl Mountbatten in 1979 (following his death in a terrorist attack), which the BBC had televised rever-entially. Like Henry V, Mountbatten was a figure of Empire; he had been the Viceroy of India up to its secession in 1948 and, thus, has a claim to be the last truly imperial figure in British history. His death was also untimely, as he had been killed by the IRA. Conse-quently, his funeral was widely interpreted as a symbolic end of Britain's imperial story. *The Daily Mail* called Mountbatten 'the last great warrior, the end of a line of heroes', and Paul Johnson, in the same newspaper, asked, 'did we bury with him more than his mortal remains – did we bury the notion of a national hero?' (6 September 1979). *The Daily Express* called the funeral 'the end of Empire' and boasted that 'the last pages in our imperial history are now being written' (6 September 1979). Commentaries on the present also emerged: *The Times* tried to capture the public mood in tones reminiscent of Gloucester's broodings about a world without Henry: 'We bury today not only a great and much loved man. We bury also a bit of our past and – what is in a way sadder still – a bit of our future.' *The Times* adumbrated Howell's own vision for *Henry VI* as a world struggling to cope with the 'death of chivalry': 'the hand of death, failing memories, bad government, growing poverty and manifest impotence have all painfully combined to rid us of our pride and illusions' (6 September 1979).

Howell drew attention to the fictionalising strategies inherent in such broadcasts. In *Part One*, the camera employed a similar technique, moving through the crowd as if it were covering a live event. By extending the dead march to three minutes – an extraordinary amount of 'dead time' for television, the length of a music video on MTV – Howell reasserted the significance of the procession as an emblem of history and its fictions. The rest of the performance was, in effect, a dismantling of this opening moment of heroic celebration and national unity. Each noble spoke his piece, but power blocks were being formed already: Gloucester against Winchester, Exeter against Bedford. They turned their comments to the assembled crowd, transforming the funeral into the stage of a political hustings: then other voices addressed the crowd, messages from France of defeat and the capture of Talbot. The people turned from mourners to anxious soldiers. The world was on the precipice of ruin, the innocent song of the chorister silenced by the clamour for death and war.

The truth behind this imperial bluster was to come. Howell revealed only slowly the full cost of war and chose to follow the funeral, instead, with a scene that ingeniously sent up those who celebrate conflict. The French were depicted as adolescents (although played by adults) who raved enthusiastically about war with preposterous naivety. In contrast to the sombre introduction of the funeral, the French army entered marching to a jaunty military tune, shifting the performance vocabulary to something more akin to that of a village fête. They smiled proudly, bouncing as they marched, swinging their arms like boy scouts on a parade, carrying their crossbows and spears like toys and waving them in the air as their generals walked on to the stage. Some even acknowledged the camera, as if the spectacle was being televised and they were being watched by their mothers. Howell captured the feeling of a live event by filming from behind the heads of the soldiers, who cheered when their generals roused them, and laughed at their jokes. All of the opening speeches were performed as public addresses: Charles shouted 'now we are victors' to huge cheers. Alençon – tall, slender and dapper, fondling a medal hung around his neck as he spoke – was the comedian, bringing down the house by comparing the English to 'a drowned mouse'; but it was the stocky Reignier who found their battle spirit, mocking 'mad brained Talbot' by twisting his finger against his head.

This was a strange kind of history play, more like children's television than period drama: Peter Ackroyd even compared *Part One* to farce (*The Times* 3 January 1983). But these counter-intuitive reference points were an ingenious response to the demands of the text. Following the commemoration of the heroic in the funeral of Henry V, the performance of heroic action as a fundamentally absurd and adolescent game was a necessary step to the play's main tragic focus, the death of Talbot. Howell soon deflated the French army's exaggerated pretensions. Charles led his troops offstage as drums and tabor played wildly; the camera paused briefly on the doors, then the music started again, this time as a mad and loose tune, and frightened soldiers ran back across the stage, the Dauphin kicking them in frustration. Creeping towards the camera, Charles insisted that he would not have retreated had not his men fled first – like a schoolboy insisting 'it wasn't my fault'. Reignier and Alençon joined him, their noses bloody, as if they had been in a playground fight. Actual war was edited out, its consequences instead reduced to the politics of schoolyard violence.

The comedy continued with Joan, who combined the Dauphin's preposterous naivety with a zealous belief in her own abilities. Joan was every inch the comedic stereotype of a blunt, industrious working-class girl. She marched on to the set dressed in peasant's clothing, her blonde hair tied back ready for business; her accent was sing-song Lancashire and peppered with colourful mispronunciations that highlighted the difference between herself and the educated nobles who winced when Charles was called the 'Dolphin'. But she was not to be fooled either: she looked straight to where Charles was hiding (and sniggering at his prank) and demanded that he 'curm, curm from b-hiiind'. Like a schoolgirl pretending to be a teacher, she put the 'Dolphin' in his place and ordered the men offstage, Reignier grumbling but nevertheless removing his helmet, giving it to Charles, and shuffling sulkily off-camera. Head girl and head boy were left to fight it out. Hilariously, Charles boasted 'I fear no woman', while putting on a helmet with a face-guard to fight Joan, who wore no armour but simply tightened her belt. When, during their duel, Charles tried to rub himself against Joan, she punched him in the groin, disarmed him and then pointed her sword victoriously at the defeated prince: Charles quickly whipped off his helmet to cover his crotch, just in case.

Howell plundered the stage vocabulary of the circus and the pantomime, popular entertainments which hinted at the plays' roots in medieval popular theatre. Ackroyd quipped that Joan had to be either Margaret Thatcher or principal boy: Brenda Blethyn played her as both, slapping her thighs and bossing the men around with exaggerated bravado. In battle, she charged around the stage wearing a helmet whose blue plume bobbed about ridiculously as she chased the English. In one scene, she stood on the stairs as soldiers attacked her, kicking or punching them backwards one by one, each blow accompanied by a crash of cymbals and a cheer from the French, who were like a crowd watching clowns at the circus. The pantomime world ended abruptly when Joan, dishevelled after her final battle, found Talbot's body propped against a cannon; as the Dauphin and his generals discussed tactics, the camera closed in on Joan's shocked face, her eyes fixed on the corpse in horror. Talbot's body drove an uncomfortable realism into Joan's fairy-tale world of chivalric heroism: now she looked grown up, staring death in the face and perhaps seeing in the corpse an image of her own impending fate.

Talbot epitomised the chivalric order lamented in the funeral scenes and toyed with by the French, but his death, in contrast to that of Henry, was not mourned. Talbot, played by Trevor Peacock, was a stocky, ageing warrior. His name was fired like cannon-shot against the enemy by his men, but in truth he was a sombre man, and Peacock introduced a lot of brooding self-doubt into the part. This was brought out early on, in Talbot's first scene: soldiers gathered about his feet, eager to hear the story of his capture, but, as he spoke, he drifted into quiet reflection. The camera closed in on his face and overlaid it with a shot of children stationed at a cannon. The juxtaposition was unsettling, as if Talbot was already beginning to confront the costs of fighting for empire – a militarised society in which children took arms.

In Talbot's final scenes, the commemoration of heroism staged in the opening procession was revisited as a requiem for a dying order. The sequence started with a heroic flourish: grim and 'moody mad', Talbot made a rousing speech, standing on a podium with his shield by his side and his sword thrust into the air. His soldiers gathered round him in a circle, the points of their swords touching his body, and shouted 'A Talbot!' At that moment, the stage grew dark except for a spotlight shining directly on Talbot's face. The tableau was broken only after York and Somerset had refused to send aid: the soldiers turned to face their enemy in slow motion, their cries of 'A Talbot!' repeated like a broken record on a loop.

With the introduction of Young Talbot, the production's wider debate between heroism and violence found its voice. Pleading with his son not to fight, Talbot found himself criticising the same appetite for war that he had previously represented. Howell described the introduction of the younger man as the key moment in *Part One*: 'When Talbot finally comes face to face with his own son who will not leave the battle although he knows he is going to get killed, then Talbot has to come face to face with his own values; because if the values of chivalry mean you have to sacrifice your son' (Fenwick *Part One* 31).

Young Talbot was introduced as a spectator to battle, the camera showing furious fighting superimposed on a close-up of a contemplative youth standing at the edge of the studio. Howell continued to shoot the scene from Young Talbot's point of view: as he found his father and started to argue with him, the camera was always looking over the younger man's shoulder. Howell's point was not to stress his story but to put the focus on the elder Talbot and his desperation. Talbot first tried to be stern and commanding, but this did not do the trick – his son wanted to be just like him. Aghast and shaking his head, he pleaded with his son, but found himself trapped by the logic of his own reputation: how could he tell his child to do what he would not do himself? As his son launched himself against the enemy, all Talbot could do was stagger after him, no longer a great soldier but a weary father.

Talbot died with his head propped against a cannon and his son in his lap. Peacock delivered his final speech quietly and slowly, choking with tears and looking away from 'my Icarus', whose head he cradled. This was a moving portrayal of a man who had been betrayed by his own value system: the commemoration of chivalric heroism staged by the opening funeral was revisited with the dying Talbot as the only mourner. The camera visualised the *Times* editorial on Mountbatten, which mourned both 'our past' and 'our future'; here, past and future were drowned in Talbot's tears. When the scene ended, Howell cut from Talbot's face to a close-up of Christ on the cross – an archetype of betrayal and sacrifice.

Part Two: two Englands

Although the series was broadcast in 1983, it was filmed from September 1981 to April 1982 (when the shoot concluded with *Richard III*), turbulent months which saw, on both the national and world stage, political assassinations, war, violent protests and jubilant street parties – all potent cultural material for any production of *Henry VI*. There were attempts on the lives of the American President Ronald Reagan, the British Prime Minister Margaret Thatcher, Pope John Paul II and even Queen Elizabeth II. None succeeded, but in October the Egyptian President Anwar Sadat was gunned down. Britain faced insurrection on two fronts.

In Northern Ireland, IRA prisoners went on a hunger strike that led to a steady tally of deaths through the summer of 1981. Meanwhile, inner-city riots engulfed the streets of Liverpool, London and many other places in Britain, creating a media panic about the imminent collapse of social order – played out on television daily: one critic called the riots a '*Coronation Street* of violence' (Tumber 304). In the midst of all this violence, two television events brought the British nation together. A fictional wedding in the soap opera *General Hospital* was the most watched marriage in television history, until 29 July, when Prince Charles, the heir to the throne, married Lady Diana Spencer. Broadcasting the event live to 750 million people worldwide, the BBC did its gloriously British best to represent a united nation celebrating its monarchy. That was July: the inner cities were still rioting come September when Howell began work on the *Henry VI* plays, and people were still talking about the wedding of Charles and Diana. There were, palpably, two Englands struggling to dominate the headlines: one enjoying the sunshine of honeymoon, the other throwing petrol bombs at riot squads.

Part Two began with a spectacular royal wedding which, over the course of several acts, turned into a riot. For Howell, it seemed, there was no real contradiction between the two Englands, for the wedding emblematised the same social injustices that caused the violence later in the play. There is, in fact, no wedding in the play – Suffolk just presents Queen Margaret to Henry. Howell turned this into a real show, a national celebration that echoed the real royal marriage that all the company would have remembered, and some participated in, only weeks before. So the nobility filed in with their banners and marched ceremoniously until they were in a formation that created a corridor for Margaret. Just above them, the balcony was dressed with the same bunting that had been used in hundreds of British street parties that summer. 'England and her lordly peers' were both represented by flags then, but here already was a sign of two Englands not quite in harmony: the stiff, formal display of the nobility centre stage versus the euphoric, gaudy commoners above who, though unseen, usurped the spectacle by cheering noisily and throwing confetti down on to Margaret as she entered dressed in a white and cream bridal dress. When the BBC broadcast Charles and Diana's wedding, it, too, edited out what cultural historians Daniel Dayan and Elihu Katz called (appropriately enough) the 'Elizabethan jocularity' of the crowd, which they contrasted with the stiff 'Victorian etiquette' and 'British arrogance' of the main procession (Dayan and Katz 82). A similar tension structured Henry and Margaret's wedding: whether consciously or not, Howell's staged ceremony commented on the politics of media events in which national identity is uncritically represented. On television, inner-city riots and the royal marriage were simply different items of news – or, to echo Raymond Williams, different segments with no apparent relationship to each other. *Part Two* subverted this separation by drawing a direct line between the commoners' role in the wedding and their subsequent uprising.

Two Englands continued to rub against each other and, on each occasion, the original spectacle of the wedding was dismantled, its political artifice revealed in newly ironic contexts. When Eleanor visited the witch Jourdain, the dynamics of the wedding were reversed. There was no spirit, no access to another world: instead, Eleanor was the dupe of the commoners, a sucker for a carnival show. Where Howell had filmed the first scene much as the BBC had filmed the real royal wedding, she now allowed the cameras to go 'behind the scenes'. This time, we saw Jourdain putting her make-up on and Bolingbroke acting much like a medieval television director, organising the set and the sound effects in preparation for their victim. By revealing all this artifice, the scene reinterpreted the wedding itself as a form of political spectacle. The ceremony was recalled again later when the disgraced Eleanor, dressed only in white (an echo of Margaret's bridal dress), was led round a darkened set to face the taunts of commoners crowded onstage.

The relationship between the two Englands was very quickly turning from celebration to something more violent; with the commoners now taunting the nobility, the transition from the 'Elizabethan jocularity' of the opening scenes to the riots in Act IV was already under way. One of Howell's real achievements was to emphasise the social and political contexts for this transition. As violent and unpleasant as it was, the Cade riot did not simply *happen*. The commoners' story simmered in the background and, with each successive act of oppression and disenfranchisement, their frustration grew. Hume's treachery, the petitioners' attempt to attract the attention of the nobility, Peter Thump's desperate fight with Master Horner, Simpcox's attempted fraud and even the pirates' capture of Suffolk were all stepping stones. Taken together, the scenes formed a sub-plot of exclusion, frustration, parody and, finally, violence that led up to, and helped to explain, the turn to rebellion following Gloucester's death. However, Howell stopped short of dignifying the commoners, whom she called the 'thickest, daftest people' (Fenwick *Part Two* 27). She saw nothing in the riot itself that could be compared to legitimate political protests; the indulgence in ignorance and cruelty was too extreme. Yet, by putting her directorial emphasis on the riot's causes, Howell avoided expressing the view, shared by many political commentators in 1981, that all such acts are the product of a subhuman intoxication with violence for violence's sake. Simpcox was unquestionably a charlatan, and those that followed him were simple-minded, but his wife's passing line, 'we did it for pure need', visibly disturbed Gloucester and suggested momentarily a more pressing sense of social hardship underlying the comedy. Howell dwelt on this for a beat, making the reduction of the scene to a simple comic episode impossible.

Comedy was also worryingly transformed into extreme class violence in the Thump–Horner scene. The fight started as a comic duel between an oafish servant and a drunken master: Horner staggered about the stage, mocked his apprentice and spat beer into his face. Suddenly, the bemused simpleton lost his temper, his face contorted, and he screamed, before launching himself at his master, whom he bludgeoned viciously. Henry and his court had been enjoying the fight in much the same way they had enjoyed Gloucester's mock trial of Simpcox. Now, however, they were silent, evidently shaken by the unexpected fury of the apprentice.

The riot itself developed imagery from the wedding scene, transforming the crowd's jocularity into the uncontained anarchy of the rebels. Howell saw Cade as a sort of neo-fascist in the mould of the National Front (Fenwick *Part Two* 27), an organisation whose mixture of fanatical nationalism and supremacist violence was a visible reminder of the thin line that can exist between patriotism and anarchy. There was an uncomfortable similarity between National Front marches coloured by Union Jacks, and the crowds who celebrated the wedding of Charles and Diana with the same flags in July 1981. In the production, flags and confetti became a repeated motif: Margaret, who had revelled in the confetti thrown on her by the crowds, now tore the commoners' petitions into similarly tiny pieces. Later, Lord Saye was dragged on to the stage and greeted with another mock celebration, but this time the confetti was made out of the charred remains of burnt books. The riot itself

8 *BBC Henry VI* (1981–83). Books are burnt by Cade's rebels

centred on a bonfire around which rebels danced and into which they threw books, chanting, 'Burn the books, burn the books!' Their anger was as much against writing as it was against the authorities who tried to suppress them. Shots of soldiers being killed were intercut with images of rebels tearing up books and throwing the shreds in the air. From the torn petition to the burning of the books, the production traced a clear line between the commoners' endeavour to be a part of their own history and their final, frustrated attempt to destroy the texts that they could not access. The riot ended with Clifford putting the rebels in chains; the camera panned across to the main stage, where Henry stood alone amidst the debris of the fighting, articles of fine clothing, cushions and jewellery scattered around him. The riots had left the set in ruins, its walls burnt and the stage a desolate, scarred environment. As Bayldon put it, 'vandals had broken into the playground' (Fenwick *Part Two* 20).

Though medieval in appearance, *Part Two* was attuned to the political dynamics and the iconography of the company's own cultural moment. The production invoked the patriotism of the royal wedding and the National Front, and the anarchy of inner-city riots, generating a forceful connection between all three. Now there was only war left: the final scenes were devoted to a weary battle between York and Clifford, who pushed each other into the timbers until both were weaponless and reduced to fighting with their bare hands in what was left of the set. Howell then showed a montage of soldiers being butchered, with the final man stabbed in the back and left draped over a cannon. The closing images were all of bodies as the camera panned across the battlefield and closed on a naked actor, his face staring as if dead, blood running across his arms and chest. This graphic depiction of conflict, so different from the pantomimes of *Part One*, was a curtain-raiser for Howell's nihilistic *Part Three*, in which she envisaged a world without any values beyond revenge and power.

Part Three: *Apocalypse Now*

With *Part Three*, which Howell considered her company's best work (Willems 86), the need to sustain the impact of so much violence gave rise to a number of experimental approaches to filming war that stretched the conservative, orthodox agenda of the series's remit. Where *Part One* had been self-consciously theatrical, Howell now turned to modern, televisual techniques such as montage and the use of colour separation overlay (a forerunner of modern 'green screen' filming).

Part Three was the most intense and, in a strange way, the most contemporary of Howell's contributions to the BBC Shakespeare series. The gaudy sets were now little more than blackened wooden posts, hardly creating an environment at all. Amidst these ruins, the values and ambitions of York, Margaret, Henry and Warwick were vainglorious and empty investments in power and tradition. One by one, characters came to realise the hollowness of their ambition, and in depicting their self-discovery, the eye of Howell's camera was harsh and unforgiving. Henry was left shocked by the sight of the soldiers killing their own kin; Margaret was steely throughout but finally broke down when her son was slaughtered in the snow. Death scenes were not sentimentalised: Clifford's body was grotesquely abused (a total reversal of the mourning rites staged in *Part One*), and the camera remained fixed on Warwick during his final speech, even when others interacted with him, in order to confront his realisation of the pointlessness of his story.

Part Three is not easy to watch, nor was it meant to be. There was no one to sympathise with, and little was provided in the way of relief from the succession of battles. Even on the page, the play is humourless and relentless, piling on battle after battle until questions of right and wrong become redundant. However, the 'alarums and defeats' found in the play (often the only stage direction for a battle) gave Howell an opportunity to struggle out of the BBC strait-jacket and inject some of her own directorial commentary. Howell could hardly be said to have been letting the plays 'speak for themselves' (as Messina had insisted they should) when she devoted so much time to fighting that is accompanied by only the sketchiest stage directions in the text; but she was not directing a work that Elizabethans would recognise, let alone understand (as Miller had hoped for). Instead, the battles became a running commentary on the main story. Whatever was happening in Shakespeare's story was undercut, and reread, by wars that were violent and increasingly strange, even hallucinatory, in the way they were filmed. Carefully choreographed by fight director Michael Ransom, the battles of Wakefield, Barnet and Towton were, in effect, mini-plays in their own right. In fact, a second company of actors was formed just for these scenes. The battles were long but not sensational, and scenes of violence were followed by shots of soldiers suffering and screaming. War was neither heroic nor romanticised.

If anything, this was much more like the 'war is hell' motif of American anti-war movies of the 1970s and 1980s. Michael Manheim argues that the 'post-Vietnam outlook' shaped Howell's approach to conflict, making her work another instance of a genre that includes Francis Ford Coppola's *Apocalypse Now* (1979) and Oliver Stone's *Platoon* (1986). Coppola's film is the most interesting one to compare with Howell's work. Using Joseph Conrad's *Heart of Darkness* as inspiration, Coppola told the story of a soldier travelling through Vietnam to find a renegade colonel. However, the film was not so much about Vietnam as about a journey into the dark psyche of America at its most extreme and violent; as the narrative draws closer to the 'heart of darkness' of the country's interior, where the colonel has his base, the cinematography becomes more hallucinogenic and interiorised. Vietnam was a modern vision of hell for an America still struggling to come to terms with its experiences there. Howell's representation of war shared this dual interest in showing the physical horrors of war and, through experimental camera techniques, suggesting a correlative interior horror, a howling madness, not just for those involved but for the nation itself. The intensity of the performance carried its own

9 *BBC Henry VI* (1981–83). Margaret (Julia Foster) cradles her son's
body; Edward IV (Brian Protheroe) looks on

psychological burden for the actors who, exhausted by the battle
scenes, complained that the battles were 'insane'. Having been first
a spectator and then an eavesdropper in *Part One* and *Part Two*,
the camera now took on the perspective of someone experiencing
a nightmare. Disorienting visuals were mixed with individual
moments of suffering and violence, and large battles were represented through unexpectedly unorthodox means.

Historical pageantry of the kind seen in the BBC's coverage of
funerals and weddings and referenced in *Part One* and *Part Two* was
now reconfigured in surreal montages. One army was portrayed
as mirror images of a single soldier, which became even stranger
when the troops marched against their own reflection. For Wakefield, Howell showed two armies played by the same actors, again
fighting each other, as if the civil war were really a fight against
one's own double or reflection. The camera made sweeps across
people fighting but showed only their legs and bodies, robbing
them of their individual humanity. On the soundtrack, drummers
beat in unison and soldiers shouted together. Towton was also
intense – its final shot was of a man on his knees, screaming madly
as he made a path through the fighting. At the conclusion of the
Battle of Wakefield, a soldier emerged from the mêlée waving a

white flag, but another man seized it and threw it to the ground, where it was trampled on by marching feet. The camera stayed with this white flag, tracking it through the whole sequence before dissolving it into an image of a red flag billowing in the wind, signifying the Lancastrian victory. In this brutal image, the ceremonial flags which had been paraded in *Part One* and *Part Two* became crude emblems of conquest.

The divisions in the kingdom, already obvious at the funeral of Henry V, were conveyed powerfully by a dismantling of the visual codes that had sustained the narrative up to this point: what had looked like a playground or an Elizabethan theatre was now transformed into something altogether less real, less stable. Henry V's funeral procession was recalled in the aftermath of the Battle of Barnet, but this time in the form of a rag-bag of limping soldiers who carried the dead from the field, amongst them the body of Warwick borne on a bier. Margaret watched the procession in determined silence – the camera closed in on her face, looking for some emotional response, but there was none. She did not even look at Warwick as he was brought past: this was a funeral procession without any mourning rites or appeals to vanished glories. The only equivalent to the chorister's song that had accompanied Henry V's cortège was the wild screaming of an injured soldier. Weary men slogged their way through a gathering snowstorm, which gradually effaced the actors until there was nothing on screen except bright light and howling winds. For Howell, 'the world came to an end there' (Willems 85); the heart of England's darkness was, ironically, an empty white BBC studio.

In the post-apocalyptic scenes that followed Tewkesbury, there was little left of the ceremonial culture of Henry VI. The set was now a blackened wooden frame pitched in snow, and Margaret's anguished mourning for her son registered a final note of despair for a chivalric past. This time, however, her emotion frightened those around her, who pulled back as she tugged frantically at their shirts, begging for her own death. *Part Three* ended wearily with a disconsolate Richard storming out of Edward's victory party.

In a climate of nostalgic parades and royal spectacles, Howell's productions of the *Henry VI* plays were an uncompromising study of the realities that underlay such apparently innocent displays. Her productions were, consequently, a challenge to the role of television and of institutions like the BBC in sustaining a heritage culture in which the past was treated uncritically as pageant. But the productions also warned spectators about the threat posed by extreme elements in society: not only royal weddings, funerals and parades but equally gaudy uses of national symbols by such far-right groups as the National Front were all part of the same political spectrum. By teasing out the plays' resonances with the present but keeping (superficially at least) within an Elizabethan framework, Howell created one of the most visually stunning and adventurous contributions to the BBC/Time-Life Shakespeare and demonstrated the theatrical vitality and contemporary relevance of the *Henry VI* plays.

CHAPTER VI

English counter-histories: the ESC's *House of Lancaster* and *House of York* (1987–89)

The English Shakespeare Company's 1987 productions of the *Henry VI* plays were part of an important, although sometimes chaotic, history-play cycle called *The Wars of the Roses*. Even for a company with a permanent theatre, to stage a seven-play cycle is a massive feat; but the ESC had no theatre of its own. Instead, Artistic Directors Michael Bogdanov and Michael Pennington took a large cast of actors, all playing multiple roles, and toured with them, first across Britain and then the world. Adapted as two plays, *House of Lancaster* and *House of York*, *Henry VI* was a vibrant and sharp satire of 1980s English patriotism, but this was underscored by a longing for an Englishness unencumbered by the taint of imperialism.[1]

Calling their company the *English* Shakespeare Company was a provocative, even ironic gesture on Bogdanov and Pennington's parts. Bogdanov had already developed a reputation in the theatre world as an *enfant terrible*. At the National Theatre, he had shown a flair for controversial interpretations of British history: the National cancelled his production of Howard Brenton's notorious *Romans in Britain* following a court action for obscenity that arose from a scene in which Roman soldiers raped native Britons. Bogdanov reworked this idea in *House of Lancaster* when English soldiers assaulted a French peasant woman. Combining sexual violence and British history was a sure way to upset Establishment figures, and Bogdanov's work on Shakespeare showed a similar irreverence for tradition that, in some ways, proved to be even more controversial. In fact, he received more complaints for his modern *The Taming of the Shrew* (RSC 1978) than he did even for *Romans in Britain* (Bogdanov *The Guardian* 22 November

2003); but his hip, rock 'n' roll version of *Romeo and Juliet* (RSC 1986), controversial at the time, anticipated Baz Luhrmann's 1996 film of the same play. After the ESC tour of the histories, Bogdanov worked on scenes from Shakespeare with the residents of council estates to show how Shakespeare could be performed by complete amateurs in the language of the street. In adapting the *Henry VIs*, his priority was to make the plays' political twists and turns accessible and pertinent. Although the resulting text was slapdash, Bogdanov had no pretensions about 'improving' Shakespeare's texts; indeed, by his own admission, he 'pasted up a version' (Bogdanov and Pennington 100), adding his own lines of 'Bogspeare' where necessary to pull together the adaptation.

The idea for a new national Shakespeare company was developed by Bogdanov when he was working at the National Theatre in the early 1980s, where he drew up a proposal for the institution to undertake more regional tours and so create (his own words) 'a link with the country' that would 'make the National Theatre truly national' (Bogdanov and Pennington xii). There was nothing new in this notion: even in the 1950s there had been calls for the National Theatre to be split across the regions (Elsom and Tomalin 116). Bogdanov's proposals were not accepted, and he eventually left the National to team up with Pennington, who had been a spear-carrier in the RSC's *The Wars of the Roses*. The new company's name impertinently placed them in the same cultural territory as the RSC and the National, as if the ESC were an alternative national theatre (originally, in fact, its founders wanted to call it the National Shakespeare Company). Regional tours were crucial to this alternative vision: in contrast to the London-based NT and the RSC, the ESC had no fixed base. It played in the towns and cities across the whole country, typically bringing plays to audiences with few opportunities to see large-scale Shakespeare productions. With a mission to perform challenging theatre for audiences outside London, the ESC could truly claim to rival the RSC as a Shakespearean institution. Even if it was, in the end, a short-lived ascendancy, the ESC's bold, mad tour of the history plays challenged the RSC's ownership of those plays and their link to narratives of national culture.

Although *Henry IV* and *Henry V* were safe choices for the ESC's first tour in 1986 (both are regular set texts in English schools), Bogdanov and Pennington's representation of history was unlike anything seen in the regions before. Punks and skinheads hung out at the Boar's Head, medieval knights duelled with modern soldiers, and, in one notorious scene, the English army marched to France shouting 'Fuck the Frogs!' over the din of Status Quo's *In the Army*. Inevitably, the ESC was criticised for not doing Shakespeare 'properly': Michael Billington found 'Bogdanov's interpretation of England's National Epic wilful, vain and historically dubious' (*The Guardian* 30 January 1989), and John Peter complained that 'this sort of rabble-rousing rubbish distorts and vulgarises Shakespeare's cool tough line on power politics' (*The Sunday Times* 27 March 1988). They were right; the ESC's histories *were* wilful, historically dubious and vulgar, and they were intended to be so. Bogdanov and Pennington styled themselves 'upstart crows' on the Shakespearean stage, wresting contemporary meaning out of Shakespeare regardless of whether or not their readings were historically authentic. The histories were, they insisted, 'plays for today, the lessons of history unlearnt' (Bogdanov and Pennington 23). As a consequence, the tour was hugely successful, allowing the ESC to extend the cycle the following year with *Richard II*, *Richard III* and the *Henry VI* plays.[2]

A constant theme in Bogdanov's work is the importance of activating contemporary associations rather than pandering to the hollow authenticity of the past. By creating visual links with the present, his productions help audiences engage with the contemporary relevance of Shakespeare's work. So important is the audience to Bogdanov's theatre that, with the council estate productions, he made the audience actors. In performance, his *Henry VI* plays confronted topical issues with postmodern means, evoking recent English history through costumes and sets in order to comment on the present. The costly war in France echoed the First World War and the Falklands, the Cade riots combined punk imagery with National-Front-style politics, and Edward's court used the media to enforce power. In this representational frame, history ran both backwards and forwards: the commoners were punks, Joan was a medieval knight; the House of Lancaster was an Edwardian autocracy, and the elders of the House of York were generals from the Second World War, with the younger brood decadent yuppies grasping at power for its own sake.

Some have taken these representational strategies as a postmodern gesture on Bogdanov's part. Barbara Hodgdon, for example, reads a sense of 'depthlessness', even 'a waning of historicity' in Bogdanov's 'cannibalisation' of historical signifiers from our 'global memory'. This 'collage of signs', Hodgdon continues, is 'a pastiche of the stereotypical past and present that recuperates history as style' (Hodgdon *The End Crowns All* 89). Hodgdon's main reference point is Fredric Jameson who, in *Postmodernism, or The Cultural Logic of Late Capitalism* (1991), also speaks of a 'waning of historicity' in the postmodern 1980s and attempts to situate postmodernism as the product of a failing capitalist system. In this respect, Bogdanov may be viewed as an artist in sympathy with Jameson, a critic rather than a practitioner of postmodernism. With the histories, he evoked and even satirised what Elizabeth Wilson describes as the 1980s 'obsession with pastiche'. Wilson continues to argue that in 'the fantasy culture of the 1980s there is no real history, no real past: it is replaced by an instant, magical nostalgia, a strangely unmotivated appropriation of the past' (Wilson 172). Bogdanov's stylistic choices mapped Shakespearean history on to an eclectic and empty nostalgia in which the engagement with the past was 'magical' rather than historical, yet his appropriations were certainly not 'strangely unmotivated'. On the contrary, history was subjected to the cultural agenda of the company. Bogdanov's reinvention of Shakespearean history as pastiche offered a counter-history to traditional representations, one which could be owned by the regional audiences for whom the tour was always principally intended.

With *House of Lancaster* and *House of York*, the ESC brought a fresh perspective to the representation of a divided England in the *Henry VI* plays. Not only did Bogdanov radically refashion history as a postmodern assemblage of medieval and modern images, he and his company interrogated 'England' as a political, social and cultural construct. In both productions, Bogdanov placed the sign-system of Englishness under pressure by contrasting it with political ambition and acts of violence. This was summed up by the logo for the company: a type of St George's Cross comprising two daubs of blood crossed on a white sheet. Although a large English flag was draped at the back of the stage for the opening scene of *House of Lancaster*, Henry V's coffin was covered in a Union Jack. The stage picture that this created juxtaposed a symbol of English national identity with a symbol of the British Empire, thereby calling into question the relationship between national and imperial identity. Englishness was dissolved in the bigger construction of Great Britain, pitching the question of 'English Shakespeare' into a complex dialectic between cultural identity and the politics of Empire.

What England was and what it could be emerged as two different issues for the company: while presenting a critique of the hollowness of a national identity evacuated by the symbolic order of Empire, Bogdanov and Pennington nevertheless made it clear in their memoir of the tour that a true Englishness, shorn of both bombastic jingoism and thuggish street fascism, was not beyond hope. Bogdanov, himself from an Eastern European family and educated in Ireland, wished for English culture the same 'sense of cultural belonging' then manifesting itself 'in Latvia, Lithuania, Romania, Hungary' and in Scotland, Ireland and Wales (Bogdanov and Pennington xiii). The name of the company was more than an ironic comment; it was a gesture towards reclaiming English culture for the regions.

As well as flags and Victorian ceremony, Englishness also emerged through the regional accents of the actors. In order to transmit Shakespeare's language through the vocal inflections of ordinary people from across the country, actors were encouraged to use their native accents rather than conform to the conventions of 'received pronunciation' (RP). History was voiced in regional accents, frustrating any attempts to homogenise the people represented onstage as a single culture. Accents were also used to make political points: the established order (Henry, Margaret, Suffolk and Somerset) spoke in measured RP but rebels spoke in thicker accents (Warwick and York were bluff Yorkshiremen, and Cade a cockney yob). Different conceptions of England emerged in all three voices: Henry envisioned England as a unified pastoral paradise, York and Warwick represented the politically disenfranchised regions, and Cade and his mob were an urban underclass alienated both politically and culturally from the national symbols that supposedly represented them but in fact took them into war.

Regionally inflected narratives of exclusion and alienation located England as much in the present as in the past. Bogdanov and Pennington insisted that England in the 1980s was 'a nation disunited, violent, trying to patch itself together' (*The Times* 27 January 1989). Dissenting from the prevailing mood of economic overconfidence, then symbolised by the young and upwardly mobile generation ('yuppies'), the ESC drew a bleak picture of a nation divided by class and region. Locating their work firmly within the turbulent politics of the 1980s, they were scathing about the Conservative government, criticising both the Falklands campaign ('a senseless war of expediency' 22) and the miners' strike (when thousands of miners facing the effective disbanding of their industry were faced down by a defiant Margaret Thatcher). In this England, to have an accent that was not RP was to be excluded from power, from history and from the symbols of national identity.

The divide was exacerbated by what Bogdanov and Pennington saw as the effective political marginalisation of the North, as the Conservative government's electoral base was firmly in the 'fat, green, get-rich-quick Yuppie haven' of the southern regions (22), leaving the North to suffer the consequences of new economic and social policies. The North/South divide was a theme throughout the *Wars* cycle; in the *Henry VI* plays, the rivalry between the diffident southerner Somerset and the bluff northerner York was cultural as well as political. The cultural politics of accent were further explored when, in *House of York*, Edward IV's Yorkshire inflections vanished into more haughty aristocratic tones following his marriage to the southern Lady Grey; for Richard Crookback, whose own fidelity to his roots was evident in his snarling accent, this was an unforgivable betrayal of family.

The locations invoked by the titles that Bogdanov and Pennington chose for their adaptations, *House of Lancaster* and *House of York*, emphasised this northern focus. The old northern capitals of Lancaster and York still use the red and white roses as emblems of civic identity. Fittingly, Bogdanov and Pennington chose York as the location for the press nights for their seven-play cycle – a choice that, in prising the press out of their usual London/Stratford axis, was itself a part of the company's self-fashioning as a regionally based national theatre. The location brought a very different focus to the history plays, as the mainly local audience was extremely aware of the investment they had in their own civic past. The audience at the York Royal Theatre watched the *House of York* as a local history play and were able to recognise within it aspects of their own local story and its relationship to broader national issues. In York, an effigy of Richard, Duke of York still has pride of place in Micklegate Bar: York still overlooks 'the town of York' (*Part Three* I.iv.180). Tellingly, the audience celebrated the end of the cycle by throwing white roses on to the stage. In this euphoric and highly theatrical gesture, they reclaimed the Shakespearean stage for a Yorkshire counter-history in which the Yorkists were (against the grain of most productions) the unambiguous heroes of the drama.

House of Lancaster: 'Done like a Frenchman!'

House of Lancaster was, in essence, a war play that Bogdanov's staging located firmly within the twentieth century through the invocation of the two World Wars. The society that mourned Henry V was a militarised one, and their new king was dressed in aristocratic military uniform. Paul Brennan's performance as Henry was unforgiving. He began as a naive schoolboy obsessed with war and with pleasing his uncles; as a national tragedy took place around him, his inaction was symptomatic of his lack of insight and his complicity with foolish imperial notions of conflict. Dressed as he was, Henry was a toy-soldier version of Henry V – he was never a holy fool. Far from living in his father's shadow, the young King relished politics and lacked any consciousness of his own vulnerability. When Talbot visited the court, Henry took him aside, eager to plan the campaign, but once again without any sense of the human cost. Easily manipulated by Suffolk and a strident Margaret, Henry's road to self-awareness was a painful one; at the end of *House of Lancaster*, having lost Gloucester, he sat alone on the throne, bewildered and frightened, before Margaret walked slowly across the stage mourning the death of Suffolk.

For Bogdanov and his English audiences, the most recent experience of 'war' (though it was never officially called a war) was the Falklands crisis. In spring 1982, the British army repelled an Argentine invasion of one of the few remaining outposts of the Empire. There were parallels with the French wars in *Part One*: this, too, was a last-ditch imperial victory. In fact, it was the last time in history that Britain used military force to defend one of its colonies. Bogdanov had already made topical references to the crisis earlier in his history-play cycle, when Agincourt was played out in 1980s military fatigues. The soldiers chanted xenophobic war slogans transparently modelled on the jingoistic tabloid headlines that celebrated the national spirit – 'Bash the Argies!' became 'Fuck the Frogs!' National identity was trivialised in order to stir up a war whose only real purpose was to secure the rule of Henry V. The same issues haunted the representation of war in *House of Lancaster*.

In *House of Lancaster*, the Falklands crisis was most directly referenced through Talbot's death. As he was directing his men in the chaos of battle, Talbot suddenly arched with pain: he had been shot in the back by an anonymous, offstage soldier. This called to mind one of the critical moments of the Falklands crisis, when Colonel 'H' Jones led the charge on Goose Green, in what became one of the bloodiest battles of the short conflict. Jones was a latter-day Talbot, 'a soldier dedicated to the point of obsession' who 'even spent his spare time playing war-games' (Eddy 220). The battle was won, but afterwards Jones's body was found on the field: like the ESC's Talbot, he had been shot in the back. It was an event which threatened to call into crisis the heroic patriotism that had so far propped up the war. Rather than confront the realities of conflict, however, the British media used it as an opportunity to trash the enemy. The inglorious death of someone who quickly (and retrospectively) came to epitomise the British bulldog spirit was presented as final proof of the cowardly, brutal nature of the Argentine army. That many, many more Argentinian soldiers died in the war was beside the point. Here was an example of the natural superiority of the British Empire, and justification for military action.

By recalling this moment, Talbot's death also reinterpreted it. This Talbot was a dying breed, a general from an Edwardian autocracy whose soldier games were so out of touch with modern warfare that he waved his sword about on a battlefield ringing with gunfire. He was a tragicomic character who blustered his way through a war he did not understand, in the face of a modern politics he was unable to comprehend. Audiences were invited repeatedly to laugh at him. When, for example, Burgundy (as played by Jack Carr in 1988–89) offered him a continental kiss on the cheek, Talbot fled the stage. Such stiffness and propriety were performed in a different key during his first encounter with Joan (played by Mary Rutherford in 1987–88 and Francesca Ryan in 1988–89), when he was brought to his knees by a spell and literally disarmed. His death was typical of the brutality of conflict, not of the French, and its meaning was simply that all war betrays the expectations of heroic fiction – or rather, that all wars are sites of political manipulation rather than heroic drama. Talbot was thrown to the wolves to support the political ambitions of the new order represented by York, Warwick and Somerset.

Meanwhile, any interpretation that contrasted the civilised English with the barbaric French was blocked by an interpolated scene in which a peasant girl was raped by English soldiers, an event that formed an ironic frame for Suffolk's 'seduction' of Margaret. Accosted by soldiers who surrounded and trapped her, the girl managed to escape and run offstage; as she did so, Margaret entered running, pursued by Suffolk. Offstage, the soldiers had evidently caught up with the girl, whose screams covered Suffolk's entrance, but it was only at the end of the scene that the nature of her experience was fully revealed. Suffolk, having mastered Margaret, turned to go, and saw the French girl, her clothing in disarray as she clutched her abdomen in pain. They looked at each other briefly, then Suffolk left and the girl hurried over the stage. As Hodgdon points out, 'it is this female figure, rather than Joan, whom Margaret replaces, and her ensuing encounter with Suffolk reprises just such a rape' (Hodgdon *The End Crowns All* 90–1).[3] There were not many battle scenes in either performance, as Bogdanov avoided turning war into spectacle, so in a sense the girl's story took the place of more traditional scenes of conflict and, in so doing, created a counter-history of warfare in which the boundaries of empire were secured through men abusing women.

In the historical logic of the production, the representation of the Falklands bled into the cultural memory of the two World Wars in which the British Empire had been contested and lost. The wars in France were performed as if they were taking place in the trenches of the Somme, while York and his men returned from Ireland in the military dress of the Second World War. Such reversals of time were deliberately political, for the production sought to remind the British public why it had abandoned the rhetoric of Empire and nationalism in the first place. By placing the First World War after the Falklands, the production illustrated the redundancy of complacent imperial triumphalism. The British generals (including the court and the king) were played either as dour bureaucrats or, as in Talbot's case, Edwardian officers in red uniform, with handlebar moustaches, proud bearings and a complete disregard for the condition of their men. Against the dominant, heroic images of conflict circulated in the wake of the Falklands, the First World War imagery highlighted the moral defeat that followed England's territorial victory.

The politics of these representational strategies were very real, as the government had already contested the way in which television had represented the Falklands and the First World War. The government criticised the BBC heavily for giving a balanced account during the Falklands, and in 1988 the Corporation was attacked again for its drama based on the conflict, Charles Wood's *Tumbledown*. In 1986, Alan Bleasedale's television series *The*

10 *The Wars of the Roses* (1987). Henry VI (Paul Brennan)

Monocled Mutineer caused an outcry in the media and in Parliament because of its depiction of a mutiny in the trenches of the First World War, a controversy stirred up further by Bleasedale's critical portrayal of the British Empire officer class as inbred, inept, contemptuous of the working classes and culpable of the atrocities of the war. (In *House of Lancaster*, a similar figure replaced the Pirate Captain, condemning Suffolk and coolly drinking champagne.) At the close of the decade, an established comedy series, Curtis and Elton's *Blackadder Goes Forth*, used the First World War to portray the British Establishment as insane and power-mad. *House of Lancaster* was, then, in good company.

To counter the imperial depiction of war, Bogdanov reinterpreted Joan as a one-woman independence movement whose spirit reflected Bogdanov's own wish to redefine English nationalism. Joan was the only character to insist on a sense of cultural belonging, this being explored most strikingly in an intriguing rereading of the scene in which Burgundy defects to the French. Shakespeare's Burgundy is a fickle Frenchman: as Joan quips, 'Done like a Frenchman! Turn and turn again!' (III.vii.85). The production, however, read against the grain of this stereotyping. As Lois Potter observed, Bogdanov cut 'Turn and turn again!' and added an earlier soliloquy in which Burgundy shows that he is already having doubts about betraying his own people (Potter 176). His defection was, in effect, endorsed as a turning away from the pursuit of power in order to embrace his own community, and Joan's subsequent intervention was neither a spell nor a seduction but a direct appeal to Burgundy's lost sense of cultural belonging. 'Done like a Frenchman!' was a compliment.

Joan was a cultural activist whose power lay in her unquestioning fidelity to her roots; she represented a force of integrity in a world consumed by decadence. By contrast, the French aristocracy, led by Andrew Jarvis as the Dauphin, were decadent and already imperialised: even their uniforms were identical to those of the English, merely dyed blue instead of green (an echo of First World War German soldiers). When escaping the English, Joan rushed onstage dressed ready for battle, while her countrymen sipped wine and wiped their brows with lingerie. Interestingly, she was the only character in either of the productions who wore fifteenth-century costume, as if her cultural authenticity brought with it a historical realism absent from the rest of the playworld.

To generate a connection between Joan's rebellious spirit and her fidelity to her cultural roots, Bogdanov turned her execution into a heroic act of sacrifice that alluded directly to recent outrages in South Africa. In 1986, anti-apartheid leader Winnie Mandela endorsed the brutal practice of 'necklacing' for suspected collaborators – a form of execution that involved lighting petrol in a rubber tyre slung round the neck. Joan was hauled behind a gauze screen, necklaced with a tyre, and set alight; the audience could only see her shadow twisting slowly in red light, her death scored by soft pipe music. Invoking South African murders was risky ground for Bogdanov, but their presence on a Shakespearean stage gave Joan's death a powerful resonance. Unlike the suspected collaborators in South Africa, Joan was never accused of betraying the rebellion; on the contrary, she was betrayed by the French generals, who finally abandoned their rights in order to capitulate to the English. As she burned, Warwick and York sipped wine at a table, apparently indifferent to the horror behind them. Their emotional disconnectedness stood in stark contrast to Joan's passion; in *House of York*, however, York's own manipulation of cultural belonging was brutally parodied by Pennington's punk Jack Cade.

House of York: abominable words

House of York began with the Kentish rebellion, but, rather than reconstruct Cade as a political hero as he had done Joan, Bogdanov stressed his empty brutality. Like Joan, Cade was a nationalist and even wore the Union Jack on his T-shirt. However, there the comparison ended. Cade was played as a vicious and amoral punk who represented, if anything, the final reduction of Englishness to the only tribal expression left to the people: violence. Cade addressed his mob at a rally in a village hall; facing a trolley draped with a Union Jack and flags, his first speech was played for full theatrical effect, his lines spat out ferociously, his gestures exaggerated. He was drunk, and so was his onstage audience, who greeted his nonsense claims and ambitions with chants and cheers. When the Staffords entered to address with contempt and disgust 'the *filth* ... and *scum*' assembled, the crowd jeered back with 'up yours' fingers, stamping their feet and shouting the hooligan chant, 'You're gonna get your fuckin' heads kicked in.' Carrying miniature national flags, the rebels' two-fingered salute was as much a gesture of tribalism as a gesture of resistance. Their strong regional accents separated them from the Received Pronunciation of the aristocrats and generals, but theirs was a language whose only meaning was found in violence. Ranting against Lord Saye, Cade rolled 'verb' and 'noun' round in his mouth as if they were strange, distasteful, 'abominable words'. By rejecting language and culture, the rebels were rejecting the weapons of the oppressor. There was no sense of cultural belonging articulated in these scenes: rather, they were about cultural dislocation and the wreckage of a working class that had had all of its forms of expression hollowed out by those only ambitious for power.

Bogdanov rejected any attempt to see in Cade a figure of protest and explicitly dissociated him from the miners' strike of 1983, which had also started in Kent. Instead, Bogdanov likened Cade and his mob to the football hooligans at Heysel (the 1985 riot at the Belgian stadium caused the building to collapse). If they were the voice of the people, it was a voice which had been brutalised by the manipulations of the powerful. Bogdanov began the play with York returning from Ireland, planning his own rebellion. Using lines culled from the Pirate Captain, York explained to his followers that the rebellion had been politically engineered by an *agent provocateur*. By adding these lines, Bogdanov made sure that Cade and his riot were discredited in advance; York had betrayed Talbot, and now he would betray the people through Cade.

With *House of York*, Bogdanov showed the nation first coming apart, then being reconfigured by Edward IV who established his power base through the politicised use of photographs and the media. History and power were no longer rooted in cultural authenticity; they were instead enacted through media management and political spin. By the end of *House of York*, the ascendant Yorkists were shown taking control of history and manipulating it for their own purposes: the final 'shots' of *House of York* were of Edward IV (Phillip Bowen) and his relatives posing for a photographer. As Edward's Queen and his two brothers in turn kissed the baby, the family portrait was captured on camera. This was a symbolic act of family unity, but it was also a photo opportunity for Edward, who displayed to the nation a new consensus at the seat of power. The images suited both Richard and Clarence's ends, too, as the pictures framed their new powers while hiding their real ambitions.

As the first strictly modern prop, the camera (which often raised a laugh from the audience amused by its incongruity in a Shakespeare history play) pointed the way to the hi-tech business world that was the setting for the ESC's *Richard III*. It was also the first symbol of modern politics – those of media management. By appropriating the family for the purposes of political aesthetics, Bogdanov brought Edward's world closer to the type of politics that dominated 1980s Britain. The imaginary nation on the stage

11 *The Wars of the Roses* (1987). Queen Margaret (June Watson)

saw the end of the Wars of the Roses being constructed through a series of publicity shots: the media had become the historiographer of the victor. However, the audience saw the reality that the camera falsified: Edward manipulating his court, Richard teasing the audience, Clarence skulking in a corner with a conspiratorial air. The brutality of history was forgotten in Edward's endless summer. The throne which York seized momentarily after the defeat of Cade did not have a place in Edward's court, and neither did ceremonial robes or traditional props of power such as crowns and sceptres. Instead, Edward ruled from what was, in effect, an ongoing cocktail party, playing the host to a gathering of interwar-years aristocracy. It was as if the violence of Towton and Wakefield had never happened.

Less ready to forget was Richard Gloucester, played by Andrew Jarvis as a critical, disenchanted aristocrat; often the villain, in this performance Richard was an unexpectedly sympathetic figure. Mediating Bogdanov's contempt for the spectacle of authority and the hypocrisy of Edward's media culture, Richard's bitter comments on his own appearance, and his withering attacks on Edward's political ineptitude, were a direct criticism of the new machinery of power. That he was a counter-force to the socialite complacency of his family had been apparent earlier in *House of York*, when Richard persuaded his father to break his word: with his arms around a worried-looking Edward, he persuaded a hesitant York into a rash decision. To blot out his doubts, York downed a glass of brandy to the ominous beat of drums in the background.

Richard's 'murder while I smile' soliloquy (*Part Three* III.ii.124–95) was delivered as a witty critique of the hypocrisy of Edward's rule. Ambling to the front of the stage dressed in a white suit, Richard held a glass of wine in one hand as the court of Edward IV continued with their party behind him, the music shifting to a snake-like jazz track. As Richard, Jarvis had an intense, uncanny look: with piercing eyes, impish face and shaven head, he seemed out of place in Edward's photogenic court, his own political talents unsuited to the media spin being created about him. Yet, this was not so much Richard the future tyrant as Richard the politician or even Richard the alternative comedian. He drew the audience to his side and wittily scorned his brother's hypocrisies in a measured and serious tone, slowing down on 'impossibilities' as he rolled his tongue around its syllables and paused for a sip of champagne. The word seemed to spark something in him, as he suddenly broke into an aggressive rant; but then he composed himself and finished the speech calmly. In this riveting, unnerving performance, such brief flashes of merciless ambition gave the audience something of what they wanted: the Shakespearean villain, the proto-Richard III. As Jarvis turned his back on the audience to hobble back to the party, the piano stopped abruptly, leaving a solo trumpet to close the scene and making the music his soundtrack more than Edward's. This was a consistent ambiguity: when the camera flashed at the end of the production, the light caught not only the royal family but Richard's psychotic smile, as the trappings of Edward's power were again used to highlight the dangerous force that was emerging to destroy it.

In the penultimate scene, Bogdanov exploited Jarvis and Brennan's physical similarities. Although they were played as opposite types – Richard was devilish, quick-tempered and comic, Henry saintly, worldly wise, and tragic – when they sat facing each other on Henry's jail bed, with Henry dressed in white, they resembled twins. Henry was resolute while Richard was initially friendly, putting his arm around his victim, then lounging in the jailer's chair twirling a flick-knife. Although Henry's face betrayed fear, he regained sufficient composure to attack Richard verbally, only to scream in surprise and pain when Richard pulled him off the bed on to the blade. Pulling Henry's head up to his own, Richard forced the saint to stare into the face of his double before giving the knife a fatal twist and throwing the body back on to the bed, going on to leap on to the corpse and stab it viciously through the neck. His final speech was performed with determination, his critical denial of society – 'I am myself alone' – spoken slowly. It was a chilling moment. Richard had finally become the monster we expected, and the link he had shared with Cade and Joan was suddenly perverted into an iconic rejection of all things social: either the epitome of Thatcherism or its apotheosis. This was a Richard who had no need of any kind of identity – regional, national, familial – beyond his own virulent will to power, a postmodern subject representing the true 'end of history'. He rejoined the party to pose with the baby for the photographer and then, as before, walked away from the festivities to the front of the stage, where he toasted the audience with champagne and the first lines of *Richard III*.

CHAPTER VII

Acts of war: the RSC's
The Plantagenets (1988–90)

In 1988, the Royal Shakespeare Company's cycle *The Plantagenets* reduced the *Henry VI* plays into two parts called *Henry VI* and *The Rise of Edward IV* (together with *Richard III, His Fall* to complete the story). Directed by Adrian Noble, *The Plantagenets* was one of the most ambitious RSC productions in a decade; with three plays performed by one cast in a run that would last two years, the cycle harked back to Terry Hands's histories in the 1970s (a link cemented when Noble asked Anton Lesser to reprise his perform- ance as Richard Gloucester) and to Hall and Barton's *Wars* cycle in the 1960s. Conscious that it was making history, the RSC published the adaptation straight away; even the white and gold souvenir programme was designed to make the event feel special – as one critic shrewdly remarked, the cycle was *meant* to be memorialised (Shaughnessy 78). But from the outset, and more explicitly than with any of the previous RSC cycles, the project was shaped by a specific cultural agenda – to make *The Plantagenets* a watershed moment that would reinvent the RSC for the modern world, and, in so doing, grapple with the social forces that had transformed the theatrical environment.

The institution was in one of its periodic financial crises, which deepened when Terry Hands stepped down as Artistic Director in 1988. Arts funding was being squeezed more tightly by the govern- ment's policy that theatre should seek funding from the private sector, thrusting the RSC into an alien world of sponsorship deals and corporate performances. Perhaps sensing that simply replacing Hands would not address the company's ability to weather and adapt to this new funding climate, the RSC appointed a *pro tem* triumvirate of directors. Among them was Adrian Noble, who was made responsible for the Stratford-upon-Avon theatre and who, with *The Plantagenets*, both responded to the crisis and pointed a way forward for the company. As the very concept of a subsidised Shakespearean theatre was under threat from the mercurial forces of Thatcherite entrepreneurialism, Noble needed to make a statement that would be noticed, and the *Henry VI* plays gave him such an opportunity.

Their rarity in performance attracted attention, as did the size of the project and its theatrical scope; the choice of plays invited comparison with the RSC's first major work, *The Wars of the Roses*, and the subject matter of the plays – a national crisis in which a world steeped in tradition is destabilised by the unchecked ambition of the Yorkists – lent itself to a study of the present crisis. More than that, the national themes of the play enabled Noble to make an implicit connection between the RSC's own troubles and wider pressures. Advertising campaigns described *The Plantagenets* as 'an epic drama of a nation torn by civil war and political intrigue' that charted 'the changing values of a civilization' – but they were careful not to specify whether this nation was England now or England in the past, leaving open the possibility that the real story told by the production was that of present society; the 1980s were full of political intrigue, and the RSC's own civil war had been brought about by the 'changing values' that followed the Thatcherite revolution. By making his 'state of the RSC' work a 'state of the nation' cycle, Noble attempted to resituate the company as a vital force in national culture. To stress the point, he talked constantly about the RSC as a 'new' company, a 'young' company reborn, and as part of this renaissance he presented returning to the plays of 'young Shakespeare' as a logical step.

There was the English Shakespeare Company to think about as well. These 'upstart crows' exemplified the new arts institution – funded through corporate sponsorship, their histories (discussed in Chapter VI) were accessible and fast-paced and cocked a snook at the traditions of playing Shakespeare. By comparison, the RSC looked stuck in the past. With the ESC tour ongoing, audiences could make up their own minds about which was the better Shakespearean theatre – at one point, the two productions even ran side by side in London.

Noble's response was to raise the stakes with superb production values that showed what a publicly funded theatre company could contribute to national culture. As the ESC rejected history, the RSC went in the other direction and revived the Victorian practice of using the history plays as an opportunity for elaborate theatrical pageantry. In Bob Crowley's brilliantly designed medieval world, courtiers were dressed in authentic-looking fifteenth-century costumes and moved on a stage decorated with colourful banners and flags. The French generals, clad in glittering gold armour, looked like 'jewels on black velvet' (*The Observer* 30 October 1988), and, throughout, large, billowing reams of silk and other materials created a lavish texture for the stage. For the commoners, Crowley added Rabelaisian touches – such as a fat Simpcox, brought in on a cart like a carnival king – to scenes that called to mind the aesthetic landscapes of Brueghel's *Kinderspiele*; and, in a significant contrast to the political realism of the ESC's histories, a sense of the supernatural was created by stage effects such as smoke hissing from grates on battlefields, as if history was 'one long dash across the crust of hell' (*ibid*).

As well as giving good value for money, these theatrical coups also reasserted the continuing validity of history, tradition and Shakespeare to the cultural life of the nation. *The Plantagenets* was, on one level, a cycle in which entrepreneurial ambition and social justice were brought together. There was considerable criticism of those who put themselves and their hunger for power before the wider interests of society. Anton Lesser's Richard was every inch a medievalised Thatcherite entrepreneur, and in his distaste for the spectacle of Henry's court the bunch-backed toad seemed to exemplify the philistinism of the new political creed that celebrated the maxim that 'there's no such thing as society' and treated culture with suspicion. Yet, the climax of the cycle offered something of an olive branch, for after Richard's death Richmond brought back to the stage the spectacular heraldic ceremony with which the cycle had begun. Noble deliberately played on the similarity of Richard and Richmond; this Richmond was also an ambitious individual and as much a proto-Thatcherite as Richard had been. Traditional culture and the new right were perhaps not so incompatible after all; by ending the cycle in this way, Noble seemed to hint that the RSC still had a role to play in national culture. In its histories, the rival ESC clung to an old-fashioned idea of radical Shakespeare (at the same time as exemplifying the Thatcherite vision of arts funding), but Noble sketched a different negotiation with the pressures of history which, with the benefit of hindsight, anticipated the reconstructed socialism of New Labour that dominated the 1990s. The RSC was not simply going to dig its heels in and resist Thatcherism: the real challenge was to accommodate it.

By moving constantly between traditional staging and contemporary themes, Noble risked being perceived as a lightweight more interested in showy spectacle than meaningful theatre. Staged in a period of institutional uncertainty, *The Plantagenets* was controversial from the beginning, not for the way in which it treated Shakespeare, but for the vision of Shakespearean theatre that Noble offered for the future. The aesthetic politics of the production confused critics – one even went so far as to compare the heraldic processions to the gaudy nationalism of the Conservative Party's triumphalist conferences in the 1980s (Shaughnessy 87). Michael Hattaway called the production 'unashamedly patriotic and heroic' (*Part One* 54), and, in *The Observer*, Michael Radcliffe complained that, amidst all the high medievalism of the staging, 'the disturbing resonances of history' were 'not sounded' (30 October 1988).

However, *The Plantagenets* was a much more ambivalent work, if anything struggling to find a way to deal with the present by being both radical and traditional. In some ways, this made for an inward-looking production; for all that the RSC seemed to be making big statements about national culture, *The Plantagenets* could usefully be read as a reflection on the company itself as it faced an uncertain future. But in tackling directly the consequences of ambition for society through characters like Richard, the cycle touched a nerve for those who shared these anxieties about the present. *The Listener* described the cycle as 'a brave, uncomfortably modern interpretation, in a trilogy whose resonances for our times are challengingly profuse' (3 November 1988). John Peter, in *The Sunday Times*, compared Henry to leading Thatcherite Keith Joseph, whose fatal flaw was his lack of media savvy, and argued that the cycle was 'political theatre as a form of deterrent' (30 October 1988). But it was, ironically, Michael Billington (the *Guardian* journalist who would later be vociferously opposed to Noble's handling of the RSC) who recognised that, far from being a vacuous spectacle, *The Plantagenets* was thoroughly contemporary in its outlook. The plays 'speak to us directly', wrote Billington, continuing that, 'a ravening, unchecked ambition for power is a danger that is permanently relevant' and noting that 'social disintegration is the overall theme' (*The Guardian* 24 October 1988).

The tension between tradition and radical reinvention manifested itself from the beginning. Noble was originally keen to match Hall's intellectually unimpeachable adapter John Barton and so commissioned Charles Wood, himself a 1960s theatrical luminary and once briefly associated with another of the RSC's defining productions from that decade, Peter Brook's anti-Vietnam play *US*. Around this time (1988), Wood also created a lot of controversy for his critical representation of the army during the Falklands crisis in his television play *Tumbledown*. So, on the face of it, hiring Wood looked like a way to reaffirm the RSC's political nerve. However, Wood's script was eventually rejected in favour of a much more conventional adaptation with most of Wood's cuts restored.[1] These earliest versions of *The Plantagenets* were strikingly ambitious. Wood more or less reduced the plays to a sequence of battle scenes connected by his own additions written in a Rabelaisian blank verse. His version began with an ironic quote from *Henry V* – 'Once more unto the breach, dear friends, once more, / Or close the wall up with our English dead' – then brought forward a choric figure who described, in a long speech, a panorama of England populated by grotesque characters such as vomiting monks, leering carpenters and bishops sitting on cats. There was no funeral for Henry V, instead the stage opened to reveal the first of Wood's many battle scenes. Political narratives were stripped away; for Wood, *Henry VI* was a war play and his rewriting focused on the experience of the soldier and the social impact of warfare. No clear reason has ever been given why the RSC did not use Wood's script; Noble simply said it was not suitable and Penny Downie (who played Margaret) and Ralph Fiennes (Henry) both hint that the company played a large role in recovering much of Shakespeare's play that had been cut.

Credited as a company adaptation, most of the actual writing was done by Noble and his assistant Stephen Raine. Downie describes the chaotic process of the development of the script by recalling heated debates between actors who wanted their lines restored and others who saw the need for cuts to make the plays coherent. Noble and Raine would then work on scenes overnight, 'sometimes to universal groan, sometimes to great excitement'. Downie continues, 'when we went back to scenes we'd worked on we would find that something had been lost from what had seemed solid, that the ground had shifted. But one had to allow it to be fluid and that, again, was an act of faith' (Downie 117). Even in the final scripts, there were some striking inconsistencies: Gloucester says farewell to Eleanor when he is meant to be under house arrest (bizarrely, Noble reversed the order of these scenes);

York's 'Cade' soliloquy is relocated to the back-end of Jourdain's execution, when narratively he should already be in Ireland; the French treaty is cut, so the story of the Dauphin is never resolved. The adaptation fragmented the narrative and then turned this fragmentation into a structural principle. The immaturity of the young Shakespeare was something to be preserved: 'We ... had a strong sense of a changing, developing style in the plays and felt that this was to be embraced rather than eschewed ... This relish of contradictions and paradoxes in the world of the Plantagenets became central to the adaptation' (Noble xiii). Despite claims to the contrary, Noble and his company conducted an operation that was no less artificial or interventionist than John Barton's had been, but it fell some way short of the ambitious meld of Shakespearean montage and new writing, a sort of *Wars* and *US* hybrid for the 1980s, that Wood and Noble originally conceived of.

Henry VI: an angry epic space

A clue to Noble's approach to the plays is offered by a story that he himself relates in the introduction to the published script, where the director recalls that, as a drama student, he had designed a set for an imagined production of *Henry VI*: 'We sought an arena rather than a theatre, and designed three leather-bound, overlapping angular stages; an angry epic space – thrilling to look at, impossible to act upon ... But those original responses have remained with me – the violence of the world, the teeming panorama of people and their politics, and most of all the extraordinary energy of the plays' (Noble vii). That Noble's starting point should be in design rather than in the text will come as no surprise to those who have criticised the director for putting spectacle before political comment. Noble's vision of history as a lethal, inhuman environment, an 'angry epic space', demanded a stage that would dominate its subjects, and, although Bob Crowley's designs for *The Plantagenets* did not revisit Noble's student design, they did construct a similarly destructive theatrical space. The sets were not only extravagant, they were large, too; against such a backdrop, the ambition of those who sought to dominate their world and determine their own history seemed absurd.

The design made the attainment of power paradoxically disempowering. *Henry VI* opened with an arresting medieval display designed to impose order on a world whose unity was threatened by the death of the king. Everything fell into confusion, however, with the unexpected arrival of the messenger, whose news of Talbot's capture brought the spectators (thronged at the back) on to the stage, transgressing the closely ordered space of the ceremony. This was only a momentary disruption: the backdrops vanished into darkness, and the commoners became soldiers marching to war.

In the court of Henry VI, the duality of power was represented by a metal throne which appeared to span the stage: its back stretched upwards out of view, but beneath it was concealed a prison. As Henry, Fiennes was dwarfed by the throne: when he entered for his coronation in France, amidst the formalities of the court procession, he crept awkwardly towards it, as if late for his own party, and sat in it sheepishly. At that moment, a spotlight brightened his face, as if to convey some sense of kingly divinity, but the king's two bodies took on a different meaning when, as Henry and his court left the stage, the throne began to rise, the lights to dim, mist tumbled on to the stage, and a cage appeared from below containing the withered body of Mortimer, the pretender to the throne. The shift from bright court to dark dungeon was a deliberately theatrical (bordering on pantomimic) transformation, signalling that Henry's court ceremonies were a mere display of power. The truth of power was, rather, figured by the prisoner below. However, Noble also established here the possibility that Henry, in his throne, was no less a prisoner than Mortimer, entrapped as he was by overbearing uncles and the abiding memory of Henry V. This idea was visualised dramatically when, at the end of *The Rise of Edward IV*, the throne-prison (which was replaced by a more modest throne for most of Edward IV's scenes) reappeared, but this time as a cage containing Henry, now no longer king.

The Plantagenets approached the *Henry VI* plays as Shakespeare's epic statement about war. An early press statement even went so far as to boast that the plays were one of 'the greatest military parables ever written' (Gore-Langton 8–9), and, with the Falklands the most recent conflict involving Britain, there were clear parallels to be made. Noble had already addressed the conflict in productions of *King Lear* and *Henry V*, where he criticised the exercise of autocratic power. With the war already part of history in 1988, Noble and his company did not so much explore it directly as examine the nature of a national identity grounded in acts of violence. Their adaptation told the story of England from England's point of view, which meant giving voice to the nation's jingoistic insularity. On the battlefield, at the edge of both territory and self-knowledge, the English confronted the unknown with a mixture of fear and the desire to conquer. This psychological approach was cleverly aligned with Shakespeare's use of the supernatural: magic, demons, prophetic spirits and providential retribution were revalued as potent forces because, to the characters onstage, they *were* real. Rather than question Joan's power, for example, the production focused on the English army's terror.

Battles concentrated on the otherness of the enemy. The enemy needed to be conquered because it was different, and, although superficially alluring, this otherness threatened the stability of national identity. Crowley made France a dark, uncertain world for the English army, who were terrified by the unknown. Lights shining through grates in the raked stage, catching a thick blanket of dry ice swirling up into the darkness, created a haunted atmos-phere that contrasted with the stiff pageantry of the English court. But like the dungeon hidden beneath the throne, this was simul-taneously a different physical place and a representation of the darker side of English national identity. Strange things happened on the borders – the English army huddled in fear as bells tolled the passing night, thunder rumbled across the stage. Hearing Joan's disembodied voice calling out to the English, Talbot (played by Robert Demeger) and Salisbury cowered in a corner of the stage, Talbot wondering, 'What stir is this? What tumult's in the heavens?' (I.vi.76), and Salisbury hazarding, 'A holy prophetess new risen up' (80; the line belongs to a messenger in the original text). With even his sense of self under threat, Talbot stammered, 'I know not where I am nor what I do' (I.vii.20).

The originality of Noble's interpretation of these scenes was one of the high points of the production. He was 'fascinated by France and determined that it should be a colony worth fighting for and keeping, not just for its wealth but for its culture, its "otherness"' (Noble xii). Rather than send the French up, as many productions have done, Noble made the Dauphin and his followers unques-tionably foreign (they spoke with French accents) with a culture of their own. Not only was France a dangerous world, but the French themselves looked very different. Crowley created a golden world as a way of signalling France as a colony 'worth fighting for'. In contrast to the English army, who were depicted as a rugged and war-weary lot trudging off to battle, the French troops were

12 *The Plantagenets* (1988). Talbot (Robert Demeger) and Young Talbot
(Mark Hadfield)

dressed in gold armour and rode golden hobbyhorses. England
was first represented by the structured ceremony of Henry V's
funeral; the French generals, by contrast, got ready for battle in a
camp of golden tents, where they were cooled by servants holding
huge golden fans. Everything about France registered luxury and
excess; everything about England reflected order and paranoia.

Joan (Julia Ford), and later Margaret, mediated between these
two worlds. As a woman-general, Joan embodied the feminine
excess which the English feared and sought to conquer. The
French were played as effeminate aristocrats, ready to be led by a
woman who more keenly understood how to exploit the jingoistic
anxiety of their enemy. Departing from stage tradition, Joan did
not send up the Dauphin's pompous Mars-like posturing, but reinforced and displayed physically the distinctive ethnicity of French
military sensibility. For Joan's first appearance, the Dauphin was
disguised as one of the banner wavers, but, when alone with her,
he took off his disguise to reveal his gold armour. This was the first
in a series of unveilings with a distinctly erotic tone to them. Later,
Joan was to be discovered in her nightclothes and stripped on the

stake, following which Suffolk (Oliver Cotton) tore away a peasant's cloak to discover Margaret dressed in a rich, olive-green dress. Such disrobings, associated solely with the French women Joan and Margaret, both stood for duplicity and suggested the desirable prize that lay within, waiting to be discovered. Joan turned this to her advantage in battle. When Talbot and Salisbury hid from the thunder, they were victims of a trick invented by Joan, who shook large bronze sheets hanging at the back of the stage. Joan was master-mistress of this world, able to turn the English desire for the golden prize of France into terror and division.

The staging of the French in this way made the audience see the whole conflict from an English point of view. As Barbara Hodgdon notices, the audience were in every sense constructed as English (*The End Crowns All* 98): this was a national performance in which the audience were scripted within the action, constructed as part of the English army looking out on to the boundaries of national reality. The first half of *Henry VI* built to a climax following Henry's French coronation, with Talbot and his men waiting in the trenches for the ensuing slaughter. Tension was constructed through a merging of scenes so that, at one point, four scenes were simultaneously available to the audience: Talbot in the trenches, York on the right of the stage, Somerset on the left, and in between, massed at the back, the French army. The tension was made all the more powerful by the position of the audience, who sat behind Talbot and his men, looking out into the dark battlefield. When the lights shifted from York (David Calder) to Somerset, they momentarily illuminated the gold armour of the French soldiers at the back of the stage: the brevity of the moment added to its threat and gave the impression of a huge army dwarfing the pitifully small band of men in the trench. As the action moved from scene to scene and the French army became more visible, the sense of impending disaster was more and more palpable. To be in the audience was also to be in the trenches, waiting for the final battle.[2]

When the battle came, national history was reduced to domestic tragedy. Noble used cinematic techniques such as slow motion and montage to foreground the Talbots' story. When the English charged desperately into the French army, the battlefield was filled with light to give the audience a god's-eye view of the battle, which was staged to represent a multitude of different locations simultaneously. The action was suddenly interrupted by Young Talbot's death: with a knife already at the young man's throat, the actors froze into a tableau. Only Talbot moved. Somehow, though it was impossible, the old soldier could see his son across the stage; crying out, he moved in slow motion to help, but he was too late – the action started again, and the boy was dead before his father could get to him.

The English were, it seemed, their own demons, and Joan's power diminished when she had no one left to fear her. Talbot, his son and the other English soldiers killed in battle remained onstage until the interval. Abandoned by the French, Joan was dumped on to the corpses – suddenly they began stirring into life and became her demons, but their reincarnation was short-lived as they slumped back on to the stage, leaving Joan to be taken by the English. With her capture, the remaining soldiers unleashed their pent-up fear and anger in a large celebration which centred on Joan's execution. Stripped and raised up high on a stake made out of scaling ladders, she became the centrepiece of a grotesque display of masculine power.[3] Jeering at her burning above (an effect created by bathing her in red light), the English soldiers celebrated their victory with a banquet – the stage image was implicitly canni-balistic for, as the fires consumed Joan, the English ate frantically below.

Before the first interval, the feminine and supernatural threat represented by the French was apparently contained by a macho victory march led by Suffolk. Joan was still on display above the stage; soldiers had mockingly drawn a red cross on her white under-dress, turning her body into an English flag of victory. To reinforce the point, a real English flag now unfolded itself from the heavens, obscuring her entirely. Joan and the French were not only conquered, they were incorporated into English national identity. As Suffolk led a triumphal victory march from the rear of the stage to the front, he succeeded in doing what Joan had failed to do, for behind him the dead soldiers stood up (among them the Talbots) and took their places in the parade, now part of the pageant of history. Yet, what was conquered was also incorporated. After the feast, a hooded figure scuttled crab-like through the battle-field, scavenging for scraps of food discarded beneath Joan's body (which still loomed over the stage) – this was Margaret.

The stage picture hinted at the turn the play was now taking: Margaret took on Joan's role as the foreigner threatening to desta-bilise English identity. Following the interval, she commanded the stage, entering the majestic court as bells rang in celebration

– the same bells that had tolled Talbot's death. Other aspects of France also permeated the English court, most notably a blue carpet decorated with fleur-de-lys. Returning from France, Suffolk brought news with him of both defeat and victory: the territories had been lost, but here was a more alluring prize – a wife for the King. Henry, awkward when having to face a woman, let Margaret command. Penny Downie played her as a petulant, passionate mistress of the court. Complaining to Suffolk about the English nobility, she stamped her feet and strutted pompously to mock Gloucester (David Waller) and Henry (an impression later echoed by Cade in *The Rise of Edward IV*). Their affair belonged more to the sensuous fields of France than to the orderly processions of the English. They grunted as they kissed – theirs was an urgent, fierce desire whose passion recalled the fury of the English army against the captive Joan.

By echoing the terror and aggression of the wars, the second half of *Henry VI* displaced the original play's focus on politics to concentrate instead on the psychological after-effects of conquest. Murder, madness, witchcraft and adultery turned the first three acts of *Part Two* into a grotesque theatre of retribution. With much of the long parliament scenes trimmed back, the emphasis was instead on Gloucester's murder, Winchester's harrowing death (in a scary performance by Antony Brown) and York's 'mad flaw'. As a consequence, one of the most important scenes for Noble was the conjuration of Bolingbroke and Jourdain, where, once again, magic was seen to be vital to the representation of history. Both Bogdanov and Howell had staged Jourdain and Bolingbroke as fairground charlatans. This Jourdain, on the other hand, was the real thing. Following York's conspiratorial discussion with Warwick, the stage was returned to the world of the battlefield with thunder, lightning, strange, indefinable noises and rolling mist. Bolingbroke was no huckster: when he struck his staff on the ground, lightning flashed – the presence of the demonic was real.

Noble departed from the text by staging Jourdain's execution; and just as Joan's death scene had been read and reread by the scenes that continued beneath it, Jourdain's body (also strapped to a stake but this time hoisted above the stage with Hume and Bolingbroke on either side in a picture which recalled the cruci-fixion) was left onstage as an ironic frame for the scenes that ended the play. With each scene marked by the tolling of a bell, York gave his 'Cade' soliloquy wearing armour and cackling like a true pantomime villain. Gloucester was murdered, and Margaret pleaded with Henry for Suffolk's life. Henry, angry at last, threw his queen across the stage, leaving Margaret sobbing spreadeagled on the floor. The bells continued to toll, but they were mixed now with the sounds of Winchester's ravings – the supernatural cacophony from the witch scene was revisited in the screams of madness. Once again, the supernatural and the psychological were run together: with Winchester, England seemed to be finally in hell.

But the play ended with a different image. Margaret, dressed in red, a white scarf covering her head, cradled Suffolk's decapitated head in her arms, her scarf stained with his blood, the image directly recalling the white cross Suffolk had painted on Joan's body. This time, the national flag was blurred and violated; the show of national unity had degenerated into a display of disunity. Henry gestured towards his broken Queen, his divided court in shock behind him and the burned body of the witch still above.

Edward IV: theatre of clowns

The Rise of Edward IV opened by deconstructing the stage space that had been mapped in *Henry VI*. Entrances in *Henry VI* had either been closely ordered to fit in with ceremonies and structures of power, or they had been perilous, as on the fields of France. Now, instead of banners, flags and attendants, there was just an empty space with a series of hand-grips running up the side. A mechanical, clanking noise preceded the opening action, echoing over the empty stage and signalling the approach of the labourers, who entered from all parts of the stage without any sense of order. Bevis appeared from the side of the stage and stood alone for a minute; then, in a moment that seemed to belong more to the theatrescapes of Samuel Beckett than a Shakespearean history play, Holland poked his head through a trapdoor beneath the stage. After their short dialogue, other rebels started to arrive – a ragged band of workers, they entered from the sides, from below and from the rear of the stage. Finally, Cade (Oliver Cotton, who had earlier played Suffolk) entered from above, swinging on to the stage on a rope and bouncing off the hand-grips. The rebels' free use of the acting space transformed the playworld from the highly structured region it had been in *Henry VI* into an anarchic, fragmented world: the stage was set for civil war.

Such acrobatics and absurdist touches demonstrated the

continuing influence of Jan Kott's seminal book *Shakespeare Our Contemporary*, in which Shakespeare's theatre was, in effect, aligned with contemporary revolutions in theatre practice and criticism. Noble's *Henry VI* had owed much to Kott's concept of the 'grand mechanism', which was represented most strikingly by the throne-prison. But this was now gone. Instead, with Beckett referenced from the outset, Noble seemed to be more influenced by Kott's influential reading of *King Lear* from the perspective of Beckett's *Endgame*, in which he argues that Shakespeare's vision of history is modern because it recognises the grotesque absurdity of existence: like Beckett, Kott suggests, Shakespeare reduces heroic tragedy, or the 'theatre of priests', to the tragicomedy of a 'theatre of clowns'. In *The Rise of Edward IV*, history belonged to the clowns, who hijacked the opening scenes with a riotously violent comedy, prefiguring the implicit absurdity of the following wars. With *Henry VI* ending on Winchester's madness, an absurdist universe had already been anticipated; but, with the riot, the play-world was shifted from Henry's theatre of priests to a theatre of clowns that began with Cade and ended with Richard.

Although the Cade scenes were trimmed and conflated, Noble actually increased the degree of violence, although, in contrast to the heavy tragedy of *Henry VI*, the tone was blackly comic. One of the most striking scenes began in darkness with a faint chattering of voices. As the lights rose, what at first sight seemed to be a group of nobles gathered at the foot of the stage was in fact Cade's men holding a multitude of heads on poles (Shakespeare specifies two heads; Noble supplied twenty). Cade himself was seated on a modern director's chair (the only anachronistic prop in the performance), indicating that even the production's rules of period representation were capable of being disrupted by the rebellion. Behind him, the rebels played with the severed heads as if they were ventriloquist dolls, ironically manipulating and giving new voices to the people who had previously ruled them. On one level, these grotesque puppets signalled the shift into a more absurdist playworld, but, at the same time, Noble used the scene to make a political point. Although angry, the commoners could do little with their anarchic power other than become puppet-masters themselves. The production developed this idea further in its staging of the Clerk of Chatham's murder, for which the commoners turned the Clerk into a living marionette by tying his arms to a rope and dragging him across the stage, humiliating him before finally stabbing him to death. As well as highlighting the commoners' story, these puppet images could be taken as a visual enactment of the way history and ceremony controlled people in other parts of the cycle: the Clerk could just as easily have been Henry, the unwilling object of many ceremonies in *Henry VI* and himself an eventual victim of the theatre of clowns.

Cade's theatre framed the following scenes, which compressed Act V of *Part Two* with the first two acts of *Part Three* to create a long act of lurid violence in which the hellish fields of France erupted in the heart of England. War was spectacular and battle scenes were long. Margaret charged from the rear of the stage like Joan in *Henry VI*, and lightning flashed as the armies of the civil war clashed. Ralph Fiennes played Henry's molehill scene against anguished cries and loud crashes of music representing the confusion of the fight. But this was still Cade's world, and among his clowns was the psychopathic Clifford who, with his father dead, immediately embarked on revenge. He made a puppet out of Rutland, who looked more than a little like Henry, by tying a rope around his neck and dragging the helpless infant round the stage before disappearing into an infernal mixture of red light and smoke, through which could be seen the dark shapes of soldiers moving wearily. It was as if the hell that had been hinted at in *Henry VI* had now overtaken the stage and consumed both Clifford and his victim. As they left, rows of white lights lit up like cats' eyes on the stage-floor to set the scene for York's death. Margaret and Clifford made York into another kind of puppet by stabbing him in the neck and using their knives to manipulate his head which, in another echo of the Cade scene, was then impaled on a pole at the front of the stage. In a later scene, the York brothers made a similar spectacle out of Clifford's body by standing it upright, moving his arms and mocking it with silly voices.

The stage was now set for the Yorkist rule: but if at first it seemed that the anarchy of Cade's rabble was gone, it quickly became apparent that Edward's stage belonged as much to the theatre of clowns as Cade's had. For a start, the vertiginous throne-prison was gone, so in effect the playworld was unmoored from the polarities of heaven and hell that had defined Henry's theatre of priests. If anything, Edward's court looked back to the golden France of *Henry VI*, which had then been the alternative world coveted by Henry. A large icon of the sun was hung at the back of the stage and children played with golden balls, while, for Edward's first scene as king, the stage was bathed in a golden light. When war returned, Edward dressed in gold and black armour, recalling the costumes of the Dauphin and his generals. Talbot's story was also alluded to, especially through the death of Warwick, whose lonely demise resembled that of the old soldier. Edward's final battle with Margaret was played in darkness, with the lights finally rising on the ragged Lancastrians and the defiant Margaret, who ended as she had begun – a refugee of war. However, her final scene did contain a moment when the pain of losing her child interrupted the ambitions of the Yorkists. In a stage picture that recalled Talbot cradling his son, Margaret clung to her Edward and had to be dragged offstage. As the scene ended, the lights dimmed on the dead bodies of Tewkesbury, which started to chatter in indecipherable female voices. We were back in the same antic theatre that had begun with Cade and his army of puppeteers. The most grotesque of them all, the biggest clown of the lot, was of course Richard.

Richard was a medieval version of the 1980s entrepreneur: on the one hand he was viciously power-hungry; but at the centre of his characterisation, according to Lesser, was an anxiety about the future. Richard's triumphant 'now' concluded the performance almost as a statement of intent to seize the moment and resist anything that might get in the way of it, including the institutions of the past and the need to look to the future. Lesser's essay on Richard for the *Players of Shakespeare* series gives important clues to understanding this anxiety about history.

> The scene of the killing of Henry VI is a moment of truth for Richard. He listens to Henry going on at length about his past; it is when he turns to the future that Richard silences him ... Richard decides he has had enough at the prospect of being told the significance of his own presence in the world. This is something that must not be uttered – like having the future read, even having one's fortune told. To know one's future destroys the sanctity of unknown destiny and for Richard (certainly the way I played him) his running condition depends upon experiencing the eternal now: every minute is fresh and full of possibilities. Prophecy always panics him. (Lesser 147)

This idea of the 'eternal now', of an existence unhinged from the future or, for that matter, the past, suggests a more than subtle swipe at the Thatcherite emphasis on the personal pursuit of wealth and power. The truly demonic became that which was outside history, which scorned and dispensed with the ideas of

[165]

tradition that the RSC itself sought to maintain. Lesser's characterisation of Richard demonised ambition as an unchecked and destabilising force. Where *Henry VI* provided problematic images of patriotism founded on war, *The Rise of Edward IV* took on the central ideology of entrepreneurial Britain. Neither of these interpretative strategies sits well with an easy dismissal of *The Plantagenets* as 'unashamedly patriotic'.

In the penultimate scene of *The Rise of Edward IV*, Richard's ascendant theatre of clowns confronted the world it had overturned. Henry's regicide was a theatrical image for the late 1980s, the slaughter of tradition by a creature who was thoroughly self-serving, a good Thatcherite for whom society had no meaning. The scene began as a bloodied white sheet (on which the final battles had taken place) was raised from the floor, forming a surreal backdrop for Richard's bloody supper. The red and white cloth recalled the mock flag the English had made of Joan in *Henry VI*, only now the stain was formless, blurred. Richard stabbed Henry in the front and back, tossing the body carelessly into the cage and snarling to the audience, 'I am myself alone.' The cage began to sink through the trapdoor and dark shapes gathered around it like demons escorting the dead king to the underworld, but, as the cage disappeared, the lights came up to reveal that the shapes were Edward and his court who, amidst bright gold lights, celebrated the end of 'sour annoy'.

Conclusion

Far from being a triumphalist staging of history, *The Plantagenets* was a dark reflection on the role of war in national culture. The dangerous world of France, both exotic and terrifying, was first of all conquered and then incorporated. With the Falklands haunting the performance of a last-ditch imperial stand, the connection with Margaret Thatcher's personal triumph against the Argentines and the subsequence discontents in 1980s society was made by Richard, whose manic, clownish individualism threatened to destabilise even Edward's golden world. Conceived at a time of institutional crisis, *The Plantagenets* asserted the primacy of theatre, and particularly of the RSC, as a cultural force capable of addressing the epic questions facing society.

With hindsight, *The Plantagenets* was a significant turning point in the performance history of the *Henry VI* plays. Publishing the script was a shrewd move and it was not long before theatre companies around the world started to use it for their own productions, most notably those staged in Ashland, Oregon in 1991–92 and directed by Pat Patton. In Ontario in 1992, Peter Hinton's *The Wars of the Roses: Henry 06, His Death* and *The Rise of Edward 04* borrowed Noble's titles and script but added some more postmodernist touches such as dressing most of the cast in ice-hockey costumes. And subsequent productions in Britain showed that attitudes to the *Henry VI* plays had moved on from the materialist interest in power politics. Both of the RSC productions that followed, in 1994 and in 2000, approached the political narratives and their resonance with contemporary events by fully acknowledging the role of the supernatural in Shakespeare's vision of history. Propeller's *Rose Rage* (2001), a two-part adaptation also discussed in Chapter IX, explored the grotesque with even more gore. Noble's vision of a human history caught on the cusp of hell, of a nation whose paranoia and insularity engulf it, pointed the way forward for productions of the plays that were not limited by the Brechtian stamp that Peter Hall had put on them and were instead open to exploring the roles of ghosts, witches, demons, madness, guilt and terror in Shakespeare's dramatisation of history.

CHAPTER VIII

Plundering in front of hell: the RSC's *Henry VI – The Battle for the Throne* (1994–95)

In 1994 Katie Mitchell directed a remarkable production of *Part Three* as a response to the civil war then being fought in Bosnia. Staged at The Other Place, the RSC's smallest Stratford-upon-Avon theatre, before being taken on tour, *Henry VI – The Battle for the Throne* (as it was retitled) performed the play as a message from the past about the horrors of civil war.

Mitchell had complete faith in the play's integrity.[1] Although cuts were made to accommodate a small cast and lines were added from other Elizabethan plays to strengthen Mitchell's main themes, the production presented the play as a story in its own right, the narrative looking neither backward to the causes of the civil war nor forward to reconciliation. (Even Henry's meeting with the future Henry VII was cut to avoid reference to *Richard III*.) Divorced from historical narrative, the play told a story of war's impact upon the people caught up in it. Their suffering and anger dominated the production and shifted the emphasis away from grotesque violence to address the marginalised voices of history, the voices of the wives, mothers, children and widows of the soldiers.

An up-and-coming but still, from the RSC's point of view, wet-behind-the-ears director, Mitchell had to wage her own institutional campaign to make her voice heard. Her vision for *Henry VI* as a production project was initially rejected by the Artistic Directorate, and, when it was eventually approved, she was put under considerable pressure to begin the play with York's return from Ireland in *Part Two*. But Mitchell had no interest in staging Cade's rebellion, nor did she see the need to break the unity of *Part Three* – the story she wanted to tell was already there. Using techniques based on the work of an experimental Polish theatre group, Mitchell turned the play into a folk story with a strong contemporary meaning.

Performing Bosnia

Mitchell brought to her *Henry VI* a distinctive vision of medieval England as a peasant culture deeply rooted in folk tradition, nature and religious ritual. But this culture was under threat. Echoing twentieth-century developments in the countries of Eastern Europe, the encroachment of a materialist modernity, represented by the Yorkists, threatened to transform and debase this culture and replace communal expression with individual ambition. Mitchell's England did not indulge in the medieval pageantry of *The Plantagenets*; instead, the director insisted on sounding the depths of Shakespeare's own association with popular traditions and folk culture. She was not interested in, and did not pander to, any sense of Shakespeare as a modern playwright, as 'our contemporary', or as a bastion of high culture. Rather, by translating Shakespeare back into the theatrical vocabulary and music of the folk, Mitchell recovered the play as a lament for a dead culture. As Barbara Hodgdon put it, Mitchell was 'less interested in history than in releasing different ways of responding to traumatic national, and global, memories' (Hodgdon 'Making it New' 16).

One striking staging illustrated Mitchell's focus on the cultural experience of civil war. For the 'father who has killed his son' sequence (*Part Three* II.v), red and white roses were substituted for the bodies dragged on to the stage by their kindred, turning the scene into an allegory of suffering. Almost side-by-side, but not seeing each other or Henry (who sat between them), the two soldiers laid their standards down and carefully examined something held clasped in their hands – speaking, they slowly opened their fingers to reveal a fragile rose from the other house. It was then that they realised what they had done. The simplicity of the staging gave the scene a poetic force that contrasted with the play's appalling violence, Paul Taylor observing that 'the fragile beauty of the flower brings home to you its incongruity as the logo for a war of butchery' (*The Independent* 12 August 1994). The objects that the soldiers brought on to the stage – the roses, their standards – were, like many props in the production, left discarded and forgotten during the next scenes, as a lingering reminder of what had happened, as if the stage were piling up metaphors of cultural loss.

Allegory inescapably connected Mitchell's production with the civil wars in Bosnia that had begun three years earlier, following the collapse of Yugoslavia. The director had a personal interest in the war and, prior to working on *Part Three*, visited the war zone, finding in what she saw there – the descent of a modern, multi-ethnic state into mayhem and savagery – a desperate situation that demanded some kind of artistic response. Mitchell knew what she wanted the production to be about before she had even chosen the play. She was not alone: Susan Sontag, too, visited Bosnia, where, in the besieged capital Sarajevo, she directed *Waiting for Godot* as an ironic comment on the failure of the West to intervene; in 1993, after seeing horrifying reports of rape camps, the dramatist Sarah Kane rewrote her play *Blasted*, setting it in a British city apparently overcome with similar atrocities (Sierz 100–1). Bosnia's culture wars were horrifically violent: women were systematically raped, a parody of a 'breeding programme', and mass murders were committed as part of a policy of ethnic cleansing. But these wars also, it seemed, were a long way from the concerns of English audiences. To bridge the gap, Sontag took herself to Bosnia, Kane brought Bosnia to England and Mitchell went back to the past, to a Bosnia-like England mired in a violent civil war.

Mitchell was driven by a very strong belief that theatre, if it was to have any artistic validity, needed to respond to the wars in Bosnia. Of course, there is an element of absurdity about a group of actors in a peaceful middle-England town addressing such issues – it can have been of only small comfort to the besieged citizens of war-torn Sarajevo to know that their plight was being contemplated by actors and audiences in a far-away theatre. But Mitchell's point was an ethical one: it would also be absurd for Shakespearean theatre to ignore the vital questions about culture and humanity that the wars raised. In Bosnia, the intellectual debate was charged by the politics of silence and of emotion in the face of international apathy towards their plight. For some, postmodernism was a smokescreen for Western culture to ignore the disaster occurring on their doorstep. Stjepan Meštrović, an American scholar with Croatian roots, castigated Western societies whose 'post-emotional types "feel" a vast range of quasi-emotions, from indignation to compassion, yet are unable to put these feelings into appropriate action' (Meštrović xii). This postmodern disengagement, or 'Balkanisation of identity' as Meštrovic puts it, was now allowing horrors reminiscent of the Holocaust to happen unchecked. Politics were failing to stop genocide; media coverage could provoke sympathetic emotions but could not translate them into effective action. It was left, then, to the arts to find a way of confronting the gap between emotion and inaction. As silence and post-emotional disengagement were part of the politics that allowed the wars to continue, a cultural response, however small and however emotionally conceived, was vital. Mitchell recognised that, through the recovery of Shakespeare's *Part Three* as a warning and a memory of civil war, there was potential for a Stratford audience to resist post-emotional apathy and empathise with Bosnia.

Making a link between Shakespeare's England and modern Bosnia was crucial, for, Mitchell insisted, Bosnia 'isn't an isolated event that happens in other countries, it has happened on our own turf' (Tushingham 90). In performance, Mitchell's England was paradoxically familiar and strange, for, while it invoked the Bosnian conflict, the production did not set the play *in* Bosnia. In fact, to locate the play firmly within an English medieval world, Mitchell set a large, faded portrait of St George as the backdrop, dominating the stage. But this was not an England familiar to anyone brought up on the romanticised vision of the medieval period typified by, for example, Laurence Olivier in his film of *Henry V* or even by the RSC's own more recent history play productions. Instead, Mitchell used European and Russian films as the main sources for the look of England's past, most notably Kilmov's Иди и смотри (*Come and See* 1985), a harrowing war film about a Byelorussian peasant boy witnessing mass murder during the Second World War; and Pasolini's *Il vangelo secondo Matteo* (*The Gospel According to St Matthew* 1964), a stark retelling of the gospel acted by Italian peasants. In both, the authenticity of a peasant culture firmly rooted in its landscape is contrasted with the corrupt and violent behaviour of oppressors.

Using visual references inspired by the films, Mitchell saw England as a nation of heroes, but of real people – peasants – whose ancient traditions were being ravaged by ambitious, amoral warriors. Rather than dress her actors in colourful costumes and steel armour, Mitchell opted for a simple look: most actors wore white tunics, recalling the disciples in Pasolini's film, but, during battle scenes, leather armour strapped on top turned the costumes into battledress. Symbols of power were simple but potent – the crown was a narrow gold band, nothing much to look at, and the throne, object of so much bloodshed, was nothing more than a wooden chair.

By affirming the Englishness of the play, and only subtly hinting at Bosnia, Mitchell recovered *Part Three* as a warning about civil war. In Brechtian fashion, the actors presented rather than represented their parts, voicing the testimony of the past and inviting the audience to share their witness, making witness a recurrent theme – the messenger's account of York's death was a moving retelling of a scene only just staged, and Henry, himself a witness in the 'father who has killed his son' scene, later sat with the huntsmen who had captured him and, by witness, taught them about the world as if he were Pasolini's Christ. Most of the minor roles – assorted messengers, huntsmen and so on – were conflated into two keepers called Gabriel and Jack Viner (played by Declan Conlon and Tam Williams), who, as atrocity succeeded atrocity, emerged as chief witnesses to the wars. Exeter (Chris Garner) played a choric role by commenting on the events as they unfolded. Usually cast as an old man, Exeter was here a young gardener who spoke to the audience directly, issuing apocalyptic warnings in a stuttering voice. Quoting *Richard II*, Exeter prophesied that 'disorder, horror, fear and mutiny' (IV.i.133) would overrun 'Miserable England' (*Richard III* III.iv.103). In another such speech, Exeter, quoting from *Gorboduc*, blasted the 'cruel flames of civil fire' that were incinerating the realm and breaking over its head 'dead black streams of mourning, plaints and woe' (*Gorboduc* III.i.189–92). Such interpolations added depth to the civil war theme and made the connections between Shakespearean England and modern Bosnia even more pointed, even more urgent, Exeter speaking as if he were the only surviving witness to the death of a world which lived only through the echo of performance. *Part Three* was not just a war play, it was a testimonial.

Gardzienice

The striking differences between Mitchell's work and previous approaches to the *Henry VI* plays were partly a matter of location, made possible by The Other Place's semi-marginal position in the RSC. A small theatre just down the road from the RST in Stratford-upon-Avon, The Other Place (TOP) was originally a corrugated-iron hut that Buzz Goodbody had transformed into a rough space for the RSC's fringe work (Beauman 230–1). Although she cut her teeth at the RSC, Mitchell had never directed in any of the company's other Stratford theatre spaces; here at TOP, relieved of pressures to fill a large theatre (either with staging or with audiences), Mitchell had so far been able to develop a theatrical vision that combined her self-effacing integrity with trenchant interpretations of classic drama such as *A Woman Killed with Kindness* (1991), *The Dybbuk* (1992) and *Ghosts* (1993). Although she had been an assistant to Terry Hands on several Shakespeare productions, *Henry VI* was the only Shakespeare play Mitchell had ever directed for the RSC.[2] Taking advantage of the theatre's marginality, its reputation for experimentation where directors could 'do anything' to the space, Mitchell turned the irreverent TOP into something church-like, laying out the auditorium with a central aisle running through from the theatre's main doors to the performance space. Space, then, literalised ideas central to the production, where orthodox ritual, iconography and music would create a thick texture of the religious, binding the spiritual life of this culture to imagery it could see, touch, taste and smell – and to a God appalled by his people. Their violence was not just murderous. It amounted to apostasy.

Bringing theatre and religious ritual together, such techniques reflected the strong influence of another practitioner who not only called his theatre a church (Allain *Gardzienice* 95) but frequently performed in churches when on tour – Wlodzimierz Staniewski, founder of the Gardzienice Theatre Association, Poland. There were already connections: Katie Mitchell had spent two weeks in Poland working with the company during a sabbatical, and movement director Paul Allain was both a member of Gardzienice and later the author of an influential account of their work (Allain *Gardzienice* 1997). Mitchell brought the Association over to the RSC in 1991 for experimental workshops with RSC actors, and early in 1994, not long before she began working on *Henry VI*, Gardzienice conducted another workshop in The Other Place (137). In this workshop, actors were confronted with an unfamiliar and highly disciplined approach to their training and performance: according to Allain, the Gardzienicean performance aesthetic, 'rooted in religious iconography, seemingly dangerous and demanding physicality and complex choral and musical work' (Allain *Gardzienice* 1), combined group activity with the

[173]

choral voice (93) to produce a profound engagement with and homage to folk culture.

Subjecting Shakespearean chronicle to Gardzienicean methods proved unexpectedly fruitful; where most directors see the history plays as testosterone-driven blood-and-guts political cartoons, Mitchell saw *Part Three* as a parable that linked the play to Renaissance popular culture. Writing in 2003, Allain explained that, although his work on movement for *Henry VI* was not trying to replicate Gardzienice directly, 'Katie and I had a shared history and vocabulary' which came out in early workshops as Allain and Mitchell collaborated with the cast to 'give a world to the play'. They explored British folk culture (such as maypole dancing) and the 'contact the people had with nature in a predominantly rural culture'. This included some striking work on how the weather (especially rain, mud and the cold) affected the physical experience of fighting. The production echoed Gardzienice by using music as a way of emphasising the oral in popular tradition. At key moments, cast members sang liturgical chants in Latin – strange, beautiful and disturbing, the high notes soaring into the flies and the bass notes reverberating through the small auditorium. This singing, which floated a layer of 'the real' upon the action, was only one form of utterance in this apparently strange, religious world, which also expressed itself in small rituals and acts of worship. One part of the set concealed a pietà, a shrine where Rutland worshipped while his father and brothers debated breaking their oath. Allain's movement work also focused on gesture, especially greetings, ways of praying and battle cries (all quotations in this paragraph are from Allain 'Correspondence' n.p.).

Gardzienice's conception of folk culture also stressed the importance of environment and ethnic identity. Staniewski insists that the earthly and the spiritual are bound together, and his work, which has sometimes been called a 'theatre of anthropology', stresses the importance of the environment to human culture (Allain *Gardzienice* 21). In *Henry VI*, religion and nature were connected. For example, Mitchell carefully researched the medieval liturgical year, and each of the psalmodies was a seasonal variation of the Mass mapped on to the production's naturalistic evocation of nature. Dark lighting, rain and swirling snow indicated winter; a brightening light and birdsong, spring and summer. In the prompt book, Mitchell gave each scene a date, the whole action spread across a year: the parliament scene was marked as November (indicated in the production by the sound of rain); York contemplated oath-breaking on Christmas Eve. York's death heralded the spring, when his sons' fortunes changed; Towton occurred on Palm Sunday; Edward's final ascent to the throne, at the height of summer. Henry was released from the Tower in the autumn, and the production headed back into winter. With the birth of Edward at the end of the play, it was Christmas again. As is often the case with Mitchell's work and with Gardzienicean theatre, this research was absorbed into the deep structure of the production and realised in performance implicitly.

The setting evoked nature, religion and death. Mitchell's designer, Rae Smith, who had worked in Yugoslavia and later illustrated Allain's book, emphasised the underlying sense of the folk which Mitchell sought to bring out in the play. Wood-chippings lay deep on the surface of the playing area, creating what Mitchell called a 'field of dirt' and filling the theatre with a woody aroma. At the rear a large wooden wall loomed, resembling the gate of a medieval city. Heavy wooden shutters hid windows above, and in the middle were two large steel doors, through which the dead walked into the afterlife. Water ran down a pipe; a bucket hung on a peg beneath two shutters; these opened to reveal the pietà. Nature was also evoked in a soundtrack of birds, rain, sheep bleating and dogs barking. The two armies slogged their way through the final battles in a howling snow-storm – impressive in a large theatre, stunning in the confines of The Other Place – as if they were fighting against nature as well as each other. Two large objects dominated the physical space. In one corner was a bell hoisted high above the stage, rung during moments of crisis and of religious observance. Opposite was a tree, to which Margaret was chained in her final scene.

Battles were a different kind of ritual, a dark coda to the liturgical songs. The rites that should have held society together were perjured and betrayed; in their worship, the Yorkists and Lancastrians appealed to spiritual truths but found unity only in death, so that, as Peter Holland shrewdly observed, 'the echoes of a genuine religion ... underlined the political manipulation of the divine for entirely worldly ends' (Holland 202). Tewkesbury began with a fade to near darkness – a heavy drum with the rhythm of a quick heartbeat set the tone. Then, from either side of the rear façade, soldiers entered in equal numbers, marching in time with the drumbeat, forming up into two lines facing the theatre exit, marching on the spot and breathing heavily, their feet striking the floor as a percussive accompaniment to the music, amplifying it to a deafening pitch (the sound, rather than any perceptible sense of the actors' bodies, filling the space created by the darkness). Making physical theatre – and theatre physical – actors were using what they had learned in Allain's workshops, turning their bodies into instruments. Deafening noise shook the seats in the auditorium, a cacophony amplified when the soldiers, each holding a banner on a wooden pole, banged them on the ground in unison. Suddenly everything stopped and a moment of peaceful silence fell – interrupted only by some birdsong which, as Taylor put it, dropped 'into the moment like an ache of nostalgia and a moral judgment on the scene' (*The Independent* 12 August 1994). This sudden contrast with nature was unexpectedly lyrical, but then the soldiers charged towards the audience, screaming as they exited through the theatre doors. In the final major battle scene of the production, set at Barnet, noise overwhelmed the action: bells and drums mixed with human cries and the sound of horses' hooves; drummers marched across a stage swamped in mist that looked like smoke: hell was opening up in a world descending into total chaos.

Battles were uproar's set pieces, the handiwork of chaos. In between them, the religious rituals and the seasonal time markers emerged fitfully as reminders of the order that war violated. But, increasingly, the production made the point that war not only subjected human and natural cycles to ambition and violence; it also transformed them. York's death, for example, was played as a strange, dismal invocation of a Christmas festival, the weary would-be monarch forced to wear a crown fashioned by Margaret from branches ripped from the leafless tree – a crown of thorns for a winter king. Rituals that should have denoted the connectedness between the English and their environment instead became rituals of individual sacrifice. York was submissive as he waited for his final blows, as if he knew his part in the ritual of sacrifice. When a tall woman, dressed in black, entered to escort the dead York off the stage, she held the napkin soaked in Rutland's blood – another sacrifice. Behind him, the crown of thorns was left onstage and, in the next scene, remained as a token of that sacrifice while his sons (standing amazed at the three 'suns' which miraculously shone on them) speculated about York's fate. When news finally came, Edward fell to his knees and wept; Richard railed and shouted at the audience.

The politics of grief

Help with interpreting this spare world was provided by the programme, which featured the central character from Brueghel's *Dulle Griet* on its cover and, on the inside, further details from the painting, including an up-close illustration of its grotesque hell-mouth. This, Brueghel's vision of an Italian peasant village teetering on the edge of doom, was clearly Mitchell's inspiration for costumes (Dulle Griet's brown breastplate over her raw linen peasant's tunic was immediately recognisable as the source for Margaret's costume), and for much more. Illustrating the proverb 'She could plunder in front of hell and return unscathed', Brueghel's painting, which depicts his warrior-woman fighting on the lip of a gaping hell-mouth with a sword in one hand and a baby and a bag full of pots in the other, surrounded by misshapen devils and backed by fire, makes Dulle Griet every bit as much an inversion as the world around her. As other women attack soldiers and loot villages, Dulle Griet stands alone, beating back the devils pouring out of hell. Mitchell was not the first theatre practitioner to be inspired by the painting: Brecht based Mother Courage on Dulle Griet, and Caryl Churchill included the warrior-woman in the opening scene of *Top Girls*. The painting offered both a visual language and an interpretative frame for approaching *Henry VI*. Although there was no hell-mouth in Smith's set, the distribution of doors and windows on the façade followed Brueghel's landscape, as if the windows were eyes and the doors a mouth out of which spilled infernal shapes. The spectator could mentally scrub the stage away and discover underneath it Brueghel's vision of hell. More tellingly, since costume design reproduced the artist's vision, all of the characters became, in effect, Dulle Griets, plundering at the gates of hell.

Both warrior-woman and mother clutching her baby, 'mad Meg' – as Griet is known in English – or 'mad Margaret' troped Henry's queen (played by Ruth Mitchell). A continental firebrand, passionately focused on protecting her son (she went everywhere with Edward in tow) and on avenging York's perjury, she entered the play ranting at Henry, who cowered. She was not someone to be controlled or tamed. Henry and York's bargain, which disinherited Edward, made Margaret more than a soldier. Unlike the rest, when she dressed for war, she wore black armour and a terrifying gold mask: like Dulle Griet's, her femininity was effaced by this militarisation of her body, the mother turned soldier furious and vindictive as the world fell apart around her.

Dark and plain, Ruth Mitchell played her part with a thick French accent, but, rather than making her exotic, her accent simply made her an outsider, difficult to understand, even harder to contain. In France, this Margaret spoke French, honouring Louis with supplications and prostrating herself before him. Warwick, on the other hand, barged in, ignored the court protocols and spoke English. The effect of this collision of actions and languages was telling: Margaret 'belonged' (but somehow to a redundant world). Warwick didn't. 'Modern', interested only in furthering his own ambition, he simply smashed culture. Mitchell understood that the key to Margaret's story was her anger at the disinheritance of her son: her fury, her crimes, sprang from her fierce desire to hold on to the past. Warwick, York and even Henry betrayed their supporters – Margaret was the only character to remain passionately true to the values she believed in. Unexpectedly, Margaret became the production's moral centre and, seemingly, the only one to recognise that there was more at stake than individual ambition.

Ultimately, the production could do little to bring Bosnia on stage, and, perhaps in recognition of this inevitable failure, Mitchell slowly separated the onstage world from the audience. With each death, a cross appeared at the edge of the playing area. Sometimes Exeter would (literally) plant the cross, digging into the earth with his trowel and leaving on the cross a piece of cloth – red or white, depending on the allegiance of the fallen. At other times, crosses appeared during the darkness between scenes as mysterious echoes of the departed, until, by the end of the performance, the actors were enclosed by the rows of graves. Gardzienice rejects Brechtian alienation, preferring to engage with its audience, and to a point, Mitchell concurred; but, in the end, this was a play and a performance about death, so inexorably the audience were pushed out of the frame, the actors disengaged, just as, on the political stage, Western eyes were similarly disengaged from the situation in Bosnia. For the Yorkists and the Lancastrians, despite the birth of Edward and the looked-for lasting joy, their culture had become little more than a communal participation in death. For Billington, the performance was 'a note of religious regret at the destruction of an English Eden' (*The Guardian* 12 August 1994), but Woddis recognised that it was also a 'powerful lament for Eastern Europe' (*What's On* 17 August 1994). They were both right: one was the image of the other.

Grief was personified by a woman in a black dress (Liz Kettle) who entered after each killing to mourn the dead. Somehow at the centre of the performance, yet neither named nor explained, she was called in the promptbook 'Mad Meg'. She never spoke to the other characters, but instead led the dead into the after-life. When Rutland was murdered, his body abandoned on the stage, she entered and sang a solo *Miserere* – a plea to God for deliverance from 'bloodguiltiness' – and then gestured to the boy, who stood up and followed her through the doors. The smell of incense crept around the auditorium, creating an atmosphere of ritual mourning; Rutland's death was transformed from a murder into a kind of sacrifice, and his rising to walk into the afterlife felt like the possibility of redemption. The appearances of Mad Meg structured the performance around each successive death scene. Her contributions were always similar, although she sang different prayers and in some scenes was accompanied by others, most notably Exeter, the only living character able to interact with her.

Sometimes, Mad Meg was accompanied by a choir played by the rest of the cast (but barely perceptible on the darkly lit stage) carrying candles, incense and ringing bells as they sang. The choir turned Meg's lonely mourning into a cultural lamenta-tion for the dead. Representing the victims of war, choir members first appeared after Tewkesbury, singing *Christe Eleison* as they led the dead York offstage. Following Warwick's death, they entered behind the woman, each member of the choir holding a skull and the standards of both houses to represent Warwick's divided loyal-ties. Another *Miserere* was sung over the body of Prince Edward, connecting his death with Rutland's, while Henry VI's death was marked by a choral *Kyrie*. After Edward's final triumph, the entire cast knelt behind Meg, singing a *Domine Deus* – 'Lord God why have you forsaken me?' Ending here, facing the audience, all of the actors participated in this concluding prayer.

Figured as Mad Meg, grief was an interruptive force able both to suspend the normal order of things in the commemoration of the past and to make a break between the trauma of the past and hope for the future. Apparently able to see both the dead and the living, Meg occupied a liminal space that was both inside and outside the play's narrative frame. In a Gardzienicean sense, she represented the persistent trace of the folk; but her role was also a way of articulating a politics of grief and particularly of the grieving mother – a powerful image in the wake of Bosnia and Rwanda. Both the Mad Meg of Brueghel's painting and the Mad Margaret of *Henry VI* were mothers as well as avengers; but, where the one held on to her child, the other finally lost hers as, chained to a tree, she was forced to witness infanticide. In Liz Kettle's Mad Meg, Brueghel and Shakespeare converged – but not, as one might expect, in the soldier; rather, in the grieving widow, an Everywoman mourning the whole world.

Meg was doubled with Lady Grey, another mother figure and grieving widow who, to begin with, even wore the same mourning dress as her spiritual alter-ego. Her story began with an attempted rape which she endured to save her children; later she fled the Lancastrians, heavily pregnant, and returned to Edward in the final scene with a baby in her arms. In that first scene, begging the new King for her dead husband's lands, she became the focus of a new kind of politics. Edward's clumsy attempt at seduction shifted the object of struggle from the throne to Grey's body. It was not enough to have martial power; Edward needed to have sexual power as well. As in Bosnia, physical violence went alongside sexual abuse in a scene that, in Mitchell's interpretation, turned Shakespeare's coy love scene into a drama of cultural degradation and feminine resistance. Grey never gave way: when Edward coaxed her with *double entendre*, she ignored it, sticking to her role as supplicant. When he pushed her down and forced himself on top of her body, she lay still and unresponsive. The battle took another turn: when he lifted her dress and then tried to force her head into his crotch, she pulled away. Only by making her his queen could Edward claim his prize.

In her next scene, Grey was doubly transfigured. Wearing white, she was no longer a mourner; but, with a bump visible beneath her dress, she also became the bearer of the next generation. Mitchell tracked her story: when Edward and his court left the stage to plan their campaign against the renegade Warwick, Grey remained, contemplative on her throne, and then got up to go, but not before leaving her crown behind her. She was obviously pregnant in her next scene, panting as she packed her possessions, weak and weary as her nurse led her away. Grey returned for the last scene of the play, entering a full stage to present her child to the king and court. But once Edward spoke the play's final line, holding the baby in his arms, he turned and disappeared through the upstage doors, the court following. Grey stayed behind. Alone, abandoned, her isolated figure watched through the doors as her infant was removed – another grieving mother, another child snatched from its natural inheritance, another woman dispossessed and abused. Grey turned, knelt, and prayed: when she did, the identities of Grey and Mad Meg fused. Behind her, the company returned, now dressed in white, and solemnly knelt to sing another psalm. Their kneeling bodies obscured the throne, but they were themselves separated from the audience by the graves which lined the stage and marked the space between them and the disinterred past the actors had performed.

Henry and Richard

The simplicity of Mitchell's approach to *Part Three* gave the play a new sense of vibrancy: perhaps for the first time, the play came into its own as a work of character drama. Unencumbered by historical pageant, 'trilogy thinking' or directorial concepts, *Henry VI* clearly brought out the stories of the main characters – Henry's loss of power, Margaret's search for justice for her son, York's self-doubts, Warwick's political fumblings and Richard's scornful desire for power at any cost. As one reviewer put it, Mitchell staged the play in 'close-up' (*The Sunday Times* 14 August 1994) – and, of course, this was crucial to Mitchell's political project. Submerging the play in monolithic spectacles would have made it more difficult to elicit empathy in the audience; instead, staged in close-up, the play's narrative conveyed the human suffering of civil war and so invited English audiences to identify both with their own nation's past and with the situation in Bosnia.

York's dramatic occupation of Parliament and the ensuing battle over the throne – enacted first through words and then through force – was, for Mitchell, strikingly resonant with the themes of politics and culture which she wished to explore. The scene was, Mitchell thought, reminiscent of the siege of the Russian White House in 1993, when the administrative centre of power became a battleground, and force looked set to determine the country's future – Mitchell even considered adding a bloody flag to her production as a reference to this event (Mitchell 'Unpublished interview' n.p.). In performance, the opening scene staged a crucial violation of the rites of power that propels the story until Edward takes the throne again by force, killing Henry's heir and allowing Richard

13 *Henry VI – The Battle for the Throne* (1994). The opening scene: George (Jo Stone-Fewings), York (Stephen Simms) and Warwick (John Keegan)

to kill Henry. When the Yorkist army broke down the doors and invaded the stage, York (Stephen Simms) hesitated for a moment, contemplating the Bible that, laid out on a table, stood in his way to the throne that stood in front of the great metal doors. It was as if he were comprehending the transgression he was about to commit – for here were the legible, visual clues to the production's main dynamic between power, inadequately represented by the throne, and peace, represented by the Bible, opened to Matthew 5:9, 'Blessed are the peacemakers' (Coursen 10).

Costumes replayed this dialectic: the Yorkists, dressed in leather armour and carrying crossbows, took up aggressive positions around the stage to face Henry and the Lancastrians, who followed moments later, unarmed, wearing only white tunics and rosary beads. But York's self-doubt and Henry's lack of courage transformed the scene from a potential *coup d'état* to the squalid political bargain struck between the King and the pretender, as Henry, with crossbows aimed at his head, agreed to disinherit his son, a bargain 'sanctified' by an oath upon the book. York and Henry clasped hands; their followers knelt and sang *Gloria in Excelsis*

[182]

Deo – a devotional rite which gave a hint of their common culture. For this one scene, the production showed the two sides worshipping together, sharing the same observances, and so adding pathos to the eventual collapse of that culture.

The cast was led by Jonathan Firth, a young actor then well known for roles in television period drama. Firth's Henry, like Pasolini's Christ, was a toughened politician with a core of idealism, a victim of his own innocence. For Mitchell, Henry 'has a very strong moral, ethical and spiritual sense of himself and the world in which he's living. He's surrounded by people whose obsessions are power and ambition' (Tushingham 91). It was always Mitchell's intention to cast a young actor as Henry, whom she saw as a compassionate innocent, destroyed by civil war and unable, until the very end of the play, to comprehend the extent to which those around him were prepared to transgress spiritual and physical values. For Peter Holland, Firth 'showed brilliantly the terrifying irrelevance of contemplative goodness in the play's politics' (Holland 202). By the end, Henry was ill, wasting away in prison with just the Bible for contemplation – the same Bible over which the two factions had sworn their oath, their ceasefire.

Richard Gloucester represented a form of power based on desire, with little time for the religious or historical structures that York had tried to preserve. Tom Smith's Richard was a modern thug, a neo-fascist, a spitting adolescent. His deformed arm covered by a metal casing during battles, Richard was a version of the strange, demonic creatures spilling out of hell in Brueghel's painting, the 'foul, misshapen stigmatic' Queen Margaret calls him. In these terms, Richard was a transgressive character, a lord of misrule, and Smith's performance played upon the pleasures of Brueghelesque inversion and diabolic carnival. Speaking directly to the audience, Richard was seductive and enticing, and certainly the most frightening character on the stage. But by the end, after all the battles, all the wind-changing shifts in allegiances, all the deaths, his was the only truth onstage – or better said, the only certainty. Richard murdered Henry over the Bible and then discarded both, because for him, family, morality and spirituality meant nothing. The only 'truth' was the power of Richard's desire.[3]

Conclusion

By approaching *Part Three* as a warning from the past that could be applied to present horrors, Mitchell created a vision of history which was radically at odds with traditional representations of medieval England, but a vision that honoured and respected the authentic experience that underpinned the drama. Although primarily addressing English audiences, Mitchell's *Henry VI* embarked on an international tour that ensured this small-scale production a large international audience. From The Other Place, *Henry VI* went to the regions, then to North America, South America, Germany (where audiences were ecstatic), the Netherlands, Japan and Austria. Mitchell travelled with the tour, and such was her dedication that she continued to make improvements to the production right up to its final performance in Austria in May 1995. This tour was not without difficulties: the pump which carried water on to the set frequently broke down; in Brazil, lighting problems turned the stage into a disco set; and in Santiago, Tam Williams knocked himself out on the steel doors. *Henry VI* was designed for The Other Place and belonged there – but, taking the play to new audiences, Mitchell strove to create global interest in her themes of politics and civil war.

Mitchell also helped to change the ways in which the *Henry VI* plays were imagined, for several productions followed in the 1990s that addressed (in different ways) the fragmentation of history and culture so much a part of the discourse of Bosnia. These included RSC associate director Barry Kyle's adaptations, *Henry VI: The Contention* and *Henry VI: The Civil War*, at the Theatre for a New Audience in New York (1995); Michael Kahn's critically acclaimed four-hour production of *Henry VI Parts I, II and III* for The Shakespeare Theatre, Washington (1996, discussed at length by Coursen, 1999); Karin Coonrod's *The Edged Sword* and *The Black Storm* (a two-part adaptation of the trilogy) for the New York Shakespeare Festival (1997); Jeremy Wechsler's two-and-a-half-hour adaptation of all three plays for the radical Bailiwick Repertory Theatre in Chicago, complemented by an exhibition of art and poetry by Robert Kameczura (1998); and Bruce Colville's one-play adaptation, *The Falcon's Pitch*, written by the award-winning playwright Jeffrey Sweet for the Illinois Shakespeare Festival (1998).

One production deserves special mention because of its affinities with Mitchell's *Henry VI*. Later in 1994, the York Theatre Royal celebrated its bicentenary with an ambitious two-part adaptation of the first tetralogy, titled *The Wars of the Roses* and directed by John Doyle. The first play in the cycle was based on *Part Three*, with extra scenes added from the other plays to provide context for the story (the very strategy Mitchell had resisted when it was suggested to her by the RSC). Like Mitchell, Doyle highlighted the contemporary relevance of the plays, but Doyle could do something that Mitchell could not – he really could claim the play as a piece of local history, as a memory of a civil war partly played out in and around York. With Oliver Cromwell's bullet holes from another civil war still visible in the city walls, York could claim a kind of kinship with besieged cities like Sarajevo. Consequently, the city was a character in the production; its walls were represented as battlements at the rear of the stage and the main character was undoubtedly the Yorkist anti-hero, Richard Gloucester. Although Mitchell's production was still touring the country, Doyle was indebted to her work: a water trough at the front of the stage added an element of naturalism, red, blue and white cloths signified allegiances onstage and the 'father who has killed his son …' scene was represented by two actors, each one speaking to a different coloured cloth as if it were his relative. Although neither as subtle nor as inventive as Mitchell's production, Doyle confirmed the resonance that *Part Three*, cut free from *Part One* and *Part Two*, now had for a world mired in civil war.

Although a small-scale production, then, Mitchell's *Henry VI* represented a significant departure in the theatre history of the plays. Without really intending to, Mitchell challenged the orthodoxy that Shakespeare's early history plays can be approached only as part of a cycle by having faith in the integrity of *Part Three* as an independent work. Further, her focus on the ethics of theatrical practice insisted that it was crucial for artists to respond directly to the political present – to the horror of events such as the Bosnian civil war. And in order to respond viscerally to the atrocities perpetrated there, she devised an original performance aesthetic by adapting the practices of radical Polish theatre to a representation of England's distant past. In the wake of Bosnia and of British devolution, the tension Mitchell invoked between tribalism and globalisation was taken up again by Michael Boyd's millennium cycle, which is the subject of the next chapter.

CHAPTER IX

Black comedies: the RSC's millennial *Henry VI* (2000–1)

The RSC celebrated the millennium with *This England*, a cycle of the two tetralogies and the first such cycle to include full-text productions of all three *Henry VI* plays. The three playing spaces in Stratford were used in turn to stage the developing cycle: *Richard II* opened in the studio theatre, The Other Place, followed by *Henry IV* in the mock-Elizabethan Swan theatre, *Henry V* in the RST, and the three parts of *Henry VI* back in the Swan (with *Richard III* concluding the cycle in London). Moving self-consciously between playing spaces, each one distinctly different in repertoire and audience expectation, the RSC seemed to be mimicking the national devolution policy which had recently created parliaments in Wales, Northern Ireland and Scotland. Where Peter Hall's *The Wars of the Roses* and Adrian Noble's *The Plantagenets* had sought to bring the company together, *This England* staged diversity, insisting upon the importance of recognising different artistic visions – four directors worked on the cycle – and different audience investments. For the *Henry VI* plays, director Michael Boyd transformed the Swan theatre into a nightmarish double of the nation, an England mired in a hellish, strange reality in which the dead refused to play dead but continued to participate in the lives of a people overtaken by madness.

Boyd first discussed the project with Adrian Noble in 1997, but both agreed then that staging all three plays was too much of a financial gamble. Even in 2000, the trilogy was budgeted to make a loss (in fact, it was a surprise hit). Not for the first time, the *Henry VI* plays were implicated in the wider politics of the RSC. Noble wanted to push through a number of reforms, among them the introduction of shorter contracts for actors and, with this, a more focused ensemble approach to production work. He also pulled out of the RSC's London base at the Barbican and started to explore the possibilities of potentially lucrative partnerships with American universities. The *Henry VI* plays exemplified the best of these reforms: performed as a true trilogy by an ensemble company, the plays ran for some months at Stratford, then relocated to the Young Vic in London and, finally, to the University of Michigan, which co-funded the production. Shortly after the history season ended, when Noble announced his resignation, Michael Boyd succeeded him and became, not insignificantly, the fifth Artistic Director to be associated with a major production of the *Henry VI* plays.

Refreshingly, Boyd never questioned the quality of the plays nor felt any artistic imperative to adapt them. He looked at medieval theatre for clues to understanding *Henry VI*, convinced that the trilogy constituted one of the high-points of what he called 'a late-flowering of medieval culture' in the sixteenth century. By approaching the plays as 'last gasps' in a lively tradition that stretched back some two hundred years, animating the medieval morality plays and mystery cycles, Boyd avoided seeing the trilogy's episodic structure and thin characterisation as symptomatic of 'apprentice' work. In medieval plays like *Everyman* and *The Castle of Perseverance*, the subject of performance is the world, and Everyman stands on a stage that sites his mortal life and immortal destiny, a hell-mouth on one side, a throne – representing heaven – on the other. In Boyd's *Henry VI*, this morality world was England – an England poised, on both its vertical and horizontal axes, precariously on the edge of hell, represented on Boyd's stage by two convex, burnished doors opening out, and a massive trapdoor opening down. Hell, then, was everywhere this production turned. Like characters in a morality play, the protagonists' struggle with temptation, desire and betrayal was personified by witches, pranksters and demons. Most strikingly, dead characters returned to the stage as revenants haunting the living. The relationship between England and 'hell' became a binding narrative for the trilogy, reflected in the subtitles advertising each play: *Part One*, 'The War Against France'; *Part Two*, 'England's Fall'; *Part Three*, 'The Chaos'. The wars of *Part One* were figured as an encounter with hell and an attempt to suppress it through the execution of Joan la Pucelle. But with Margaret (played by Fiona Bell who doubled Joan) infecting the playworld of *Part Two*, England fell into the same chaos it had tried to contain in *Part One*. Hell worked as both a medieval and a modern idea for Boyd. Paintings by Hieronymus Bosch, used for some of the poster art advertising the trilogy, were echoed by the demons, ghosts and rebels who overran the stage when Cade and his crew rioted – hell let loose. Equally, though, hell worked as a way of thinking about the pernicious aspects of the devolutionary impulses then engaging both the nation and the RSC.

Boyd faced competition as, at almost the same time, Edward Hall (son of Peter Hall) opened his adaptation of the *Henry VI* plays, brilliantly retitled *Rose Rage*, at the Windmill theatre in Buckinghamshire. Sparky, bloody and intense, Hall boasted a 'new look at the *Henry VI* plays' in his programme and what he gave audiences was an edgy horror film set in an abattoir. As audiences entered, the all-male cast were already on the stage, wearing white coats and masks with animal-like snouts, sharpening knives with a slow and sinister scrape as the audience took their seats. Behind the cast, a set of mesh lockers were arranged like cages as if to tell everyone, there's no way out. Claustrophobic and frequently gory, *Rose Rage* was also very funny. An overdone performance of the hymn 'Jerusalem' opened the production and, throughout, violence was represented not through mutilated bodies, but mutilated food. Cabbages stood in for heads; a sack of blood was drained into a bucket to represent Warwick bleeding to death; in other scenes, meat was cut up on a table. Hall made intense and irreverent theatre out of the plays which challenged the solemnity of past productions.

For the first time, audiences could make up their own mind about whether the *Henry VI* plays were better taken whole or adapted, in three parts or two. Although Hall denied following in his father's footsteps, he and his co-adapter Roger Warren conflated the plays just as Peter Hall and John Barton had done nearly forty years before. If anything, Edward Hall was more savage with his cuts, as each part of *Rose Rage* ran to a tight two hours. Some critics applauded Hall for his bold and uncompromising modernisation of the plays; others, among them Michael Billington, compared Hall unfavourably to Boyd, in effect celebrating the achievement of Shakespeare's trilogy and regretting any reduction of its epic scope – a neat and ironic reversal of their critical reception of Terry Hands's 'full text' trilogy back in 1977. For Billington, Boyd's vision of a society enacting self-immolation was simply bigger and richer than Hall's, who reduced the plays to a 'Marlovian blood-bath' when, played full, they were really about greater themes such as 'nationhood, politics and time'. Not all critics agreed. Those who saw them as plodding apprentice work welcomed Hall's visceral, irreverent pantomime; those who saw more ('more' than many of them had been shown by Hands) rightly accused *Rose Rage* of turning back 'the theatrical clock' (*The Guardian* 17 June 2002). It was Boyd, ultimately, who produced the more challenging work.

This England? Oh, that England …

By its title, *This England* called attention to the whole question of representing England on the stage. Was 'this England' to be the one set in a silver sea or the one whose lands had been leased out? In fact, rather than making a definitive statement about England, the cycle posed a question, as if the title should really have been '*This England?*' For the first time at the RSC, staging English history was not driven by one artistic vision: instead, each director working on the cycle was given a brief to interpret Shakespeare's England his own way. Boyd's England was a dark, troubled nation falling into the chaos that engulfs it in *Part Three*. He made no attempt to make history recognisable: his England was a strange place, alien to modern audiences. But, in one respect, Boyd's production choices reflected a very contemporary theme, for he brought to the RSC its first-ever black king, David Oyelowo, Henry, in a process of colour-blind casting that saw several parts go to actors from minority backgrounds. Even if the world onstage was a medieval one, the ethnic mix in the cast placed it visually within the politics of the present.

Scare-stories in the press earlier in the year had shown how sensitive English society could still be about its multi-ethnic identity. A rumour circulated that the government was proposing to get rid of the racist connotations of nationalism by changing the name of the country, and even the broadsheets took the bait, publishing editorials both attacking and defending the proposal. The rumour, which was not true, sprang from a report by the Commission for the Future of Multi-Ethnic Britain recommending that Britain should declare itself multi-ethnic, as many other countries around the world had already done. According to the Labour peer Lord Parekh, such a move would make 'a statement of who we are. It is a way of saying to ethnic minorities and the world that we not only tolerate but cherish our diversity', and he added that it would also be a way of rethinking Britain's 'national story' (quoted in *The Guardian* 11 October 2000). *The Daily Telegraph* countered by discarding ethnicity as a category defining Britishness: while it was true that 'our nationhood has been shaped over the centuries by waves of settlers, each bringing his [sic] own contribution to British identity', the more important fact for the *Telegraph* was that 'our common nationality ... allows us to define Britishness in civic, rather than racial, terms'. Framed in 'civic, rather than racial' terms, the whole question of 'who we are' was very much in the air when the RSC launched its *This England* season. Boyd was the only director in the cycle to suggest that 'who we are' could be responded to with a colour-blind cast production of Shakespearean history. Inevitably, the press picked up on this too.

For the first time in the RSC's history, audiences watched a staging of the nation that not only included non-white actors, but even seemed to privilege them – though Boyd disputed this, countering press curiosity about his casting by claiming that, since his casting was colour-blind, in this production colour did not signify.[1] An idea that dates back to the 1960s, when Joseph Papp's New York Shakespeare Festival started casting roles on ability rather than race, colour-blind casting is a practice that has become standard in America, but Britain has been slower to implement it, and another three years would pass before the National Theatre followed the RSC by casting Adrian Lester as the first black, British Henry V to appear on the NT's stage. For Libby Appel, the American producer whose mixed-race *Henry VI* played at the Oregon Shakespeare Festival in 1991–92, colour-blind casting is never truly blind, as it forces 'a challenge to audience expectations' (Pao 15). And the controversy cuts both ways, for black communities have not automatically embraced the concept either. Indeed, in North America the widespread use of colour-blind casting has been controversial within African-American intellectual communities. Most notably, as Angela C. Pao reminds us in her balanced study, the playwright August Wilson criticised African-Americans who played Shakespearean kings: 'As far as Wilson is concerned, an African American actor who plays the role of a Shakespearean English king allows his body to be used in "the celebration of a culture which has oppressed [black people]"' (Pao 3). In such an assumption, Shakespeare and English history are indivisible from the imperial, white mythologies which have produced inequalities in society.

In the case of the *Henry VI* plays, whether consciously or not, the total effect of mixing white and non-white actors in a history play subverted (or perhaps exposed) English history as a white mythology. Where the Commission's recommendations had proved an easy fall guy for editorials to rant about 'politically correct garbage', the casting of a black actor as an English king was a more confrontational way of exposing latent prejudices and of exploring the true meaning of Britain's multi-ethnic status. Press reviews of the productions reflected this unease; and, though there were exceptions, many reviewers drew attention to the conjunction of Oyelowo's racial identity and Henry's historic national identity. Oyelowo himself remembers an article in *The Daily Telegraph* which said that 'moves like these open us up to ridicule' (Oyelowo 28). *The Mail on Sunday* conceded that Oyelowo did well with the part, yet remarked: 'I'm not sure you could have a black actor playing a monarch with a familiar face, but with *Henry VI* it's fine because your average theatre-goer starts with a pretty blank slate' (*The Mail on Sunday* 7 January 2001). To paraphrase: because 'we' are not familiar with the image of Henry VI, because we do not (nationally, historically speaking) identify with him, it is acceptable for him to be played by a non-white actor. Another review in *The Daily Mail* found a subtextual meaning in Oyelowo's performance, noting how, by the end of the trilogy, 'he becomes culturally indifferent to his own story, ending his life in a white dhoti, face down in a pool of spreading blood' (*The Daily Mail* 15 December 2000). The phrase 'culturally indifferent to his own story' is particularly problematic. What can it mean? How can a character be 'culturally indifferent to his own story'? Is it the character or the actor who becomes culturally indifferent, unable or unwilling to identify with the mythology which constitutes 'his own story'?

The effect of the colour-blind casting policy was not in any real sense an appropriation of British history for a new, multicultural agenda; there was no effort to translate a white mythology into a new national history of which a multicultural audience could claim ownership. Yet, the controversy over the casting of an 'English' king was indicative of the radical potential inherent in any real incursions on the territory of national identity by the 'pc garbage' of non-white communities. This audience of press reviewers was confronted with an image of its own history which it claimed not to recognise. Henry and the world which he ruled were unfamiliar, even disconcerting.

[191]

Haunted histories

The controversy over David Oyelowo's casting is of interest only in retrospect because of the worrying conservatism of some of the commentators who reacted, as we have seen, with a questionable insistence upon preserving the white mythology of English history. Boyd's reinvention of England went much further, alienating all audiences who brought with them the baggage of being British. Whatever positive image of the nation may or may not have underlined the mixed-race production, the *Henry VI* that opened to audiences in late 2000 boldly turned on its head the romanticised notion of the past evoked by the 'this England' umbrella title. Race was not an overt concern – blackness, one of the key colours of this dark production, came from a different place entirely. The aesthetic register was keyed to blackness, as if a shadow had been thrown not only over England but over the theatre and the audience: the stage was black, many of the costumes were black, and when white did appear – in Henry's costume, in York's and in Margaret's white-blonde hair and in bright lights that cut into the darkness – it was only to put into relief the intense blackness that pervaded all three productions.

Boyd took inspiration from Shakespeare's own imagery in the *Henry VI* plays where black is the colour of both mourning and congealed blood: in *Part One*, Exeter cries 'We mourn in black; why mourn we not in blood?' (I.i.17); the murdered Gloucester's face is 'black and full of blood' in *Part Two* (III.ii.168); in *Part Three*, Richard exhorts his brothers not to 'wrap our bodies in black mourning gowns' (II.i.161) but to fight on the battlefields to avenge their father's death. By opposing mourning with ritual, Shakespeare stages a series of interrupted and unresolved episodes of grief in which, rather than honouring the memory of blood kin, mourners choose to fight and so perpetuate cycles of death. *Henry VI* begins with an unresolved mourning ritual, as Bedford's invocation to the ghost of Henry V is interrupted by messages from France; later, Talbot sheds tears over the bodies of Salisbury and his son; Clifford pledges to avenge his father's death, and York dies with his son's blood smeared across his face. Gloucester, on the other hand, dies with his face blackened by blood, as if wearing the mourning weeds abjured by Bedford and Richard: he literally mourns in blood.

Responding to this imagery rather than to the narrow agenda

of colour-blind casting, the productions staged a world caught in a perpetual cycle of mourning, so that death, not race, shaped the representation of 'this England'. The first line of the play offered a starting point, as Bedford gestured to the flies and intoned 'hung be the heavens with black', and, to the sound of discordant music, Henry V's corpse was lowered from the ceiling, down through a large trapdoor out of which light shone, cutting through the darkness. Mourners stood all about the stage and also in the auditorium, as if the audience was also caught up in the ritual – not just spectators but participants in the memorialising of the dead King. Gloucester, angry and passionate, addressed these offstage mourners, at the same time implicating the audience in the mourning ritual. But the ritual was not completed: messengers divided the ceremony by shouting from all three points of the stage so that the spatial order of the funeral, as well as its speeches, was interrupted.

Shakespeare's reference to the heavens is theatrical as well as metaphysical. In an Elizabethan playhouse, the heavens was the underside of the canopy which stretched over the centre of the stage. It was perhaps with this in mind that the *Henry VI* productions restructured the stage and auditorium of the Swan. Not just the heavens but the entire theatre was 'hung with black', the familiar honey-coloured timbers of the Swan wrapped in black muslin: and the stage was extended bizarrely into the shape of a spread-eagled corpse – a move Boyd described as an 'aesthetic protest'. He replaced the Swan's Elizabethan-style thrust stage with a massive 'in the round' platform – not so much round, however, as polygonal, jagged – that cut through and divided the auditorium, so that even spaces in the gallery were invaded by the stage. Two large convex metal doors were the only onstage entrance. Action on all four sides of the galleries ensured that no one in the audience ever had anything more than a partial view of the action; sometimes bright floodlights were shone directly at different sections of the audience, making them unwilling participants in the national spectacle, an uncomfortable experience for both the watched and the watchers. For Joan's capture and York's final scene, the Swan was made claustrophobic, the sense of approaching threat an acoustic effect: from outside, actors pounded on the doors and walls, the noise running around the auditorium, escalating, accelerating, deafening. If this theatre bore any relationship to the historic Swan playhouse of Shakespeare's age, it was only as its Mr-Hyde-like double, its evil twin.

Appropriately, this re-dressing of the Swan theatre enacted a strategy of doubling that characterised the whole production. Several parts were played (in effect) by the ghosts of previous characters. History began to resemble a ride on a ghost train as zombies lumbered wide-eyed and pale about the stage and intoned lines in wretched voices. Sometimes these ghosts took on minor parts, effectively parodying the whole process of doubling required by the large-scale casts of Shakespeare's history plays. Actors did not just play two roles; they played their second role still dressed as the ghost of a previous character. Such strategies were a reminder that theatre, unlike history, exists only in the present: all of the protagonists of a history play are, in effect, ghosts. Boyd rewrote the rules for performing history plays; this England was haunted by past atrocities and by characters who continued to influence events beyond their deaths. Traumatic events refused to be trapped by the contingencies of time. Instead, they echoed through the rest of the story, shaping and defining the ensuing chaos.

More than any other event, the performances were haunted by repetitions of the Talbots' final moments, which re-enacted again and again the elder Talbot's failure to save his son. Ambushed and slain, Young Talbot swung like a butcher's carcass, suspended from the flies in a harness, his face vacant and bloody, as the old soldier, wounded, desperately tried to reach him. In *Part Two*, Young Talbot reappeared as Jourdain's Spirit, but he wore the same clothes, he was hoisted above the stage in the same way, his wounds still bled, and a ghostly Old Talbot swung his sword below, still trying to get to him. Later in the same play, Talbot became the Pirate Captain and Young Talbot was Whitmore – now the ghosts started to enact a form of historical retribution as they executed Suffolk and joined in Cade's rebellion.[2] But in *Part Three*, they lost each other again: they were the ones who played 'the father who has killed his son' and the 'son who has killed his father'. In a gut-wrenching theatrical coup, all the more uncanny for its utter simplicity, when the old man finished his speech over the corpse of what he discovered was his boy, the pair, literally embracing death, rolled over – the corpse coming alive as the live man crumpled: so Old Talbot became the dead father, and the reanimated Young Talbot grieved, recognising him killed. The scene attracted criticism from reviewers who missed its strange poetic symmetry, but, by doubling Talbot and his son with other fathers and sons, Boyd tied their story emblematically to the biggest ideas the trilogy staged, binding up in them numerous other moments of retribution, betrayal and grief across the three plays.

Despite its emphasis on death and mourning, the production was not relentlessly grim. In fact, the company performed with genuine generic ambiguity, tapping into profound emotion in some scenes, while always aware that, with evil villains cackling in the shadows and ghosts stumbling across the stage, their work bordered on Hammer Horror. Given Boyd's interest in the plays' echoes of medieval theatre, this mix of the serious and the comic is not so surprising. England's fall was dark, macabre and scary, but it was also funny as it plundered the theatrical conventions of popular drama, medieval theatre and even pantomime. The most nightmarish scenes came in the middle of *Part Two*, when a pasty Gloucester haunted the deranged Winchester on his deathbed and then when he and Winchester, both now ghosts (along with the Talbots and a comically headless Suffolk), joined in the commoners' revolt. Gloucester, *post mortem*, was impassive and silent, like a stern figure of death; but Winchester, whom Gloucester kept on a leash like a dog, joined the rabble. Cade (Jake Nightingale) was a lanky, bearded and mad agitator who scaled the walls and lorded it over the stage on a trapeze. For some, this carnivalesque image recalled Peter Brook's seminal *A Midsummer Night's Dream*, which married Shakespearean comedy with circus-style performance. In a way, Brook did haunt the production, but, in Boyd's theatre, people were beasts, not clowns, and Boyd himself described the scenes as 'more John Milton than Peter Brook' (Boyd 'Unpublished interview' n.p.).

The riot was a dark carnival, a Hallowe'en parade that owed more to popular entertainments than to political theatre. There was little in the staging that gave any insight into the reasons *why* the commoners revolted: on the contrary, the production stressed the demonic aspects of anarchy. Audiences were invited to loathe the rebels, who in turn taunted members of the audience as if they were the lords and ladies whom they hated. The scene started with Aidan McArdle and Tom Beard playing Bevis and Holland as hawkers at a fairground or baddies in a Christmas pantomime. They went out of their way to alienate the audience, railing at them as if *they* were the enemy. The actors improvised by targeting audience members and upbraiding them as the educated aristocrats Cade's rout sneers at. It was, of course, extremely funny, but the politics of this playing of the rebellion meant that it was never

[195]

going to offer a *subversive* image of history. On the contrary, it was a spectacle which deliberately recalled the shenanigans of the medieval Vice figure, entertaining the audience but also maintaining the crucial difference between the educated RSC patron and the ragged, ignorant lot onstage. The countercultural rebellion that Hands and to some extent Hall directed was not present here. Boyd even avoided the political ambiguities that underpinned Howell's, Bogdanov's and Noble's interpretations of the riot. Boyd's commoners were not oppressed, poor and disenfranchised people trying to have their voices heard; they were just plain nasty.

Cade as Vice, his rebellion as carnival, provided relief – not least by radically changing the performance tempo – for spectators who were in the theatre for the full time, nine hours, it took to play the trilogy. But the comedy was dark at its bloodstained edge. Civil war after Bosnia and Kosovo could hardly be unknowing for either spectators or actors, and Boyd's inspiration was to use these scenes to plant seeds for the next plays – the actors playing Bevis and Holland returned in the next act as Richard and Edward, in effect making the two commoners ghosts of the future, devils from a medieval pageant ready to play history at its own game. On the production's transfer to London, Boyd added an unnamed character, played by Rashan Stone, later Clarence, thus strengthening the thematic link between the commoners and York's own insurrection. Linking York with Cade's fairground rabble made the Duke a pantomime villain who emerged from the shadows with a 'mad flaw' twitching across his face. But, accompanied by his sons (familiar from the riot), dressed in black and armed with steel, York was also a villain of a different order. Both comic and vicious, York brought together the anarchy of the riot and the brutal politics of the court. The world he inhabited was literally another England, a nightmare vision of the nation haunted by the victims of history, just as the staging of English history itself was haunted by recent violence in the name of the nation state in the Balkans.

Boyd's haunted histories showed an England unable to break free from the shackles of past transgressions and caught in a cycle of dynastic ambition in which the integrity of bloodlines was called into question. With the theatre itself taking on a role in this strange double of the nation, and the audience cast as, variously, mourners and aristocrats facing Cade's rioters, there was a clear implication that the theatre – maybe even the RSC itself – was not a passive spectator, but a participant in this tragedy of nation. Indeed, one image went even further: when audiences left the Swan theatre, they had to step over a large pool of blood left by Henry's murder, as if the 'national' theatre itself was bleeding. Was it England, or the RSC itself, that was hurt? In 2004, looking back on this period, Boyd described the RSC then as an 'unhappy company' suffering from a 'gradual erosion of faith in the very primitive driving impulses behind the founding of the RSC' (Boyd 'Unpublished interview' n.p.). The productions' strangely resistant approach to the nation may, after all, have been more about the 'State of the RSC' than the 'State of the Nation'.

Hissing-red: Joan and Margaret

As well as bringing together mourning, murder and war, blood (red and black) in the production was forcefully associated with sexual sadism. Violence was not only brutal, it could be erotic, too. In the 1970s, Terry Hands had been the first to recognise the importance of the plays' sexual politics, but Boyd went further by inscribing a dark eroticism at the heart of the cycle, based not on the sex appeal of an actress like Helen Mirren (who played a sensuous Margaret in Terry Hands's productions) but on a deviant obsession with violently mistreated bodies. It sometimes seemed as if political ambition were merely a symptom for some kind of barely containable, irrational impulse to violate other people. This connection was made during Joan's trial and execution, staged with Joan bound to a ladder and hoisted over the trapdoor that slowly opened, discovering hell just beneath England's brittle surface. Up to this point, *The War Against France* had been a war play; but now the whole drama came down to York's persecution of a trapped woman. Joan had already made a mocking pass at York when, earlier in the same scene, seeming to yield to capture, she leaped at him like a tiger for the jugular, wrapped her legs around his body and forced a kiss on to his lips, and he recoiled, spitting the kiss off and rubbing his polluted mouth. Now, suspended over the abyss, with every turn she made to resist her captors sending the ladder swinging sickeningly, Joan pleaded her belly to escape burning. 'The holy maid with child?' shrilled mocking York. As he spoke, he jumped across the pit and on to the bottom rung of the ladder, pressing his body against hers; then, cool, arch, scientific, he slowly pushed his dagger under her skirts, up between her legs, twisted it, brought it out again and inspected its tip, covered with blood.

14 *The Chaos* (2000). A battle-scarred York (Clive Wood) bargains with Henry VI
(David Oyelowo)

Was this blood from the virgin's hymen it had just penetrated and,
ironically, spoiled? Or from the foetus it had just aborted? 'And
yet', York feigned hurt protest, reaching under her clothes, 'she is
a virgin pure!' When he pulled away, he held a handful of blood.

The episode looked backwards and forwards to place both Joan
and York in a psychosexual construction of rebellion. York was
predatory and possibly mad, his face twitching as he fantasised
about power; and Joan, too, was driven by a bitter sense of disempowerment that contextualised her battlefield bravado. Abandoned
by her compatriots and pleading with her demons to give her one
more victory, Joan ripped away the twisted cloth that bandaged
her wrists to expose the deep scars across her veins – evidence
that she had, indeed, fed her 'familiar spirits' 'with my blood', with
'blood-sacrifice' or had attempted self-slaughter. Joan's power, it
seemed, was an appalling form of self-harm.

York was deviant not just politically, but sexually as well: he
enjoyed abusing Joan. Dressed in black, his corpse-white hair
cropped, his demeanour frighteningly focused, Clive Wood called
to mind a shared cultural memory (or stereotype) of the Nazi as

sexual sadist, whose fantasies, identified and studied by Klaus Theweleit, share qualities evident in this York's attitude to Joan: as Theweleit has shown, many Nazi soldiers fantasised about the 'proletarian woman as monster', a 'fantastic being who swears, shrieks, spits, scratches, farts, bites, pounces, tears to shreds; who is slovenly, wind-whipped, hissing-red, indecent' (Theweleit 67). Indeed, Fiona Bell brought out Joan's proletarian character by playing her in her native working-class Scots accent – another aspect of the cycle's 'devolution' of national culture, but also an indication of class that placed this shrieking, spitting, indecent monster within the frame of York's own extreme fantasies. Theweleit is quick to point out that such Nazi imaginings have little to do with reality: rather, the threat posed by the sexually active proletarian woman was a function of some unnameable horror feared by Nazi soldiers (70). Read in this light, Joan acts more as an exposé of York's delusions than as an appraisal of the peasant girl turned warrior: it is as if spectators see Joan only from York's point of view. When York pulled his hand from under Joan's dress, his mocking smile was a triumph, the blood representing his ability to conquer the unnameable horror and subject it to the penetration-logic of the battlefield; and, lowering Joan into the pit, York buried that horror deep below the surface of consciousness.

Joan had already placed herself in a narrative of sexual possession that only now made sense. During her fight with the Dauphin, she was losing, when behind her appeared three women, dressed gorgeously in red crushed velvet. Boyd's innovation, these 'demons', as they were identified in the promptbook, mimicked Joan's actions – or rather, their parallel play *directed* them and tripled her feminine power. The conceit raised the stakes in the fight, intensifying its violent eroticism as if it were segueing into a deviant form of courtship. When Joan, a warrior woman in skirts, beat the Dauphin to his knees and then, locked in a clinch, struggled with him on the ground, he finished on top, but even as he proclaimed himself her 'thrall', he reached for her crotch (foreshadowing the 'abortion' later on). Joan won the local combat, but the Dauphin won the juicier prize, the sexual trophy: this Joan would never be chaste or saintly.

Joan's 'demons' were like repressed memories, haunting her and giving her a peculiar kind of strength. They joined Joan again when she fought Talbot, helping to trap him with their swords before letting him go. And they also played a role in the conversion of Burgundy, which was performed as another kind of seduction, another kind of deviant wooing. As Joan enticed him, the demon-women stood about the stage and discordantly echoed her invocation to 'come, come' – itself, perhaps, a sexual pun disclosing the erotic dimension of Burgundy's transgression. The power of these women was also linked to sexual desire in the Countess of Auvergne's house, when (now wearing blue) they became the Countess's handmaidens and with her tried to seduce Talbot, suggesting a continuity between Joan's power and the Countess's. But Talbot's easy victory made for a poor foreshadowing of York's much darker and difficult triumph over Joan. The women reappeared a final time, back in their red costumes, to desert Joan. But then, in a stunning *coup de théâtre*, seconds after she was executed as Joan, Fiona Bell ran back on to the stage, transformed, dressed in red velvet like Joan's vanished demons, fused with them in a new role: Margaret.

This latest French woman was also, initially, shaped by obsession and infatuation. For Henry, Margaret was little more than an idealised vision of femininity, an idea Boyd literalised by introducing Margaret to Henry as a living picture. A large gilt frame descended from the flies with the young princess stood, frozen, within it. Henry was immediately drawn to the image and kept his eyes on her as he talked to Gloucester, looking but not touching. This established a physical distance between Henry and Margaret, with only the suggestion of an unfulfilled sexuality in the King that would come to characterise the choreography of their relationship in the subsequent plays. Henry was both already under her spell and yet unable to comprehend her as anything other than a strange presence dropped from the heavens. Either way, from this moment on Margaret owned the stage: she remained in the frame as Suffolk gave the final speech of *Part One*, but after he left, Margaret stepped out of the painting and walked confidently across the empty stage, leaving the lights to fade on the still-glowing picture frame. This theatrical coup established Margaret's importance and her mysterious ability to inhabit different worlds. Even Suffolk, the Machiavel who tries to capture the story at the end of the play with his bid for power, had that story usurped: Margaret claimed the end of the play and the territory of the stage as her own, a territory Joan had fought for and lost.

Having first contemplated Margaret as a picture of aesthetic beauty, Henry never fully understood the true complexity of her character. Where he wavered in the face of York's revolt, Margaret captured the spirit early embodied by Joan. She broke out of the frame of the demure wife implied by the living picture, just as she broke out of the frame of history by becoming a general and leading an army. Boyd stressed that he wanted the relationship between Margaret and Henry to be a genuinely loving one, pointing out that Margaret only ever criticises Henry in *Part Two* when she is with Suffolk. Boyd and Bell avoided caricaturing Margaret. She was no apprentice version of Lady Macbeth, as Sir Barry Jackson once presumed. Bell's Margaret was both a force of history and a woman fighting for her family.

Yet she was also, in *Parts One* and *Two*, sexually active and unable to be satisfied by the voyeuristic sexual immaturity of Henry. With Suffolk, Margaret found a different kind of love – and one that, under Boyd's direction, hinted at a more transgressive sexual relationship than is usually staged. For example, in an early scene in *Part Two* (*England's Fall*), Margaret and Suffolk were apparently aroused by their confrontation with the commoners. In fact, Bell's Margaret went further than the written text by not only tearing up the petition against Suffolk but also dragging the poor commoner across the stage. With the commoners gone, the pair embraced and kissed, clearly enjoying their sadistic behaviour, and broke their embrace only as the court filed in, risking everything until the last possible minute. In their last scene together, Margaret stood some distance away from Suffolk, her back to him, while he railed at his misfortune. Margaret evoked some pity from the audience, but Suffolk was nothing more than a lunatic. In her next scene, the relationship turned macabre as Margaret stood in a doorway cradling Suffolk's head while Henry paced the stage. (Strangely, it really *was* Suffolk's head. The effect was achieved by dressing both actors in black and placing them against a black background, Suffolk kneeling, his body disappearing into Margaret's dress as she caressed what looked like his decapitated head.)

Boyd continued to explore Margaret's sadistic eroticism in her relationship with York, who had already shown how vicious he could be in *Part One* (*The War Against France*). Boyd created an interesting rhyme by, in effect, replaying York's capture, torture and execution of Joan – with the roles reversed. Bell's performance in both roles strengthened the notion that York, in his final death scene, paid the price for that earlier transgression. After Tewkesbury, alone onstage, York was hemmed in by an army whose approach was terrifyingly represented by deafening pounding around the perimeter walls, as if the theatre itself were finally closing in on him. In this direct recollection of Joan's final scene, Margaret was the force of historical retribution; Rutland's blood smeared on York's face remembered Joan's blood on York's hands; and his final humiliating death, railing (as Joan had done) against the barbarity of his captors, served to underline the hollowness of York's ambitions.

Exploring the metaphysics of Shakespeare's 'order of things', Boyd's trilogy refused to allow spectators to see Shakespeare's history in terms of a modern, rationalist, materialist world that informs, underpins and writes the modern national self. Rather, it showed spectators a disconcertingly strange vision of national history. There was no 'us' in this history – *we* were not affirmed, celebrated, or comforted by actors performing these roles, speaking these lines. It was an unusual choice Boyd (and the RSC) made to mark the millennium with such a problematic representation of the nation and perhaps also of itself. While spectators were on one level fully engaged by the artfulness of the spectacle, on another, Boyd's productions insistently divorced spectators from a sense of recognition or identification with *this* England. The master-narrative of 'This England' was the very postmodern reflection that there are no master-narratives any more, and the *Henry VI* plays destabilised this national identity by portraying the nightmare of a world that has surrendered to 'The Chaos'. In this respect, the zombies and demons who stalked the stage suggested a view of history shaped by the irrational and the unexplainable; in the main characters, too, the performances focused on madness and irrational sexual transgression. Ironically, for a production so rooted in an understanding of the plays' medievalism, the last word was 'Now!', spat out by crookbacked Richard and triggering the final blackout. It was as if, after nine hours of relentless black comedy, Boyd wanted to turn it all back on the audience, to remind them that these plays had staged their history, their England, after all.

APPENDIX

Major actors and staff for productions discussed in this volume

The Shakespeare Memorial Theatre, Stratford-upon-Avon, 1889
Henry VI Part One

Director: Osmond Tearle   Script: Charles Flower

Henry VI	Erskine Lewis	*Gloucester*	Robert H. Owen
Bedford	Hewitson Porter	*Warwick*	Herbert Sheridan
Margaret	Ellen Cranston	*Talbot*	Osmond Tearle
Burgundy	Dermot O'Neill	*Winchester*	Phillip Gordon
York	Edwin Lever	*Dauphin*	F. B. Conway
Joan	Mary Kingsley	*Suffolk*	A. Clifton Alderson

The Shakespeare Memorial Theatre, Stratford-upon-Avon, 1906
Henry VI Part One, Part Two and Part Three

Director: Frank Benson   Script: Frank Benson

Henry VI	George Buchanan	*Gloucester*	H. O. Nicholson
Richard	Frank Benson	*Warwick*	B. A. Pittar
Margaret	Constance Benson	*Talbot*	Frank Benson
Edward IV	H. O. Nicholson	*Winchester*	Frank Benson
York	Clarence Derwent	*Cade*	C. A. Doran
Joan	Tita Brand	*Suffolk*	Cyril Keightley

The Birmingham Repertory Theatre, Birmingham, 1953
Henry VI Part One, Part Two and Part Three

Director: Douglas Seale   Script: Sir Barry Jackson

Henry VI	Jack May	*Gloucester*	Edgar Wreford
Richard	Paul Daneman	*Warwick*	Bernard Hepton
Margaret	Rosalind Boxall	*Talbot*	Alan Bridges
Edward IV	Alan Bridges	*Winchester*	Alfred Burke
York	John Arnatt	*Cade*	William Avenall
Joan	Nancie Jackson	*Suffolk*	Richard Pasco

The British Broadcasting Company, London, 1960

An Age of Kings (Episodes 9–13)

Director: Michael Hayes   Adaptation: Peter Dews

Henry VI	Terry Scully	*Gloucester*	John Ringham
Richard	Paul Daneman	*Warwick*	Frank Windsor
Margaret	Mary Morris	*Duchess of*	
Edward IV	Julian Glover	*Gloucester*	Nancie Jackson
York	Jack May	*Winchester*	Robert Lang
Joan	Eileen Atkins	*Cade*	Esmond Knight
		Suffolk	Edgar Wreford

The Royal Shakespeare Company, Stratford and London, 1963–64

The Wars of the Roses: Henry VI and Edward IV

Director: Peter Hall, John Barton and Clifford Williams
Adaptation: John Barton

Henry VI	David Warner	*Gloucester*	Paul Hardwick
Richard	Ian Holm	*Warwick*	Brewster Mason
Margaret	Peggy Ashcroft	*Talbot*	Clive Morton
Edward IV	Roy Dotrice	*Winchester*	Nicholas Selby
York	Donald Sinden	*Cade*	Clive Swift
Joan	Janet Suzman	*Suffolk*	William Squire

The Royal Shakespeare Company, Stratford-upon-Avon, 1977–78

Henry VI Parts One, Two and Three

Director: Terry Hands
Full Text

Henry VI	Alan Howard	*Gloucester*	Graham Crowden
Richard	Anton Lesser	*Warwick*	Julian Glover
Margaret	Helen Mirren	*Talbot*	David Swift
Edward IV	Alfred Lynch	*Winchester*	John Rhys-Davies
York	Emrys James	*Cade*	James Laurenson
Joan	Charlotte Cornwell	*Suffolk*	Peter McEnery

The British Broadcasting Company, 1981–83

Henry VI Parts I, II and III

Director: Jane Howell
Full Text

Henry VI	Peter Benson	*Gloucester*	David Burke
Richard	Ron Cook	*Warwick*	Mark Wing-Davey
Margaret	Julia Foster	*Talbot*	Trevor Peacock
Edward IV	Brian Protheroe	*Winchester*	Frank Middlemass
York	Bernard Hill	*Cade*	Trevor Peacock
Joan	Brenda Blethyn	*Suffolk*	Paul Chapman

The English Shakespeare Company, Touring, 1987–88

Henry VI: House of Lancaster and *Henry VI: House of York*

Director: Michael Bogdanov
Adaptation: Michael Bogdanov and Company

Henry VI	Paul Brennan	*Gloucester*	Colin Farrell
Richard	Andrew Jarvis	*Warwick*	Michael Cronin
Margaret	June Watson	*Talbot*	Michael Fenner
Edward	Phillip Bowen	*Winchester*	Clyde Pollitt
York	John Castle/	*Cade*	Michael Pennington
	Barry Stanton	*Suffolk*	Chris Hunter/
Joan	Mary Rutherford/		Michael Pennington
	Francesca Ryan		

The Royal Shakespeare Company, Stratford and London, 1988–1990

The Plantagenets: Henry VI and *The Rise of Edward IV*

Director: Adrian Noble   Adaptation: Adrian Noble and Company

Henry VI	Ralph Fiennes	*Gloucester*	David Waller
Richard	Anton Lesser	*Warwick*	David Lyon
Margaret	Penny Downie	*Talbot*	Robert Demeger
Edward IV	Ken Bones	*Winchester*	Antony Brown
York	David Calder	*Cade*	Oliver Cotton
Joan	Julia Ford	*Suffolk*	Oliver Cotton

The Royal Shakespeare Company, Touring, 1994–95

Henry VI – The Battle for the Throne

Director: Katie Mitchell   Adaptation: Katie Mitchell

Henry VI	Jonathan Firth	*Grey*	Liz Kettle
Richard	Tom Smith	*Clifford*	Jamie Hinde
Margaret	Ruth Mitchell	*Warwick*	John Keegan
Edward IV	Owen Lloyd	*George*	Jo Stone-Fewings
York	Stephen Simms	*Exeter*	Chris Garner

**The Royal Shakespeare Company, Stratford, London
and Michigan, 2000–1**

*Part One: The War Against France, Part Two: England's Fall,
Part Three: The Chaos*

Director: Michael Boyd
Full Text

Henry VI	David Oyelowo	*Gloucester*	Richard Cordery
Richard	Aidan McArdle	*Warwick*	Geoff Francis
Margaret	Fiona Bell	*Talbot*	Keith Bartlett
Edward IV	Tom Beard	*Winchester*	Christopher Ettridge
York	Clive Wood	*Cade*	Jake Nightingale
Joan	Fiona Bell	*Suffolk*	Richard Dillane

NOTES

Introduction

1 Post-fascist Europe was also explored in the Italian director Giorgio Strehler's free adaptation *Il gioco dei potenti* (1965) (usually translated as *Power Games* or *The Game of the Mighty*). Strehler's adaptation added some powerful images to Shakespeare's text. For example, the production began with Henry's coronation but the crown was too heavy for Henry, here played by a child, and so it was placed back on a shrine close by to Henry V's bier. As the child left the stage, an adult Henry VI entered 'with the same posture, in the same dress' (Director's Note – here and throughout this discussion I have drawn heavily on Christian Jauslin's remarkably vivid account of the production's promptbook in his essay 'The Game of the Powerful'). Strehler mixed *Henry VI* with elements from Shakespeare's more well-known works. *Macbeth* was invoked when Strehler depicted the Duchess of Gloucester sleepwalking. Two gravediggers appeared in several scenes based on *Hamlet* and *King John*. In one strikingly absurdist alteration, the battles in France were staged as a play-within-a-play performed by a touring company before the King, echoing both *A Midsummer Night's Dream* and *Hamlet*.
2 There have been many productions of the plays, most coming out of the United States's rich festival circuit, where the plays have usually been staged to complete a cycle of Shakespeare's canon. Ashland, Colorado, Antioch, the Great Lakes, New Jersey, Champlain and Los Angeles have all produced one *Henry VI* or more, as has Stratford Ontario in Canada. The most exceptional have been in Ashland for the Oregon Shakespeare Festival where *Henry VI* has been staged several times both in Ashland's remarkable recreation of an Elizabethan playhouse and in its well-equipped modern studios.

Chapter II

1 For more on Nugent Monck, I recommend Franklin J. Hildy's excellent *Shakespeare at the Maddermarket*.
2 The nursery rhyme is medieval in origin; the Lion and the Unicorn (which marries the heraldic symbols of England and Scotland) was designed for James I, to serve as the symbol of his project to unify Great Britain.
3 In the 1957 revival at the Old Vic, Barbara Jefford played Margaret and made an equally memorable warrior-queen, adding an extra dimension of 'vulnerability and humour' (Martin 87).

Chapter III

1 Barton's 'fakes', wrote Roger Gellert in *The New Statesman* (22 July 1963) were 'invisible, I'd swear, to all but the most obsessional scholar. I jotted several fishy-sounding lines down on my programme; they all turned out to be genuine Bard.'

2 Given a try-out in *The Tempest* earlier in the season, 'gunk' revolutionised some aspects of costume design but didn't make older technologies entirely redundant. For as *The Birmingham Post* reported on 27 June 1963, 'The women who work in the Royal Shakespeare Theatre ... have a curious occupation for their spare moments. Twenty-one of them, from Dame Peggy Ashcroft to the office secretaries, are knitting balls of butcher's string into 5ft-long strips.' Painted silver, the knitting looked like chain-mail – one of the oldest theatrical dodges for making actor-friendly armour.

3 The part, originally played by Michael Craig, was recast for the quatercentenary season and the television film. I use Squires's performance because it is the one students can consult in the BBC film, a copy of which is held in the RSC's archives in Stratford-upon-Avon.

4 The part was originally played by John Welsh. Hardwick's performance is preserved on film in the RSC's archives, Stratford-upon-Avon.

5 The part was originally played by Derek Smith. Swift's performance is preserved on film in the RSC's archives, Stratford-upon-Avon.

Chapter IV

1 Hands's aim, he said, was to present the trilogy 'without any reshaping, without any tailoring, without any adapting – in fact with less than we would do with any other productions'. He wanted 'to put it all very crudely, very naively down on the stage – everything that was there, warts and all' (quoted in Swander 148–9). His ambitions have consistently been read by academic writers on these productions after the event as textually 'naive'. For Barbara Hodgdon in *The Ends Crowns All*, Hands's 'expressed trust' in the plays' 'alleged capacity to speak for themselves ... shares the naïveté Hands ascribes to the plays' (82); for Robert Shaughnessy in *Representing Shakespeare*, it demonstrated Hands's 'avowed policy of textual *laissez-faire*' (66–9). At the time, however, Hands's intent to 'trust Shakespeare' was actually a deep-dyed Machiavel's innocent-seeming subterfuge. Invoking 'Shakespeare' to his project, Hands was manoeuvring like a politically astute Hermione appealing to Delphi in *The Winter's Tale*, effectively casting the perennial debate about authorship, adaptation, cutting and rewriting – a debate whose theatrical authority was, of course, John Barton – into a higher court, beyond mere mortal judgment, most critics having forgotten that Hall and Barton had described their own project of adaptation as perpetrating 'the ultimate literary heresy' (Hall and Barton vii).

2 To begin with, Alan Howard was deeply reluctant to take the part. Eventually Hands persuaded him by promising him Coriolanus later that season. To make absolutely sure that Hands wouldn't 'forget' the deal, Howard, in the border scene in *Part Three* (III.i, Scene 62) sat cross-legged on the stage studying a book – an octodecimo edition of *Coriolanus*.

3 See Beauman 340. Rehearsals began in April 1977; the press nights were 12, 13 and 14 July. My citations refer to the texts used by this production, the three parts of *Henry VI* edited by G. B. Harrison for the Penguin series in 1959. I cite also the scene numbers from the promptbook, which will give readers a better sense of the whole performance project.

4 In conversation, April 2002. This comment perhaps modifies Hodgdon's critical judgments in *The End Crowns All* that Hands's performance text 'risks masking political analysis with aesthetics by presenting history as a pictorial discourse', and that, while 'there is no denying the success and value of his project, its mannered representational strategies tend, perhaps inevitably, toward what might be called an archaeology of mystification' (87).

Chapter V

1 Critics have been divided over whether the *Henry VI–Richard III* sequence was the most 'theatrical' or the most 'televisual' episode in the BBC Shakespeare. Stanley Wells, Neil Taylor and Graham Holderness all admire the way in which Howell translated Shakespeare into television. However, Michèle Willems, Hardy Cook and Dennis Bingham argue that Howell's Brechtian stylisations emphasised the theatrical over the naturalistic conventions of most television drama.

2 Snow was used for these scenes also in *The Wars of the Roses* (1963) and *Henry VI – The Battle for the Throne* (1994).

3 Harry Fenwick made a similar observation that the battlements were 'equally images of modernity and shadows of a medieval castle' (Fenwick *Part One* 24).

4 See Willis 63 for a full account of the debacle. Willis described the final product as the 'nadir' of the Shakespeare series in America.

Chapter VI

1 The main sources for this discussion of the ESC productions are the films shot by Bogdanov in Swansea towards the end of the tour and subsequently released on video. The cycle went through many changes during its two-year tour; the Swansea performances were at the end of the run and so represent the cycle in its 'finished' state. Nevertheless, some details which I build my interpretation on may clash with readers' own memories of the performances that they attended: tracking every change would have been an unwieldy task. Unfortunately, the Swansea productions were not filmed from a fixed point of view: rather, Bogdanov wanted to make a film out of the stage performance and so introduced filmic devices including close-ups that make it difficult to see what an audience would be seeing. These close-ups and some battle scenes were filmed during the afternoon and edited into the film of the live performance. Because it was a live performance, some of the scenes were not filmed satisfactorily and were cut in the final edit – in the videos, sudden cuts in the soundtrack are clues to where these edits were made. In particular, the important scene between York and Mortimer was cut entirely from the film of *House of Lancaster*,

even though it was performed. Despite these problems, the videos remain the best record of the detail, design and ambition of the ESC productions. The promptbooks, held by the Theatre Museum, were also consulted, and I have made use of a number of reviews and critical studies, as well as my own memories of the cycle, to supplant what is available on video.

2   The radical agenda and subversive style of the ESC productions have attracted a number of academic studies. Barbara Hodgdon and Lois Potter discuss the *Henry VI* plays specifically, both drawing attention to the representation of gender, whilst Jackson, Armstrong, Manheim and Hattaway look more generally at the ESC project, its politics and its reception. The best work on the ESC is, however, Bogdanov and Pennington's own memoir of *The Wars of the Roses*.

3   Hodgdon recalls that, as they dragged Joan offstage, one of the soldiers started unbuttoning his trousers. This had been cut by the time of the Swansea performances.

Chapter VII

1   This gave rise to the unique credit in the programme, 'based on an adaptation by Charles Wood'. *The Plantagenets* is then an adaptation of an adaptation of *Henry VI*.

2   The 'trench' was the same space that Henry V's coffin had been lowered into at the start of the performance.

3   In the first performances, Joan was raised on top of a pyre built around the cell used for Mortimer's (and later Henry's) incarceration, i.e. the actress actually sat on the English throne, although this was obscured.

Chapter VIII

1   It is often said that Mitchell's script included materials from *Part Two* but this is not the case. This misunderstanding arose because of an early press release which announced the then forthcoming production as an adaptation of *Part Two* and *Part Three* at a time when Mitchell was still insisting that *Part Three* could be staged as a play in its own right. Mitchell's final script did contain small additions from *Richard III* and several non-Shakespeare plays, but nothing from *Part Two*.

2   In fact, it was only under pressure from the RSC that Mitchell staged Shakespeare at all. Her original intention for her civil war production was to stage Euripides' *The Phoenician Women* (which she directed the following season) but the RSC insisted that the production be Shakespearean. Mitchell thought of *Macbeth*, but Adrian Noble was already planning a production; then she dallied briefly with *Richard II* and resisted pressure to take on *Romeo and Juliet*. Apparently, her initial suggestion to stage *Part Three* was greeted with laughter.

3   Mitchell originally intended to end the production with Henry's body laid out on a table in the centre of the stage, watched by Edward's court. The actors would have left the stage, leaving Richard alone, sitting on the arm of the throne, and looking in horror as the corpse started to bleed.

Chapter IX

1 The practice of colour-blind casting has been unevenly instituted at the RSC, and the *Henry VI*s were the only productions in the cycle really to embrace it in a positive way. Boyd has himself been one of the leading advocates of a Peter-Brook-style multi-ethnic cast. One of his productions, *A Midsummer Night's Dream* (1999), blended African theatre styles with Western forms.

2 In one of Boyd's few substantial alterations, Suffolk's death was rewritten to bring out the workings of prophecy and retribution. Rather than play with Shakespeare's pun on 'water', Walter engulfed Suffolk in a sea of blue cloth brought out of the main door – into which Suffolk strode, laughing.

BIBLIOGRAPHY

Addenbrooke, David. *The Royal Shakespeare Company: The Peter Hall Years*. London: Kimber, 1974.

Allain, Paul. *Gardzienice: Polish Theatre in Transition*. London and New York: Routledge, 1997.

—— unpublished correspondence with Stuart Hampton-Reeves, 2004.

Armstrong, Isobel. 'Thatcher's Shakespeare?' *Textual Practice* 3 (1989). 1–14.

Ashcroft, Peggy. 'Margaret of Anjou.' *Deutsche Shakespeare-Gesellschaft West Jahrbuch* (1974). 7–9.

Barrault, Jean-Louis. *Memories for Tomorrow: The Memoirs of Jean-Louis Barrault*. Trans. Jonathan Griffin. London: Thames and Hudson, 1974.

Beauman, Sally. *The Royal Shakespeare Company: A History of Ten Decades*. Oxford: Oxford University Press, 1982.

Benjamin, Walter. *Illuminations*. Trans. Harry Zohn. New York: Knopf Publishing Group, 1969.

Bingham, Dennis. 'Jane Howell's First Tetralogy: Brechtian Break-Out or Just Good Television?' In Bulman and Coursen, eds. 221–9.

Bloom, Harold. *Shakespeare: The Invention of the Human*. London: Fourth Estate, 1999.

Bogdanov, Michael and Michael Pennington. *The English Shakespeare Company: The Story of The Wars of the Roses, 1986–1989*. London: Nick Hern Books, 1990.

Booth, Stephen. 'Shakespeare in California, 1974–75.' *Shakespeare Quarterly* 27.1 (Winter 1976). 94–108.

Boyd, Michael. Unpublished interview with Stuart Hampton-Reeves, 2001.

Brandow, Elizabeth S. C. 'History, Royal or English: A Study of the Royal Shakespeare Company's *The Plantagenets* and the English Shakespeare Company's *The Wars of the Roses*.' Unpublished M.A. dissertation, University of Birmingham, 1989.

Brown, John Russell. *Free Shakespeare*. London: Heinemann, 1974.

Bulman, James C. 'The BBC Shakespeare and "House Style".' *Shakespeare Quarterly* 35 (1984). 571–81.

—— and H. R. Coursen, eds. *Shakespeare on Television: An Anthology of Essays and Reviews*. Hanover and London: University Press of New England, 1988.

Burden, Dennis. 'Shakespeare's History Plays 1952–1983.' *Shakespeare Survey* 38 (1985). 1–18.

Chambers, E. K. *The Elizabethan Stage*. Vols. 1–4. Oxford: Clarendon Press, 1923.
—— *William Shakespeare: A Study of Facts and Problems*. Vols. 1–2. Oxford: Clarendon Press, 1930
Cook, Hardy. 'Jane Howell's BBC First Tetralogy: Theatrical and Televisual Manipulations.' *Literature and Film Quarterly* 20.4 (1992). 326–31.
Coursen, H. R. *Reading Shakespeare Onstage*. Newark: University of Delaware, 1995.
Cox, John D. and Eric Rasmussen, eds. *King Henry VI Part Three*. Arden Shakespeare 3rd Series. London: Arden Shakespeare, 2001.
Crosse, Gordon. *Shakespearean Playgoing 1890–1952*. London: Mowbray, 1953.
Daniell, David. 'Opening Up the Text: Shakespeare's *Henry VI* Plays in Performance.' *Themes in Drama* (1979). 247–77.
Dayan, Daniel and Elihu Katz. *Media Events: The Live Broadcasting of History*. Cambridge, Massachusetts: Harvard University Press, 1992.
Déprats, Jean-Michel. 'Shakespeare in France.' *Shakespeare Quarterly* 32 (Autumn 1981). 390–92.
Derrida, Jacques. *Specters of Marx: State of the Debt, the Work of Mourning and the New International*. Trans. Peggy Kamuf. London and New York: Routledge, 1994.
Dessen, Alan C. 'Shakespeare's Scripts and the Modern Director.' *Shakespeare Survey* 36 (1983). 57–64.
—— *Recovering Shakespeare's Theatrical Vocabulary*. Cambridge: Cambridge University Press, 1995.
Downie, Penny. 'Queen Margaret in *Henry VI* and *Richard III*'. In Smallwood, ed. 1993. 114–39.
Eddy, Paul and Magnus Linklater with Peter Gillman. *The Falklands War*. London: Sphere, 1982.
Ellis, John. *Visible Fictions: Cinema, Television, Video*. London and New York: Routledge, 1992.
Elson, John and Nicholas Tomalin. *The History of the National Theatre*. London: Jonathan Cape, 1978.
Fenwick, Harry. 'The Production.' In John Wilders, ed. *The BBC-TV Shakespeare: Henry VI Part One*. London: BBC Books, 1983. 21–31.
—— 'The Production.' In John Wilders, ed. *The BBC-TV Shakespeare: Henry VI Part Two*. London: BBC Books, 1983. 18–29.
—— 'The Production.' In John Wilders, ed. *The BBC-TV Shakespeare: Henry VI Part Three*. London: BBC Books, 1983. 20–31.
Foulkes, Richard. *Performing Shakespeare in the Age of Empire*. Cambridge: Cambridge University Press, 2002.
Fukuyama, Francis. *The End of History and the Last Man*. New York: Free Press, 1992.

Gore-Langton, Robert. 'The Plantagenets.' *Plays and Players* 421 (October 1988). 8–10.

Hall, Peter and John Barton. *The Wars of the Roses*. London: BBC, 1970.

Hampton-Reeves, Stuart. 'Alarums and Defeats: *Henry VI* on Tour.' *Early Modern Literary Studies* 5.2 (September 1999). 1.1–18. URL: http://purl.oclc.org/emls/05–2/hampalar.htm

Hattaway, Michael. 'Shakespeare's Histories: The Politics of Recent British Productions.' In Hattaway et al., eds. *Shakespeare in the New Europe*. Sheffield: Sheffield University Press, 1994. 351–69.

—— ed. *The First Part of King Henry VI*. New Cambridge Shakespeare. Cambridge: Cambridge University Press, 1990.

—— ed. *The Second Part of King Henry VI*. New Cambridge Shakespeare. Cambridge: Cambridge University Press, 1991.

—— ed. *The Third Part of King Henry VI*. New Cambridge Shakespeare. Cambridge: Cambridge University Press, 1990.

Hildy, Franklin J. *Shakespeare at the Maddermarket: Nugent Monck and the Norwich Players*. Ann Arbor, Michigan: University of Michigan, 1986.

Hinchcliffe, Judith, *King Henry VI, Parts One, Two, and Three: An Annotated Bibliography*. New York: Garland, 1984.

Hirsch, Foster. 'The New York Shakespeare Festival 1970.' *Shakespeare Quarterly* 21.4 (Autumn 1970). 477–80.

Hodgdon, Barbara. *The End Crowns All: Closure and Contradiction in Shakespeare's History Plays*. Princeton: Princeton University Press, 1991.

—— 'Making it New: Katie Mitchell Refashions Shakespeare-History.' In Marianne Novy, ed. *Transforming Shakespeare: Contemporary Women's Re-visions in Literature and Performance*. London: Palgrave, 1999.

Holderness, Graham, 'Radical Potentiality and Institutional Closure: Shakespeare in Film and Television.' In Sinfield and Dollimore, eds. 206–25.

—— *Shakespeare Recycled: The Making of Historical Drama*. London and New York: Harvester Wheatsheaf, 1992.

—— '"What ish my Nation?" Shakespeare and National Identities.' *Textual Practice* 5 (Spring 1991). 80–99.

Holland, Peter. *English Shakespeares*. Cambridge: Cambridge University Press, 1997.

Honan, Park. *Shakespeare: A Life*. Oxford: Oxford University Press, 1998.

Hortmann,Wilhelm. *Shakespeare on the German Stage: The Twentieth Century*. Cambridge: Cambridge University Press, 1998.

Howard, Jean and Phyllis Rackin. *Engendering the Nation: A Feminist Account of Shakespeare's English Histories*. London and New York: Routledge, 1997.

Innes, Christopher. *Modern German Drama: A Study in Form.* Cambridge: Cambridge University Press, 1979.

Jackson, Sir Barry. 'On Producing *Henry VI.*' *Shakespeare Survey* 6 (1953). 49–52.

Jackson, MacD. P. '*The Wars of the Roses*: The English Shakespeare Company on Tour.' *Shakespeare Quarterly* 40 (1989). 208–11.

Jameson, Fredric. *Postmodernism, or The Cultural Logic of Late Capitalism.* London and New York: Verso, 1991.

Jauslin, Christian. 'The Game of the Powerful: Giorgio Strehler's Adaptation of *Henry VI.*' *Deutsche Shakespeare-Gesellschaft West Jahrbuch* 112 (1976). 15–22.

Jenkins, Harold. 'Shakespeare's History Plays: 1900–1951.' *Shakespeare Survey* 6 (1953). 1–15.

Joughin, John J. *Shakespeare and National Culture.* Manchester: Manchester University Press, 1997.

Kennedy, Dennis. *Foreign Shakespeare.* Cambridge: Cambridge University Press, 1993.

Knowles, Ronald ed. *King Henry VI, Part Two.* Arden Shakespeare 3rd Series. London: Arden Shakespeare, 1999.

Kott, Jan. *Shakespeare Our Contemporary.* Trans. Boleslaw Taborski. London: Methuen, 1965.

Leiter, Samuel L. ed. *Shakespeare Around the Globe: A Guide to Notable Postwar Revivals.* London: Greenwood Press, 1986.

Lesser, Anton. 'Richard of Gloucester in *Henry VI* and *Richard III*'. In Smallwood, ed. 1993. 140–57.

Manheim, Michael. 'The English History Play on Screen.' In Anthony Davies and Stanley Wells, eds. *Shakespeare and the Moving Image.* Cambridge: Cambridge University Press, 1994. 121–45.

Martin, Randall. *King Henry VI, Part Three.* Oxford World Classics. Oxford: Oxford University Press, 2001.

Meštrović, Stjepan G. *Postemotional Society.* London: Sage, 1996.

Mitchell, Katie. Unpublished interview with Stuart Hampton-Reeves, 1994.

Myers, Norman J. 'Finding "a Heap of Jewels" in "Lesser" Shakespeare: The Wars of the Roses and Richard Duke of York.' *New England Theatre Journal* 7 (1996). 95–107.

Nashe, Thomas. *The Works of Thomas Nashe.* R. B. McKerrow, ed. F. P. Wilson, rev. 5 vols. Oxford: Blackwell, 1958.

Nichols, Nina da Vinci. '*Henry VI.*' *Shakespeare Bulletin* 15.2 (Spring 1997). 10–12.

Nietzsche, Friedrich. *Untimely Meditations.* 2nd edition. Daniel Breazeale, ed. Trans. R. J. Hollingdale. Cambridge: Cambridge University Press, 1997.

Noble, Adrian. 'Introduction.' In Royal Shakespeare Company *The Plantagenets* vii–xv.

Nora, Pierre. 'Between Memory and History: Les Lieux de Memoires.' *Representations* 26 (1989). 7–25.

Oba, Kenji. 'Shakespeare in Japan.' *Shakespeare Quarterly* 33.4 (Winter 1982). 498–9.

Oyelowo, David. *Henry VI.* London: Faber, 2003.

Pao, Angela C. 'Recasting Race: Casting Practices and Racial Formations.' *Theatre Survey* 41.2 (November 2000). 1–21.

Phelan, Peggy. *Mourning Sex: Performing Public Memories.* London and New York: Routledge, 1997.

Potter, Lois. 'Recycling the Early Histories: *The Wars of the Roses* and *The Plantagenets.*' *Shakespeare Survey* 43 (1991). 171–81.

Rackin, Phyllis. *Stages of History: Shakespeare's English Chronicles.* Ithaca: Cornell University Press, 1990.

Roach, Joseph. *Cities of the Dead: Circum-Atlantic Performance.* New York: Columbia University Press, 1996.

Royal Shakespeare Company. *The Plantagenets.* London: Faber, 1988.

Ryan, Lawrence V. '*Henry VI* on Stage and Screen.' In Sylvan Barnet ed. *Henry VI 1, 2 and 3.* The Signet Classic Shakespeare Series. New York: Signet, 1989. 230–50.

Salgado, Gamini. *Eyewitnesses of Shakespeare: First Hand Accounts of Performances 1590–1890.* London: Sussex University Press, 1975.

Sanders, Norman, ed. *King Henry VI Part One.* New Penguin Shakespeare. Harmondsworth: Penguin, 1981.

—— ed. *King Henry VI Part Two.* New Penguin Shakespeare. Harmondsworth: Penguin, 1981.

—— ed. *King Henry VI Part Three.* New Penguin Shakespeare. Harmondsworth: Penguin, 1981.

Schama, Simon. *A History of Britain III: The Fate of Empire 1776–2001.* London: BBC Books, 2002.

Shaughnessy, Robert. *Representing Shakespeare: England, History and the RSC.* London and New York: Harvester Wheatsheaf, 1994.

Sierz, Aleks. *In-Yer-Face Theatre: British Drama Today.* London: Faber, 2001.

Sinfield, Alan. 'The Government, the People and the Festival.' In Jim Fyrth, ed. *Labour's Promised Land? Culture and Society in Labour Britain 1945–51.* London: Lawrence & Wishart, 1995.

—— and Jonathan Dollimore, eds. *Political Shakespeare: Essays in Cultural Materialism.* 2nd edition. Manchester: Manchester University Press, 1994.

—— 'Royal Shakespeare: Theatre and the Making of Ideology.' In Sinfield and Dollimore 182–205.

Smallwood, Robert, ed. *Players of Shakespeare 3.* Cambridge: Cambridge University Press, 1993.

—— ed. *Players of Shakespeare 6: Essays in the Performance of Shakespeare's History Plays.* Cambridge: Cambridge University Press, 2004.

Swander, Homer D. 'The Rediscovery of *Henry VI*.' *Shakespeare Quarterly* 29 (1978). 146–63.

Taylor, Neil. 'Two Types of Television Shakespeare.' *Shakespeare Survey* 39 (1987). 103–11.

Theweleit, Klaus. *Male Fantasies 1: Women, Floods, Bodies, History*. Trans. Stephen Conway et al. London: Polity Press, 1981.

Thomson, Peter. *Shakespeare's Professional Career*. Cambridge: Cambridge University Press, 1994.

Tillyard, E. M. W. *Shakespeare's History Plays*. London: Chatto and Windus, 1944.

Trewin, J. C. *The Birmingham Repertory Theatre 1913–1963*. London: Barrie & Rockcliffe, 1963.

—— *Going to Shakespeare*. London: Allen and Unwin, 1978.

Tumber, Howard. *Television and the Riots: A Report for the Broadcasting Research Unit of the British Film Institute*. London: British Film Institute, 1982.

Tushingham, David. 'Katie Mitchell: Keep Working. Keep Open. Keep Learning. Keep Looking.' In David Tushingham, ed. *Food for the Soul: A New Generation of British Theatremakers*. London: Methuen, 1994. 81–91.

Vivis, Anthony. 'Shakespeare Without the Shadows.' *Gambit International* 3.10 (1965). 96–9.

Wagner, Cosima. *Cosima Wagner's Diaries. Vol. 1 1869–1877*. Martin Gregor-Dellin and Dietrich Mach, eds. Trans. Geoffrey Skelton. London: Collins, 1978.

Warren, Roger and Edward Hall. *Rose Rage*. London: Oberon Books, 2001.

Wells, Stanley. 'The History of the Whole Contention.' *Times Literary Supplement* 4 February 1983.

—— *Shakespeare in the Theatre: An Anthology of Criticism*. Oxford: Oxford University Press, 2000.

Wikander, Matthew H. 'The Spitted Infant: Scenic Emblem and Exclusionist Politics in Restoration Adaptations of Shakespeare.' *Shakespeare Quarterly* 37.3 (Autumn 1986). 340–58.

Willems, Michèle, ed. *Shakespeare à la Télévision*. Rouen: Publications de l'Université de Rouen, 1986.

—— 'Entretien avec Jane Howell, réalisatrice de la première Tetralogie, de *The Winter's Tale* et de *Titus Andronicus*'. In Willems *Shakespeare*. 79–81.

—— 'Verbal-Visual, Verbal-Pictorial, Textual-Televisual? Reflections on the BBC Series.' *Shakespeare Survey* 39 (1987). 91–102.

Williams, Raymond. *Television: Technology and Cultural Form*. London: Fontana, 1974.

Williams, Simon, *Shakespeare on the German Stage*. Vol. 1, 1586–1914. Cambridge: Cambridge University Press, 1990.

Willis, Susan. *The BBC Shakespeare Plays: Making the Televised Canon.* Chapel Hill and London: University of North Carolina Press, 1991.
Wilson, Elizabeth. *Adorned in Dreams: Fashion and Modernity.* London: Virago 1985.

INDEX

We have not indexed individual productions where they are the main subject of a chapter. Illustrations are indicated by page numbers in italics.